WOMEN'S TWO ROLES

HOME AND WORK

BY

ALVA MYRDAL & VIOLA KLEIN

LONDON
ROUTLEDGE & KEGAN PAUL LTD

First published in 1956
by Routledge & Kegan Paul Limited
Broadway House, 68–74 Carter Lane
London, E.C.4

Second impression 1962
Second edition (revised and reset) 1968

© *Alva Myrdal and Viola Klein 1956, 1968*

Printed in Great Britain
by Butler & Tanner Limited
Frome and London

SBN 7100 2894 6 (P)
SBN 7100 3489 X (C)

CONTENTS

TABLES

TABLES

PREFACE TO THE SECOND EDITION

Ten years have passed since this book was first published. The occasion of a new reprint has offered us a welcome opportunity to re-read and, if need be, revise the arguments put forward a decade ago.

In an era of rapid social change ten years seem a long time indeed. Can a social analysis, undertaken in 1956, still bear the light of day in 1966? Developments have been very marked in the field under discussion here; have they been in the direction we then envisaged? Much of our argument was based on demographic data which can now be supplemented by more recent ones, and on an interpretation of economic trends—notoriously uncertain foundations for predictions.

Scrutinizing our book with the hindsight of ten years' experience and with the detachment which is the fruit of so long a time-lapse, we feel convinced that its reasoning is no less valid to-day than it was in the first place. Some of the ideas which then were new may have become commonplaces by frequent repetition (the 'Four Phases of a Woman's Life-Span' is one of them; the fact that married women are the 'last relatively untapped reserve of labour' is another).

If we were to write the book afresh to-day, we should no doubt change some of its emphases a little, underlining some more recent developments (such as the growing proportion of married women over the age of 35 in the workforce, or the correlation between the level of education and the employment rate of women); we should omit some arguments (e.g. the discussion as to whether the employment of women has an effect on the fertility rate); and we should, of course, make use of more recent research findings. We should also be less inclined to be on the defensive than we were at a time when the employment of married women still was a less general and more controversial phenomenon. However, these are minor details, not affecting the main outline: a transposition from one key to another, perhaps, not a change of tune.

Both in the economic and the demographic spheres the trends we first observed have continued in the same direction—only more decisively so than we could then envisage.

ix

The proportion of the population in 'non-productive' age groups, for instance, has grown at both ends of the age scale in three of the four countries discussed in this book. The percentage of the population aged 65 and over, as well as that under 15, has considerably increased; and, in addition, a higher proportion of young people stay on at school or college longer.

PERCENTAGE OF POPULATION OF NON-WORKING AGES

	Under 15 years		65 years and over	
	1950	1962	1950	1962
	%	%	%	%
United States	26·8	31·2	8·1	9·3
United Kingdom	22·3	23·0	10·7	11·8
France	22·7	28·2	11·4	11·8
Sweden	23·4	21·5	10·3	12·1

Source: *Manpower Statistics 1950–1962*, OECD, Paris, 1963.

This trend is continuing and is growing in importance. To quote only one example: According to existing projections[1] the section of the population aged under 15 and over retiring age in England and Wales should rise to 39·9 per cent in 1970, and to 41 per cent in 1980 (not allowing for the rise in school-leaving age from 15 to 16, due in 1971, which will add a further 1·5 per cent to the non-productive population). Similar trends can be observed in the other industrial countries.

The marriage rate has further increased, and the average age at first marriage has further declined. More than a quarter of all brides in the U.K. are under twenty; well over one-third are 19 or under in the U.S.A. The child-bearing age has correspondingly been lowered so that—even allowing for the slight increase in the birthrate which has meanwhile taken place—the 'post-active motherhood phase' has been further extended. The increasing employment rate of women over the age of 35 is, in part, a reflection of this development.

In the economic field, full employment, with attending man-

[1] *Registrar General's Statistical Review of England and Wales, 1963*, Part II, Population Table, 1965.

power shortages, particularly in skilled occupations, has continued. Mainly as a result of the high marriage rate at early ages these shortages have been acute above all in occupations which are traditionally feminine, such as nursing, teaching, social work, and in the ever-expanding 'service' sector of the economy.

Our highly industrialized society is geared to the ever-growing production of a vast range of consumer goods, most of which help to simplify domestic management. At the same time, they act as a spur for married women to seek gainful employment in order to increase the family income and be able to purchase these consumer goods. In this way, our economic system has, by its own momentum, set into motion a spiral effect: More household gadgets set more women free for employment, and more wives in paid employment increase the need—and provide the cash—for more and better domestic appliances. The pressures of mass production and competitive advertising have created a situation in which the employment of married women is, for large sectors of the population, the key to a share in the much publicized 'affluence' of our society, and the conditions of the labour market are such that jobs of one kind or another are not difficult to find.

One by-product of these developments is a noticeable change of public opinion. Prejudices against employing married women, although still persisting in some quarters, are on the wane, and the practice of going out to work, at least part-time, has become so widespread among women in their thirties and forties, irrespective of social class, that those who fail to do so now almost have to give an explanation for staying at home.

In this sense, the development which we foresaw in dim outline ten years ago has come full circle. We may be forgiven for feeling gratified with the correctness of our assessment.

In view of what has been said, we do not think it necessary greatly to revise our text. We have brought the demographic data up-to-date by replacing, or supplementing, some of the existing tables and have largely rewritten chapter 4 ('Women in the Labour Force To-day') in the light of recent information.

We have also expanded our bibliography to include relevant literature published during the last decade.

As to other parts of the book—for instance, chapters 6 and 7— we felt that, although a number of newer investigations have been carried out which we should, naturally, have quoted in place of the earlier ones had we written this book to-day, their results have not substantially altered the picture nor added new certainties which would impel us to revise the views expressed here. The serious student of the subject will be able, with the help of the bibliography, to supplement the information contained in these pages.

Both in method and in aim this book is a study of social change, not a blueprint for an ideal future society. We have endeavoured to analyse reality such as we found it, to understand the social forces at work, and to deduce some consequences likely to follow from the trends we could observe. We have also attempted in our conclusions to point out some ways in which society might help those most directly affected by the process of change to adjust to the new conditions of life.

To those concerned with a reform of society such a 'minimum programme' must fall disappointingly short of expectations. At the same time, it is bound to antagonize those wishing to preserve the *status quo ante*.

However, as sociologists we see our task neither in providing an imaginative vision of a new and better society nor in a vain attempt to arrest the inevitable processes of change. Our job is strictly to study and to describe the conditions such as they exist at a given time and place and, on the basis of the observed facts, to make limited predictions about probable developments in the near future. This may be a less 'exciting' undertaking than actually manipulating events in an endeavour to change their course; it is nonetheless an essential task. Without a realistic appraisal of the current situation and the underlying processes all social action must remain futile.

A. M. & V. K.

Spring, 1966

FOREWORD

This book has a rather long history. It originated in a suggestion, made to me shortly after the end of the last war by the International Federation of University Women, to make an international survey of the needs for social reforms if women are to be put into a position to reconcile family and professional life. Through the various national branches of the I.F.U.W. questionnaires were distributed, and some information was collected showing that in many countries there was a growing interest in, and understanding of, the problem, and that in some parts of the world first steps had been taken to make it easier for women to pull their weight in the economic life of their country.

However, the material available was much too heterogeneous to be used with any pretension to scientific accuracy and, further, the war was still too close to allow generalizations as to what conditions might be accepted as normal in peace-time. Moreover, my service first with the United Nations and then with UNESCO involved more than merely the physical interruption of the work begun in 1946; it impressed me so strongly with the overwhelming problems in the underdeveloped countries that I found it intellectually impossible to proceed with a manuscript which could only concern a few highly favoured nations.

When pressed to continue the interrupted work on the manuscript I found the solution to my difficulties in associating with Viola Klein. Approaching the problem of Women and Work, as we did, from different angles, we happily found ourselves in basic agreement on all the major issues involved.

This book, then, is the outcome of our harmonious co-operation. For reasons of geography, and because each of us had a full-time job besides writing this book, our progress was not as fast as we might have desired. There were moments, we confess, when a life with only two responsibilities, one job and one home, appeared to us a 'leisurely' existence to which we were eagerly looking forward. May we therefore plead extenuating circumstances should some of our readers on occasion feel that we have underrated the difficulties of their dual role?   A. M.

INTRODUCTION

Whether married women should be employed outside their homes has become the most topical issue concerning women in recent years and the controversy is carried on with much spirit and profound conviction on both sides. Since so many questions of vital concern to individual lives are involved, it is not surprising that the discussion is, by and large, mainly conducted on a level of personal opinions and emotions rather than on the basis of sociological facts. Such facts are, however, essential for a rational assessment of the situation and a sober evaluation of the pros and cons of the case; to supply the relevant data for such an assessment is the intention of this book.

Our readers will be left in no doubt as to the side to which we lean in this controversy; but they will, we hope, credit us with impartiality in the collection of facts and in the presentation of the real issues involved.

The problem of 'women and work', and of women's role in society generally, has completely changed its complexion during the last few decades. It is no longer a question of what women are physically and mentally capable of doing. Experience has settled the long controversy about feminine abilities and has proved that women are fit for a much wider range of activities than merely those compatible with the commonly accepted idea of the 'weaker sex'.

The emphasis has now shifted from the discussion of: 'What *can* women do?' to one of: 'What *should* women do?' Implicit in this question is an interest both in women's individual well-being and in the welfare of society.

What to do with our lives is a problem which poses itself more acutely in regard to women than to men, partly because women are relative newcomers to important sectors of the social scene, partly because their lives are more intricately linked with the existence of the family and the continuation of the race.

At this juncture in our social history women are guided by two apparently conflicting aims. On the one hand, they want, like everybody else, to develop their personalities to the full and to take

xv

an active part in adult social and economic life within the limits of their individual interests and abilities. On the other hand, most women want a home and a family of their own. At a time when most social and economic life was carried on at home these aims did not conflict with each other. They appear to do so to-day.

The claims of society on women are, likewise, twofold, and these, too, appear under present conditions of life and work to contradict each other. The need of society to perpetuate and re-generate itself, which puts a relatively greater share of respon-sibility on women than on men, imposes demands on women which compete with other claims arising from society's need for economic progress. The realization of the latter is to a con-siderable, yet often underrated, extent, dependent on women's co-operation.

This clash of conflicting interests has stirred public discussion during the last generation or two, and has resulted in varied interpretations of women's 'true' social role. By now, women are becoming weary of listening to contradictory exhortations about their duties. Different cultural traditions make their influences felt, and contrasting political ideologies have clouded the issue. There is no uniform ideal which could apply to styles of life, or family patterns, as unlike each other as those of a village in Central Europe and a suburb of Los Angeles. Yet all are part of our con-temporary world and have come within easy reach of each other.

In the old days, women knew where they stood and their lives were spent in the care of their families. Their world was bounded by the walls of their homes. From there, a resolute minority thrust out into the world of business and public affairs and succeeded in being admitted, largely to the extent that they were willing to turn their backs on home and family.

Those pioneering days are now over. With them has gone the need for women to make a fatal decision between irreconcilable alternatives. The Gordian knot of a seemingly insoluble feminine dilemma has been cut. The technical and social developments of the last few decades have given women the opportunity to com-bine and to integrate their two interests in Home and Work—if we may thus, in short, characterize the two spheres of interest. No longer need women forgo the pleasures of one sphere in order to enjoy the satisfactions of the other. The best of both worlds has come within their grasp, if only they reach out for it.

To make this a reality for more than the chosen few, something in the nature of a mental revolt will be needed. There is no doubt that society can be organized in such a way as to give practical scope both for family life and the gainful employment of women. But more clear thinking both about ends and means, and a courageous facing of facts, will be required before these two roles will be fused into one harmonious whole.

In discussing this contemporary problem of Women one qualification has to be made: we are speaking here only of women in Western societies. We are fully aware that there is no uniform 'Woman Problem' which equally applies to all countries. Within the limits of this study it would, however, be impossible to include a comparison between the social roles of women all over the world, or to discuss the great variety of difficulties affecting women in different cultures and various stages of social development.

For the purposes of this study emphasis has been placed on the situation which presents itself in the most highly industrialized countries of our time. We must, nevertheless, remember the fact that to the vast majority of women in the present world—to all those in the underdeveloped countries with their rapidly increasing populations, their patterns of large families, and their pre-industrial economies—the problems as here presented simply do not apply at the present time. Yet, although this study only deals with one particular phase in the process of social evolution, the subject of women's dual function in society has a universal application; for similar problems to those at present experienced in industrialized countries are likely to arise elsewhere at some later time, when other countries reach phases in their economic development corresponding to those reached in the industrialized West.

It is hoped that the experience and wisdom so dearly bought by a century of trial and error in the modern, industrial societies will be of some benefit not only to the young people of these countries but also to people of all ages in the younger communities of the world.

CHAPTER ONE

A REVOLUTION IN TWO STAGES

During the present century the social position of women has undergone a series of profound changes, in which we can distinguish two main phases. The first is characterized by the admission of women to an increasing variety of hitherto 'masculine' jobs, provided, on the whole, that the women were unencumbered by family ties. The outstanding feature of the second phase is the endeavour of a growing number of women to combine family and employment. Altogether, this social change amounts to a gradual recapture of positions which were lost when women were squeezed out of the economic process by the Industrial Revolution.

Before that revolution women had at all times played a very active part in the economic life of society, as they do in agricultural communities to this day. Their two roles, raising a family and doing economically productive work, were fused into one way of life, work at home. When industrialization forced these to be separated, it was at first thought that women could carry on only one, namely, the family function. They had, therefore, first to assert their right to work alongside men; and now they have to prove that they can carry on both functions in one and the same lifetime, which is so much longer now than it was.

The process of eliminating women from economically active positions of course affected different social groups in different ways, as does the complementary process of bringing them back into paid jobs. In both the urban and the rural proletariat the latter was an immediate effect of industrialization, and the exploitation of women and children in its early phases was one of the blackest spots in the social history of the nineteenth century. Later, as wages rose, many working-class women left the labour market, since it was felt to be an important element in a higher standard of living that wives and mothers should be able to stay at home, like the women in more privileged social groups.

It eventually fell to the women in the urban middle class to symbolize the more systematic return to economic productivity, by entering paid employment.

The recovering of women's lost territory is a long and uneven process, as yet incomplete. The most painful part of the readjustment is caused by the fact that habits of thought that belong to past phases of these complex developments, and frequently to particular social groups, become established as absolutes in situations where they no longer apply.

Proving Women's Abilities outside the Home

The first lingering misconception which had to be cleared up was that women did not fit into the world of industry, of paid employment, in short, of 'men's jobs'. The sweated labour of women during the early period of industrialization, and their continued employment in several sectors of light industry, was not appreciated as proving their competitive qualifications.

It was left to the pioneers from the middle and upper classes, fighting their way to individual recognition against heavy odds, to demonstrate women's fitness to do 'masculine' work under the same conditions as men. To prove their case the pioneers were mostly quite willing to ignore the fact that they were women, and satisfied that this fact should also be ignored by others. Women's share in the economic life of the past had been forgotten, and it appeared to many that in their claim for a place in the scheme of economic production women had to break completely new ground. Whether hesitant or defiant, every new step seemed to provide a new test case. Every professionally active woman felt herself to be continually on trial.

This, in fact, the pioneers of women's emancipation were, individually and collectively. The period was characterized by the publication of countless comparative studies and measurements testing the relative aptitudes and traits of men and women—from their genius for mathematics to their ability to walk the tight-rope.

These investigations, carried out by psychologists and sociologists, have proved that most women are as good as most men on most scores; that individuals of one sex always vary more between themselves than any averages for the sexes as a whole differ from each other; and that any measurable differences in average performance of one sex in a particular field are balanced by the differences in another. If men show a somewhat greater inclination towards one capacity, such as mechanics, women compensate by excelling in another, such as languages. If men more often excel in physical strength, women correspondingly excel in dexterity.

The issue of comparative performances can be regarded as settled to-day, both scientifically and practically. Though differences in attitudes between men and women still form a favourite topic of drawing-room conversation and popular quiz-programmes, women's abilities are no longer seriously in doubt. These discussions rather seem to be a kind of rearguard action carried on after the main battle has been decided. In a world of so much accepted sex equality they perhaps represent a last unconscious protest against standardization and uniformity.

In the meantime, women's achievements have become evident to anyone. This process was undoubtedly accelerated by the two world wars in which necessity compelled society to use women in occupations which previously were the monopoly of men. At some time during the 1939 war a most impressive poster could be seen all over Britain. It showed the photograph of a young woman in uniform and steel helmet carrying a crying child out of the flames of a bombed house. In her composed and matter-of-fact way she symbolized the courage and determination of Britain under air bombardment, and her attitude had beneath its efficiency just that touch of motherliness and sentiment that made so direct an appeal to the heart. There could be no doubt in anybody's mind that the photograph was genuine. For everybody knew from personal experience that countless women had faced, and were facing, similar dangers with equal courage and equanimity. It was no longer necessary for women to 'protest too much', as the early feminists did in their exaggerated imitation of men.

The first phase of the revolution was concluded and women had met the demands made on them.

It must also be admitted that the demands came half-way to meet women. In our highly complex and diversified economic structure there is scope for all sorts of natural gifts. Physical strength is no longer an essential prerequisite for most jobs. Many operations formerly imposing great strain on the workers are now performed by machines requiring the attendant's skill rather than muscular force; better hygienic conditions and reduced hours of work have made both industrial and clerical jobs less exhausting;

3

and improved means of communication have helped to bridge the gulf between home and workplace. Changed also is the attitude of employers: modern industrial management in Western Europe and North America no longer pursues the short-sighted policy of getting the most out of its workers by methods of sweated labour. Instead, it tries as far as possible to adjust the working conditions to human needs. Good labour relations are considered essential to successful production. Scientific investigations are carried out in the fields of industrial psychology and personnel management, as well as in the sphere of production techniques, in order to discover the material and psychological conditions leading to the highest productivity.

Thus the setting for participation in the processes of economic production is much more favourable to women than at any time since the beginning of the Industrial Revolution. Moreover, our society has begun to accept the fact that women are in jobs to stay.

Defining Women's Family Role

However, there is often a lack of clarity in present-day generalizations about women's economic function. We know now that the highly important contribution of women within the old type of home, which was the centre of productive processes, has been changed in a radical way. Nevertheless, this domestic setting as the accepted framework of women's life and work still underlies the pattern of women's 'roles' to an irrationally large extent. Memories of a long obsolete social pattern linger on, and as well as colouring our dreams they distort our attempts at rational thinking.

Up to the beginning of the nineteenth century spinning, weaving and making cloths, baking bread, curing meat, making soap, brewing beer, preserving fruit and many other processes now usually carried out in factories, as well as a good deal of teaching and nursing, were part of a woman's household routine. Thus, the importance of a woman's contribution could not be in question. Even the bearing of numerous children, who were not merely a liability as additional mouths to be fed, but also, from an early age, an asset as additional hands to help earning the family's income, enhanced women's economic value and filled them with a secure sense of purpose.

When the equilibrium of pre-industrial society was upset by

new technical and social developments the external conditions of women's lives were radically changed. Small-scale family handicrafts decayed and were superseded by large industries employing individual workers, not families. The employment of children in factories and mines had soon to be stopped by legislation, for humanitarian reasons; elementary education became general, and before long the law enjoined on parents the duty to support their children fully, at least up to the age of 10. Thus from the economic point of view children became a burden instead of an asset to the poorer section of the population, while at the same time a large part of the responsibility for their education was taken away from the home. Many working-class wives went to work in factories and, with their ten- to twelve-hour day, neglected their children and homes to a degree which shocked the social conscience of the later nineteenth century. This is the background against which married women's employment outside their homes came to be regarded as a social evil, and their concentration on home-making as an improvement of their standard of living.

That the workload in the home meanwhile drastically diminished—for a variety of reasons, the most important being the reduction in the size of the family—was never fully recognized. It is still, in some quarters, considered almost blasphemous to point out this historical fact.

Side by side with the ideal of the hard-working housewife another, quite different, feminine ideal, related to the privileges of the aristocracy, became more important as the middle classes grew in size and prosperity, the 'Lady of Leisure'. This ideal, cultivated more in the last century than in the present one, in point of fact put parasitism of women at a premium. The task of an upper-middle-class wife was chiefly to be an ornament to her husband's home and a living testimony to his wealth. Her idleness was one of the prerequisites. Up to this day, the two contrary ideals vie with each other in the columns of every woman's journal. There are on the one hand the domestic virtues with the fragrance of freshly-made bread every day, together with the statistics showing a fourteen- to sixteen-hour working day. But there are also the costly cults of the lily-white hands, of lavish entertaining, and of changing one's highly fashionable clothes oftener and oftener—the much advertised dreams of all that goes with being 'well provided for', once one is married. There is a curious causal relationship (though this is not necessarily appreciated) operating in the advertising columns of modern fashion magazines. While on the one hand more and more gadgets are offered to save time and labour, more and more time-consuming beauty treatments are recommended to keep in control a feminine figure which shows the effects of too little exercise and too much leisure.

There is no use denying that, even to-day, the twin ideals of the hard-working housewife and of the leisured lady exist in an unholy (and as a rule unrecognized) alliance, jointly circumscribing woman's role as one to be acted out within the home. The worst of this ideology is not that it is irrational and out of harmony with the facts of contemporary life, but that it presents our young girls with a thoroughly false picture of the practical choice they have to make for their lives. An honest scrutiny should be made to differentiate between productive and necessary work in the home and what is only a time-consuming pretext; a distinction must also be made between well-earned leisure and sheer waste of time.

Women become Citizens

Yet, while the nineteenth-century ideal of bourgeois women has been kept alive to this day and has become accepted in all social classes, the futility of feminine existence in the upper middle class was the very mainspring which motivated the social revolution usually called the emancipation of women. This movement was not simply a revolt of the weaker sex against the shackles imposed on it throughout the centuries by the strong, free male—effective though the emotional appeal of this image may be. The fact is rather that women lagged one step behind men in the process of social evolution. This is true both in the fields of economics and politics.

A social group can only achieve representation in parliamentary government when it is strong enough to enforce its demand. The middle classes in France were admitted to a share in political power only after the Revolution, and in England, only after the passing of the Reform Bill in 1832. While in Sweden the farmers, like the merchants, had their place in the 'four estates' from the inception of parliamentary democracy more than 500 years ago, the working class became a partner very late, in the first decades of this century, through gradual reforms. Only in the U.S.A. was

6

universal male suffrage tried out very early on. In Europe, the gradual extension of the political franchise to cover all the adult population except lunatics, convicts, and women, followed after the social changes created by the Industrial Revolution. Women were not enfranchised until the end of the first world war in the U.S.A., the United Kingdom, and Sweden, and until the end of the second world war in France.

It took women longer than men to achieve political freedom and democratic rights, access to education and opportunity for employment, as women were generally retarded in their adjustment to the Industrial Revolution. In their clamour for the 'Right to Work' their aim was to regain the position of economic productivity and the sense of social usefulness they had lost when the centre of production was moved from the home to the factory. However revolutionary women's demand for the right to work may have appeared at the time, in fact they were not striving for a new thing but for the restitution of their lost share in the scheme of economic affairs. If women now made an articulate and conscious request to go out into the world, they were not driven by a sudden wave of perversity, or fashion, but by the simple logic of economics. The work had been moved from the home, and women wanted to move after it, as men had done not so long before.

Discrimination against women in the field of property rights was another consequence of the new economic developments of the nineteenth century. Among the landed gentry and in the families of independent craftsmen, women had often wielded considerable power, but they were handicapped when it came to the new types of investment in industry and commerce. The servitude against which they now protested was a more recent growth than was generally recognized.

The Right to Education, another important issue in the emancipation of women, was granted to women somewhat later than to men. But here, too, they should be regarded as latecomers in the evolutionary process rather than as one half of mankind kept in subjection by the other half. Education, previously a privilege of the few, was gradually put on a broader basis during the nineteenth century. Beginning with some States of the U.S.A., where a system of free, tax-supported State schools, open to all, was already established in the first quarter of the century and spread to all the Northern States before 1850, compulsory general education was introduced in Sweden in 1842, in Britain in 1870 and in France in 1882 (to confine our examples to the four countries which will provide our illustrations throughout this study).

In some past societies, for instance, the aristocratic culture of the Middle Ages, education, particularly in the 'humanities', was more women's domain than that of men. This situation became reversed as economic developments affected the two sexes differently, for with general education went professional training. While medicine, for instance, was often in the hands of women as long as it was a humanitarian art, women became excluded from its practice as soon as conditions of competence were officially regulated—because women could not get the basic training. Thus it was logical that one of the earliest reforms women fought for should have been the right to higher education. The dates when they won the right to enter universities mark the pioneer victories for the efforts to set the world right again for women.

Conflicting Roles and Ideals

The Woman with a Career is a creation of distinctly middle-class origin, and is symptomatic of the second phase of the social revolution which we have been describing. The acceptance of this feminine role shows that it is possible for women to envisage the idea of work outside the home as a career for life without any feeling of self-denial or resignation, and to plan for it as a positive gain.

Admittedly, the ideal of 'career woman' has until recently been held by women only—and by a very limited number of women at that. To this day the term has such an unpleasant connotation for many people that professional women often hasten to assure you that they are not 'career women'. Men have, for a variety of reasons, found it difficult to adjust themselves to the idea of a wife who so radically differs from their mothers. The other two ideal feminine roles—that of the hard-working housewife and that of the lady of the salon—continue to thrive together in the minds both of men and of innumerable women, and this confusion brings a great deal of unreality into the life plans of young girls. While woman's external conditions of life have changed drastically, the ideal picture of her future is still visualized by the young girl as if these changes had never happened. In this case there is an unusually

8

long time-lag between the emergence of new realities and relationships and the acceptance of their full implications.

It is, of course, neither accurate nor fair to make general statements about women as if they all belonged to one class or one type.

Take, for example, the desire of women to share in productive social processes which we discussed before, and their demands for the 'Right to Work' and the 'Right to Education'. These, clearly, were middle-class ideologies. While to women condemned to the passivity and languor of a Victorian drawing-room the chance of going out to work, like their menfolk, might seem exciting and enriching, work was a necessity, often hardly bearable, for working-class women.

To-day, a few generations later, with women's education fairly well established, the difference in the attitude to work is still quite marked between different strata—which do not necessarily coincide with social classes. Women with higher education or a specialized training who have known the satisfactions of responsibility or of skilled work are, naturally, more loath to give up their jobs on marrying than girls who have done semi-skilled or routine work. Pearl Jephcott, in her studies of factory girls[1], was struck by the absence among them of any sympathetic relationship to their work. She found that employment was considered by these girls as an unavoidable but temporary phase in their lives and the sooner it came to an end the better. Their imaginations having been fed on Hollywood pictures and the weekly magazines which form their chief reading matter, they wait for the day on which they will enter the blissful state of matrimony, happily to live in it ever after. In the same way, most shorthand typists, shop assistants, and women employed in jobs of a similar routine nature, with little prospect of advancement, long to escape into a world in which they will have neither a boss nor a fixed time-table. Though the change may in effect be the substitution of one routine for another, it replaces one which is imposed from outside—either by the impersonal workings of the machinery or by the will of a superior—with another which the woman can to some extent manipulate herself and which therefore gives her the feeling of freedom.

In contrast, the highly skilled or the professional woman who has to give up her career for domestic routine is likely to feel frustrated after some time if she cannot use her abilities. Her

[1] A. P. Jephcott; *Girls Growing Up*, London, 1942, and *Rising Twenty*, London, 1948.

frustration may express itself in various forms, the most frequent of which is the complaint about the drudgery of domestic work.

To-day, when families have generally been reduced to manageable size, when public services and factory products have taken over many functions previously performed at home, and when labour-saving devices, even if they have not considerably reduced the number of working hours, have at least taken the backache and sweat out of a good deal of housework, the word 'drudgery' in connexion with domestic duties is more frequently used than ever before. Just as the rising standards of living have made poverty, though generally less acute, psychologically more frustrating, so the availability of labour-saving gadgets on the one hand, and of an alternative way of life as independent income-earner on the other, have made the domestic routine more irksome to the housewife. Housewives, in our time, have become a discontented class and are on that account—and because they have votes, too—constantly courted, appealed to and glorified by governments and politicians.

During the last generation or so, an interesting shift in feminine discontent has taken place. Much of women's envy of men, which undoubtedly was a strong undercurrent in the earlier feminist movement, has changed its direction and turned into envy of one group of women against another: working women begrudge housewives their freedom to do things in their own time and in their own way, and possibly also the prestige that tends to go with greater leisure; whereas housewives envy employed women their financial independence, the greater variety of their social contacts, and their sense of purpose. This is one result of the present stage of partial emancipation in which two feminine ideals, two distinct ways of life, continue uneasily side by side.

There exist, it is true, many individual differences of emphasis and also, more important, varying degrees of consciousness of aims. But on the whole it seems true to say that human beings—women no less than men—need for their happiness both emotional fulfilment in their personal relations and a sense of social purpose. Even to the most ardent feminists it is clear to-day that work is no end in itself and that the past over-emphasis on careers at the expense of marriage and family has done great damage to the women's cause.

On the other hand, the widespread discontent among urban housewives to-day bears witness to the fact that looking after one man and a family of two—however attractive a pattern of life this may seem to the young girl spending her days at the typewriter or behind a shop-counter—is, under present conditions, not enough to fill the many years of a woman's life and to give her the satisfaction of feeling that she is pulling her weight. Although this is unpleasant to accept, many women have begun to wake up to the realization that their children will not remain children all the time and that husbands, however ardent in their courtship, cannot be expected to remain the same for the half-century that their married life is now statistically likely to last.

Some Basic Facts

These are some of the dilemmas to be discussed and examined in this book. The necessity to make generalizations will, naturally, constitute a drawback, which this study shares with so many other discussions on social problems. One cannot hope to do more than give a rough outline of the principles involved. The picture drawn up loses in detailed accuracy what it gains in universality. It may be possible to give a general idea of the *roles* held up before women; but when it comes to comparing them with the ways in which women actually live, there are too many individual variations for the sketch ever to be quite true to life.

We thought it necessary to make this reservation and to warn our readers beforehand that they may expect to find here an anatomical drawing rather than a portrait of themselves. For statistical purposes women are too large and heterogeneous a group to be treated as a unit. General statements about them can be made only with reference to a few objective, measurable facts which are independent of social and individual background, such as, for instance, average expectation of life, years of adulthood, normal reproductive patterns, etc. But to put down an average age at which people start work would already give a misleading picture, because full-time education generally comes to an end later among the higher income groups. And wherever such subjective factors as attitudes, opinions or habits enter, a statistically constituted 'average woman' becomes a mere phantom. In an age which has made family limitation increasingly a matter of choice, even such apparently objective figures as fertility rates are dependent on personal attitudes, on education, and on social values, and reflect class differences and religious and other influences. If we care to take different countries into account, the situation becomes even more complex.

Certain facts, however, apply universally, and they are sufficient to serve as starting points for a rough analysis of present conditions as well as a basis for a discussion of future possibilities. The following five points will throw the problem into relief:

(1) Women, as the child-bearing sex, present specific social problems. This fact has, in particular, to be taken into account in the evaluation of their creative contribution to society.

(2) As a result of their maternal function women's adjustment to the social changes brought about by the Industrial Revolution, especially to the separation of work from home, has been retarded.

(3) The mental health and happiness of coming generations depend, to an extent which we have to-day only begun to understand, on the love and security provided during early childhood. In this sense women bear a special burden of responsibility for the future quality of our people.

(4) The general increase in longevity which characterizes this century has had a more marked effect on women than on men. Women to-day have a longer average expectation of life compared with their grandmothers, and also compared with their male contemporaries.

(5) Under present conditions, with an average family of only slightly more than two children, and reasonable amenities, an average housewife can be considered to be employed full-time on tasks which are necessary for home-making only during a quarter to one-third of her normal adult life.

CHAPTER TWO

WOMEN IN AN AGEING SOCIETY

Two developments have largely been responsible for initiating the second phase of the social revolution which has brought the equality of women an essential step nearer to becoming a reality: one is the greatly increased average expectation of life, and the other is the change in the size and structure of the family. It is these demographic changes which make a radical re-thinking of women's role in society imperative.

Increased Expectation of Life

In terms of previous generations the women of to-day have not only one but two adult lives to dispose of.

Expressed in the sober language of population statistics the historical fact is that during the last hundred years the average expectation of life at birth has nearly doubled. A baby girl born to-day in the advanced countries will on an average reach the age of 70 or more.

The gain is due, in the first place, to the enormous reduction of infant mortality; but the progress of the medical sciences, improved hygiene, etc., have diminished the dangers to life also in the later years. While, for instance, the expectation of life at birth of a girl born in Britain has increased by 70 per cent during the last hundred years, the corresponding increase at the age of 25 is 35 per cent. In net years the gain at birth is 30 years, at the age of 25 about 13 years. Even within the ten years since the first edition of this book another year or two has been added in all countries to the average length of life.

At the average age of marriage a woman to-day has half a century, or more, in front of her. The full measure of this advance is best seen in comparison with the last century. While in 1850 one half of the female population died before the age of 45, nearly 90 per cent survive that age to-day, and 70 per cent reach the age of

13

65, which was reached by only one-third of all women a hundred years ago. This is a considerable achievement. Moreover, these additional years do not mean a prolonged period of senility and dying off, but genuinely represent an increase in years of health and vitality.

This extension of life has not, of course, been limited to one sex only, but as the following table shows, it is more marked for women than for men in all the countries under consideration:

Table 1

EXPECTATION OF LIFE AT VARIOUS AGES IN FOUR COUNTRIES

Age: Sex:	0 M	F	25 M	F	40 M	F	60 M	F
U.S.A. (1962)	66·8	73·4	45·1	50·9	31·4	36·7	15·9	19·6
France (1962)	67·29	74·14	45·19	51·37	31·47	37·13	15·68	19·61
Sweden (1961)	71·56	75·35	48·99	52·09	34·86	37·60	17·56	19·63
U.K. (England and Wales) (1960–62)	68·0	74·0	48·8	51·0	31·6	36·6	15·1	19·0

Source: *Demographic Yearbook*, United Nations, New York, 1963.

New Attitude to Ageing

The increased expectation of life is having far-reaching consequences which make themselves felt in the economic, social and psychological spheres. One of its effects is a gradual change in the general attitude to ageing. This change is expressed in the new and more sanguine way in which people evaluate their own abilities and prospects in advancing years, and also in objective recognition of these improved possibilities. The idea that a person's age cannot simply be assessed by the number of years he, or she, has been alive, is gradually gaining ground, at least among sociologists, gerontologists, etc. The notion that 'a man is as old as he feels' is, of course, not new; but only recently has science taken note of the reality underlying this popular saying. The term 'biological age' has been introduced, in contradistinction to 'chronological age', to give expression to the dichotomy.

In a paper read to the International Population Congress in Rome, in September 1954, Professor Henri Laugier of the Sorbonne spoke of 'chronological age' as 'a concept of ridiculously insufficient character' which, he said, 'has no other merit except that of being susceptible to precise measurement, at least in our Western societies'. He suggested that researches should be carried out, as a matter of high priority, with a view to establishing a scale by which the real 'biological age' of a person can be measured, analogous to the system by which the 'developmental age' of young children—i.e. their advance or retardment in relation to the norm of their particular age group—can be ascertained. For, as Professor Laugier pointed out, the margin of uncertainty about the 'real, biological age' of a person increases with the number of years and is particularly great at a time when chronological age is taken as the criterion by which an individual's usefulness in his field of work is estimated. At the chronological age of 70 the divergences in biological age may in fact be as wide as between chronological ages of 50 and 90.

Physical and mental fitness determine a person's biological age only in part. Another part is played by an individual's own assessment of his, or her, age role. In this respect the changes in people's attitudes have been very great and are particularly marked in the lives of women.

To-day a young woman of 36 feels herself in the prime of life. She would be amazed to read on the seventeenth-century portrait of a stately and mature lady the melancholy inscription:

> My childhood past that bewtiffied my fleshe
> and gone my youth that gave me colour freshe,
> I am now come to those ripe years at last
> that tell me how my wanton days be past
> and therefore frinde so turnes the time me
> I once was young and now am as you see.
>
> AETATIS XXXVI.

A hundred years ago, in Balzac's days, *la femme de trente ans* had reached a critical phase in her life. If she was not yet resigned to middle-aged respectability she was a figure either of tragedy or of ridicule. In the eyes of the world, and most likely also in her own eyes, she was definitely *passée*.

As recently as a generation ago it still appeared to a scientific observer of women such as Freud that the age of 30 was a deadline in their lives. 'I cannot refrain from mentioning,' said Freud in his lecture on the Psychology of Women, 'an impression which one receives over and over again in analytic work. A man of about thirty seems youthful and, in a sense, an incompletely developed individual of whom we expect that he will be able to make good use of the possibilities of development which analysis lays open to him. But a woman of about the same age frequently staggers us by her psychological rigidity and unchangeability. Her libido has taken up its final positions and seems powerless to leave them for others. There are no paths open for further development; it is as though the whole process had been gone through and remained inaccessible to influence for the future. . . .' Freud thought that this psychological process was the result of a constitutional disposition.[1]

It may seem idle to speculate whether Freud would have made the same observations thirty years later. His interpretation, that we had to do with a constitutional difference between men and women, would certainly meet more criticism to-day. At any rate there are many indications that the 'deadline' has moved up by at least ten years, if not more, since he published his *Introductory Lectures*, and that even at 40 many women to-day feel they have not yet 'exhausted the possibilities of further development'. We find more and more individuals who demonstrate their lust for life for considerably longer periods. Colette, the French novelist, may be quoted as an extreme case of the 'new' mentality: on the occasion of her 80th birthday she gave an interview to the newspapers, the essence of which was that she found it hard to adjust to old age. 'If only one were 58,' she sighed, 'because at that time one is still desired and full of hope for the future.' And now Dr. Kinsey, supported by massive statistical evidence, tells us that even in the sphere of sexual development, where women were always thought to mature younger and to fade more quickly than men, these general assumptions are out of date and the converse of the facts.[2] Women in our Western civilization, it appears, reach the height of their sexual maturity later and retain their capacities far longer than our social mores have given them credit for.

Do most women subjectively adapt themselves to the full realization of their altered physical condition? It is difficult to say, because the old stereotypes continue to exist, very much unchanged,

---

[1] Cf. also Viola Klein, *The Feminine Character*, London, 1946.
[2] A. C. Kinsey, *Sexual Behavior in the Human Female*, Philadelphia and London, 1953.

side by side with the new ideals. 'Grandmother' is still pictured in advertising as a sweet, slightly decrepit old lady with white hair—the favourite pose being that during the hour of story-telling to curly-haired grandchildren. The fact that women become grandmothers in their forties or early fifties and that they need not, as an age-type, look much different from Marlene Dietrich, will probably influence mass clichés only fifty years from now—despite contemporary advertisers of cosmetics, hair-tints, etc., who try to persuade women that they can look 20 at 65.

On the other hand, there are hosts of publications with titles such as *Life Begins at Forty*, *Youth after Forty*, *Glamour for the Over-Forties*, etc., whose very element of pep-talk must make one suspicious. But they are, no doubt, evidence of a widespread desire to extend the period of continued development and growth of personality and bear witness to a still somewhat nervous and self-conscious refusal to 'take up one's final position'.

Allowing for the unavoidable time-lag in adjustment to the new social condition of a longer and healthier life, a great psychological change has nevertheless already taken place. It affords, in fact, an excellent illustration of the intimate correlation between objective social reality and subjective individual reaction.

People's personal attitudes are a reflection of the social situation and, at the same time, an important factor in it. They are a reflection, because in their innumerable individual, subjective ways people react to the same objective social fact—for instance, in our example, to the phenomenon of increased longevity. Individual attitudes are themselves a social factor, because these personal reactions become active ingredients of the social situation, contribute to its mental climate, and may influence its change. To be more specific: the changing attitude of women to the process of ageing—itself, as we have seen, a function of a demographic fact—in its turn has a bearing on such questions as employment, social customs and behaviour patterns. In this way social fact and psychological correlative are two different aspects of the same total situation.

Even such 'impersonal' data as population figures and employment statistics find an expression in personal attitudes. They are reflected in the opinions of people who are hardly, if at all, aware of the social facts underlying and conditioning their conscious thought. The restlessness and sense of futility among middle-class women of the Victorian era, which we mentioned earlier, is an example. It was the subjective counterpart of the economic and social changes wrought by the Industrial Revolution. The 'clinging vine' ideal, in fashion then, was the unconscious expression of a social situation in which women had lost their economic usefulness and had to rely exclusively on their 'charms' to catch a husband, and on public morality to retain him.

Examples like these could be multiplied indefinitely. Indeed, it would make a fascinating game—or the material of a number of dissertations—to consider the psychological correlates to a series of statistically established facts; one could take for example the surplus number of women, or the small size of modern families, or mass migrations, and many others.

In dealing with the situation of women in our society it will be necessary to adopt a method which does justice both to its subjective aspects and to the measurable, objective data. Scientific facts and statistics must be included to the extent that a fair description of the present-day situation can be rendered. At the same time, it must be realized that the psychological problems and dilemmas arising out of this situation, the conflicting ideals and contradictory aims typical of a society in transition are a part of the whole and probably just as important as the more measurable data. Furthermore, they always appear with a greater or smaller time lag, so that a rational adaptation to a changing situation is slow.

The Ageing Population—a Burden or a Reserve of Labour?

The problem of our ageing population has in recent years been given much thought by the social scientists and administrators of all Western countries. Serious concern has been expressed at the fact that, given present rates of reproduction and mortality, an increasing number of old people will have to be supported by a shrinking proportion of working people. For example, at the time of the 1911 Census in Great Britain, one person in fifteen was of pensionable age (over 65 for men, and over 60 for women); however, the proportion was twice as high (two in fifteen) in 1947. It has been estimated that in 25 years the proportion of elderly pensioners to adults of working age may be as high as one to three.

In France, where the problem is most acute, the proportion of adults of working age to old people has within a hundred years been reduced from 9:1 in 1851 to 5:1 in 1951.

The situation is similar in all Western countries, as Table 2 shows.

Table 2

PROPORTION OF PEOPLE AGED 65 AND OVER IN TOTAL POPULATION

Country	1900 %	1950 %	1960 %
U.S.A.	4	8·1	9·3
United Kingdom	5·3	10·7	11·8
France	8·4	11·4	11·8
Germany	4·9	9·2	10·9
Sweden	8·4	10·2	12·1

This table and the subsequent figures are taken from Jean Daric, 'Vieillissement de la Population. Besoins et Niveau de vie des personnes agées', published in *Population*, No. 1, Janvier-Mars 1952, Paris, and supplemented by the figures for 1960, taken from *Manpower Statistics*, O.E.C.D., Paris, 1963.

When we consider, in addition, that with rising educational standards an increasing number of young people, as well as the old, fail to contribute to the national economy, the shrinkage of the proportion of economically productive persons becomes considerable.

In view of this situation attempts are now being made to extend the working life of the population within the limits of existing legislation. Measures to keep people at work beyond the legal retiring age have recently been taken in various countries. The U.S. Department of Labor's Bureau of Employment Security, for instance, has inaugurated a specialized employment programme for older workers which is based on the findings of a survey of job problems of 342,000 older workers in five States. It has published a guide to local employment offices providing for specialized assistance in advising and placing older people.[1]

In Great Britain people who stay on in their jobs after the retirement age qualify for a bigger pension. The Ministry of Labour, like its American counterpart, is trying to encourage the employment of older people. An example is to be set by the Civil Service. In February 1952 the Chancellor of the Exchequer announced in Parliament the general aim to employ all Civil Servants for as long as is practicable. This means that, in fact, the statutory

[1] Cf. also Stephen Grieur, *Job Re-Design*, O.E.C.D., Paris, 1964.

retiring age has been abolished in the Civil Service. It is note-worthy that this decision was taken at a time when it was proposed to reduce manpower in the Civil Service by 10,000 within the next six months in view of the financial and economic situation. Some first steps were also taken, e.g. by the General Post Office and later in other branches of the Civil Service, to raise the upper age limit for recruiting.

To prolong the active period of life is one way of dealing with the problems raised by an ageing population. It may also con-tribute towards a solution of many economic and psychological problems of old age. Chiefly, however, it is an attempt to increase productivity by enlisting the services of superannuated people.

Old people are, however, by no means the only labour reserve available. Women constitute another one, for they have long 'under-productive' periods in their lives.

It was stated in the previous chapter that women's life is still geared to a role which can no longer be their only one. However perfectly a woman fits into the part of a devoted mother at a certain time, she cannot continue to act it for ever. Whereas fifty years ago a woman spent on the average fifteen years of a con-siderably shorter life in actual child-bearing and nursing of babies, the corresponding average is three-and-a-half years to-day. Assum-ing she marries at the age of 22, this represents only 6–7 per cent of the remaining years of her life. The family function of women, for which, according to the old rules, women 'were set aside', has diminished radically.

The Smaller Family

First, and most conspicuously, the size of their families has been reduced. While in the Victorian era six, eight, or more, children (and still more births) in a family were by no means a rare occurrence, the average being 5·8 to women married in 1870, only one married woman in three has more than two children to-day, the average being 2·5 to women married in 1920. These are British figures.

In Sweden, of all married women of working age (i.e. under 65) only 10·4 per cent have three or more children under the age of 16, according to the census of 1960. Over one quarter of all married couples have no children under 16, and an additional 25·3 per

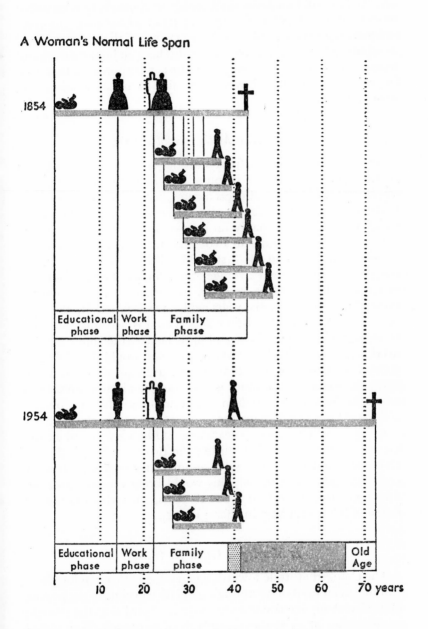

A Woman's Normal Life Span

1854

Educational phase | Work phase | Family phase

1954

Educational phase | Work phase | Family phase | Old Age

10   20   30   40   50   60   70 years

cent have no children under the age of 7. If women may be regarded as free from child care if they have no children under 15 years of age living at home, no less than 71 per cent of all women counted as adults are 'free' in this sense. As this takes in both married and unmarried women, one might venture an approximation that three-quarters of all adult women are free from actual occupation with children.

How long is a Mother needed at Home?

Any argument derived from statistics is open to the criticism that it ignores the wide variation of individual situations. Bearing this in mind, let us nevertheless assume, with all due reservations, that the families of the future may arrive at an average of three children (which is probably an over-optimistic assessment, since the present ratio is closer to two) and, further, that the interval between marriage and the first child will be two years (which is longer than the present average) and, finally, that the interval between children will be, roughly, two years. At the birth of the third child, therefore, six years will have elapsed. If, then, we take it that continued full-time supervision is necessary until the youngest child reaches the age of 9, this makes the active motherhood period 15 years. Our 'average woman' would then be about 40 (i.e. assuming, over-generously, an average marriage age of 25), and would have another 35 years of life ahead of her. Some may consider that the children would need her until the youngest child is 15; this would bring the mother's age to 46 before the new era begins, with another 28 years to go. Others may consider that she need not give up work during the two years before the first child and that she could well resume outside work when the youngest child starts school; this would bring the period of full-time motherhood down to about 10 years, after which her expectation of life would be a further 40 years.

Is Marriage a Career for Women?

The changed attitude towards ageing, the increase in longevity, and the social need of stemming the relative decline of the population of working age combine to make it absurd that the youthful grandmother of 45 to-day should, in perpetuation of an out-of-date pattern, feel that she is entitled to rest on her laurels for the rest of her life like her grandmother who, at that age, had brought up at least half a dozen children and was prepared to settle down to old age. Modern mothers who make no plans outside the family for their future will not only play havoc with their own lives but will make nervous wrecks of their overprotected children and of their husbands.

Another cliché in public thinking which has kept company with the previous one, and which is equally false, gets recurrent publicity in newspaper headlines such as:

CAREER OR MARRIAGE?
FILM STAR GIVES UP FAME AND $100,000 A YEAR

with the rider: 'When it comes to a choice a woman will always decide on a home.' The idea that being in love is a full-time occupation has, of course, a great romantic appeal, but it perpetuates a false dilemma. Marriage is a civil and legal state in which a certain division of functions has been an accepted norm. At its best, it means love and companionship and a sharing of life's pleasures and sorrows—a state of affectionate partnership rather than a time-consuming drudgery or a 'job'. Running a home is an occupation incidental rather than essential to the state of being married. After all, it is done also by many unmarried women as well as by and for bachelors.

The organization of a home, and the division of labour within it, are matters dependent on existing facilities, on personal arrangements and on convenience. Having small children certainly is a full-time job, but this, as we have said before, takes up a relatively short and transient phase in a woman's life. To identify this phase with the married state as such is an error of thinking for which society, and men in particular, pay dearly. It has led to the establishment of a social pattern in which men are to 'provide' for women and women are 'to be provided for'.

The Changed Structure of the Family

Moreover, the structure as well as the size of the family has considerably changed during the last few generations. There are no longer maiden aunts and grandmothers living within the close circle of the family, and the separation of generations has become a generally accepted pattern. Daughters as well as sons leave the parental home as soon as they grow up, either when they go to college, or in order to take up jobs elsewhere, or merely because independence is high in our scale of social values.

We cannot here explore the cobweb of cultural mores and psychological attitudes which this has created, although it is of great sociological interest, but certain aspects are relevant and will be discussed.

Matrimonial Uncertainties

In the figures on longevity at the beginning of this chapter, we saw that women have a longer average expectation of life than men. The numerical preponderance of women in most countries is largely due to their lower mortality rate, for in general rather more baby boys are born than girls. Thus in younger age groups the proportion of men and women is more or less equal, but women as they grow older increasingly outnumber men, the ratio passing 2:1 at extreme ages. This means that the number of women who survive their husbands is considerable. If we make further allowance for the fact that, as a rule, men are two or more years older than their wives, the unavoidable conclusion is that many women have to face years of widowhood without either a provider or an object for their wholehearted attention. This eventuality may be too unpleasant to envisage at the outset of adult life, when plans for the future are made, but it is a contingency that should be taken into account.

In addition, an increasing number of marriages break up by divorce, separation, or desertion. In England, which has a conservative divorce legislation, the ratio of divorces to new marriages is roughly one to eleven (1963), or 0.6 per thousand of the population. Divorce rates in France are about the same; in the U.S.A. they are nearly four times as high (2.26 per 1000 of the population in 1961). In Sweden, there is one divorce per six new marriages (1964), or 1.2 per 1000 of the population.

In addition, the economic instability of our time renders it more than desirable that women should be able to stand on their own feet and earn their living. No longer is it true, as in Jane Austen's days, that 'marriage was the only honourable provision for well-educated young women of small fortune and, however uncertain of giving happiness, must be their pleasantest preservation from want'. To-day, matrimony is no more a guarantee of 'preservation from want' than it ever was a guarantee of happiness.

Fortunately, there are now many other 'honourable provisions' available for well-educated young women of whatever 'fortune' or class, even though the chances of 'happiness' still largely lie in the same sphere as before. But this is, after all, not a particularly feminine characteristic.

There are, then, at least three different factors which call for a re-definition of women's role in society: First, the considerable increase in the average life-span; secondly, the reduction of the period entirely devoted to maternal duties; and thirdly, the factors of uncertainty relating to the later, and possibly lonely, years of married life.

CHAPTER THREE

THE PHASES OF A LIFE-SPAN

Some of our readers may object that our attitude to life, and to women's life in particular, is too utilitarian. Why are you trying, they may ask, to press-gang women into jobs? Why this puritanical attitude towards work as the soul's salvation? Would it not be better to preserve, as long as possible, the vestiges of a leisured group, or at least a category of people who are able to arrange things in their own time, to do the many odd and unremunerative jobs that need doing, and to enjoy what is really worth-while in life, friendships and books and art?

To such readers we would like to say two things: Firstly, our modern economy cannot afford, nor can our democratic ideology tolerate, the existence of a large section of the population living by the efforts of others. Whether we like it or not, the leisured class has passed into history, together with the coach-and-four, the home-brewed ale, and other symbols of the 'good old times'. The gentleman of leisure, who spent his time travelling, educating himself, and enjoying the good things in life has disappeared, and the lady of leisure is bound to follow. With changed technical means our social aims, too, have altered. If we want to live in a fairly just, fairly rational society; if we want the living standard of our population to improve and its children be educated; if we want to free old age from the anxieties of dire poverty—we shall all have to contribute according to our best ability.

Secondly, far from preaching a gospel of hard work, we hope for increased leisure so that more people may have a share in the 'good life'. Leisure must, however, be understood in its true function: as a period of rest and re-creation within a full life.

We, too, like our critical reader, want to live in a world in which people are, first of all, human beings and not only 'good citizens'. We, too, abhor the ant-hill State in which the value of a person is assessed only in terms of his, or her, share in the fulfilment of a predetermined plan of production. We hold that a life of nothing but work would be too dull to be worth living.

THE PHASES OF A LIFE-SPAN

Home and Work—Two Worlds?

It is for this reason that we have become convinced that a fairer re-distribution of work and leisure between the sexes is necessary, as has already begun between different social classes. If men and women are to live in one world, as they are to live harmoniously within one home and one family, their share in the rhythm of activity and rest, and their centres of interests and enjoyments, must become more evenly balanced than they are now. It cannot be healthy to join together in a life-long partnership two human beings whose lives run at such an unequal pace and whose interests are in fields as far apart as has become customary in our society during this last century or so.

The fact that so many women—mainly unmarried women— have entered the 'masculine' sphere of work may have helped to gloss over the true state of affairs; but it is no exaggeration to say that the cleavage between the two worlds of job and home is, for the majority of people, more complete to-day than it ever was in the past. Work and home are separated not only locally, sometimes by many miles, but in atmosphere, interests, speed and intensity of life. How many children have the faintest idea, or can imagine, how their fathers spend the greatest part of their waking hours? Moving from factory or office to his dormitory suburb man changes as from one planet to another. He is awaited by a wife whose life is geared to an entirely different rhythm. Their home, which they ideally share, has become almost exclusively her domain and their children are chiefly her responsibility.

Yet, marriage, home life, and children, ought to be enjoyed by men and women together. Nobody—and least of all the child— is served by the present tendency to put these things all on one side as 'Woman's World'.

Those who oppose the extension of married women's work outside their homes in the name of tradition, have fixed their eyes on one phase in our social history, namely the nineteenth century. Such traditionalists would be well advised to look a bit further back to a time when there was a more stable equilibrium between the demands of the community and the needs of the individual. In those days of more harmoniously integrated families work and leisure were shared much more evenly between men and women, between parents and children, between young and old. The

27

companionship thus provided and the smoother transition from one age-group to another is something very different from to-day's pattern, with its separate compartments for husband and wife and for each generation. This more recent pattern has caused so much tension that it is well worth asking whether we could not recapture in new forms some of the valuable features of the old way of life.

Once upon a time the family was the natural environment for both men and women. Husband and wife took part in the education of their children; each shared the other's worries and successes, and all carried their respective share in the joint load of work, even though that share differed between the individual members of the family according to their strength and ability. Probably, very great cultural values were lost when that partnership was broken up. Most certainly we have not again found any similarly balanced way of life.

It should, however, be noted that it was the partnership of men and women which created that equilibrium. There is no use in lamenting the loss to-day, but there is perhaps even less use in raising romantic hopes that women could create that richness of life if left alone to guard the remaining tokens of the old-time atmosphere. Those who assert that home-making is women's exclusive role commit the fallacy of leaving women alone to do a thing which should be done jointly by men and women if the ideal of a happy home is to become a reality.

Many people instinctively feel this to be true. The fact that an increasing number of men use their leisure time for hobbies which allow them to make a constructive contribution to their homes is evidence for it. In the most highly mechanized country of the world, the United States, more people than ever spend their spare time as amateur painters, carpenters, paper-hangers, gardeners, etc. No doubt, the high cost of skilled labour accounts for this to a large extent. But, apart from this financial incentive, most men positively enjoy these creative hobbies; not only as a counterpoise to their routine or sedentary occupations but because it establishes their share in the 'nest-building' activities of their wives and creates between them a unity of purpose which was largely lost when the functions of husband and wife were strictly divided almost to the exclusion of the man from the home.

A comparison with old times brings to light yet another disparity between the lives of men and women to-day. Under pre-industrial conditions, labour and leisure were not as definitely separated as they are now. Children were soothed with fairy tales while hands were busy on the loom. The father cutting the hay could take time off to teach his son to put pins into the rake or to distinguish the songs of different birds. Certainly, the nights were set aside for sleep and rest, but this was broken when a cow was about to calve. This gliding from one occupation to another, from work to play and back again, is totally foreign to the industrial world. It is, however, still typical of the home milieu. It is this fact which makes illusory all attempts of measuring housework in terms of 'women-hours'. It also gives rise to unfair comparisons between the work-load of housewives and others whose work is subject to a controlled and time-studied forty-eight hours week— a comparison which usually results in discontent on both sides. Again, it is only in hobbies that men—and, of course, also women who earn their living—can take part in this pre-industrial mixture of work and leisure, of which it would be impossible to say where the one begins and the other ends.

The Specialization of Age Groups

An important characteristic of life in contemporary society seems to have gone almost unnoticed: the division of life into more or less clearly defined phases. Specialization, now characteristic of all sectors of society, takes place also within the lifetime of each individual and separates one period from another. In each of them he assumes a different social role, and they may be termed educational, working or 'retired' phases.

In pre-industrial times not only was there less division of labour between one individual and another, but also the different periods in the life-time of one person were less clearly marked off from each other by special social functions. Youth was not as definitely as now set aside for education; old-age was not as distinctly as now regarded as a period of rest.

Women's lives, too, ran along a straighter course. Household duties and a comprehensive scheme of domestic activities filled many of their hours while they were still children. Training itself belonged to the home. Married life was a continuation on a more responsible level of the life they had been used to in their parents' homes, with the addition, of course, of child-bearing. Finally, death came, as often as not in the fullness of their lives, not long after their children had stopped clamouring for their attention and certainly very rarely at such a late age that they could not be useful, in one way or another, in the chores of their homes.

The pattern of life of unmarried women was not very different. According to prevailing custom the household was the natural frame for their activities, too, be it the home of their parents or of one of their relatives.

Now, functionally different phases have been added at either end of a normal working life. The problems posed thereby have, so far, received little attention. While the distribution of labour has been investigated extensively, the distribution of energy over a normal life-span, and the questions arising from it, have been given relatively little thought. True, there are special sections within the sciences of psychology and sociology solely devoted to the study of problems associated with the period of education. The introduction of old-age pensions and the setting of age-limits for various jobs have, in their turn, created problems of adjustment, sociological and psychological as well as economic, many of which have been the objects of *ad hoc* investigations. We have a new science, gerontology, devoted to the problems, medical, psychological, and sociological, of old people. Yet, so far, social psychology has not dealt with the more general question of time sequences in human life; more especially, it has paid no attention to what we might call the psychology of 'non-participation'. This would, in many respects, be a rewarding subject for investigation. Among others, it might throw a new light on some aspects of feminine psychology.

It is time, too, for systematic studies of the way in which the social changes aforementioned have affected men and women differently and caused so great a divergence between their ways of life. This gulf has only recently begun to be bridged—a development which is a healthy sign of regeneration and, as such, most welcome.

The Chronology of Women's Lives presents a Special Problem

The occupations of women are of course specialized in the same way as those of men; their youth has been freed from chores in favour of education, and their old age spared the duties of productive work. But, in addition to this, the central, adult period of their lives is split into two entirely different phases by the cleavage which now exists between the style of life of single and married women. For a varying number of years preceding marriage women are now prepared for, and conditioned to, a way of life which is in marked contrast to the existence most of them are likely to lead later on. A minority of them continue in this first phase throughout their lives. The vast majority, however, experience a complete change of social role.

(*a*) FIRST PHASE OF ADULTHOOD. Between school-leaving and marrying most women pass through a phase which lasts for five to seven years on the average in the European countries, rather less in the United States, in which they earn their own living. As many as 82 per cent of all single women between the ages of 15 and 60 in England are gainfully employed. The comparative percentages in the U.S.A. are 51 per cent (where the average age for first marriages is 20·8 compared with 22·1 in Great Britain, and where, moreover, school-leaving age in most States is considerably higher, namely 18, the interval between school-leaving and marriage thus being much shorter in the U.S.), in Sweden 75·9 (average marrying age of single women 26·1) and in France 65·2 (average age for first marriages 22·9).

This period has undoubtedly an important formative influence on their personalities. At this time they are colleagues of men. Being in contact with the activities of their community, they become members of societies and reach political maturity—all in the same way as their fellow workers of the other sex. They gain leisure in exchange for their labour, and they get used to spending it freely, without much more parental supervision than grown-up boys. They also earn an independent income and develop their habits of spending it themselves.

It is for this period of their lives, as a rule, that women receive their higher education and acquire their technical skills or professional training if they do. From society's point of view this means a considerable investment even though women have, to this day, made comparatively little inroad into the places of higher learning in most countries. Table 3 on the following page illustrates this.

While on primary and secondary school level the enrolment of boys and girls is roughly equal, in higher education and most types of vocational training the percentage of girls is still much lower, although, compared with the figures given in Table 3, the proportion of women has increased in recent years. Among the entrants to college in the United States in 1962 there were 42 per cent women; among those gaining a B.A., M.A., or first professional degree, however, women were only one-third at the same period. In England and Wales, according to the Robbins Report, women

Table 3

PERCENTAGE OF WOMEN STUDENTS IN HIGHER EDUCATION, 1953 AND 1937

	Percentage of Females in total number of students, 1952/53	Percentage of Females in total number of students, 1937
U.S.A.*	35	40
Great Britain	24	22
France	36	29
Sweden	26	17

* The relative decline of the proportion of women students in higher education, in comparison with 1937, is due to the post-war veterans' enrolment scheme.
Source: UNESCO Statistical Division.

were 40 per cent of the entrants to full-time higher education in 1961; if all types of higher education were taken together, however, including part-time and private study, women were only 25·5 per cent of the entrants during the same year. In France, the proportion of women among the total number of students rose to 40 per cent in 1960, in Sweden to 35 per cent in 1962/63 (and was estimated to be 38 per cent in 1965/66).

After completing their education a period of employment follows for practically all girls. That women should enter the world of employment is to-day taken for granted, as a rule, and their rights to do most jobs are hardly queried. Their segregation in unskilled domestic work, either in their parents' or somebody else's home, is already a thing of the past. To-day most of them are becoming vocationally trained and financially self-supporting.

Economically speaking, girls before marriage live a man's life, though they are often handicapped by inequality of reward and by the still more important lack of opportunity of real advancement. Most of them can as yet hardly be called 'career women', since careers are still largely the prerogative of men. But then—and this really is the crux of the matter—most girls have no intention of carrying on in a vocation throughout their lifetime.

(*b*) SECOND PHASE OF ADULTHOOD. After a period of employment the road forks. The group of women that continues as wage-earners is composed, mainly, of women who do not marry. Their number has been shrinking since the war.

The census figures give only a poor indication of how many women marry, since they show the distribution of all women into single and married from the age of 14 or 15 onward, thus including age groups below the normal marriage age and thereby weighting the scales heavily on the side of the single women. Nevertheless, as an indication of how many women above school-leaving age are unmarried, they may be quoted here:

Table 4

PERCENTAGE OF FEMALE POPULATION AGED 15 AND OVER BY MARITAL STATUS

	England & Wales (1961)	U.S.A. (1960)	Sweden (1960)	France (1962)
Single	21·8	19·1	27·7	22·4
Married	64·4	65·9	65·2	59·3
Widowed	13·0	}15·0	}7·1	16·3
Divorced	0·9			2·0

A clearer picture of the marriage ratio may be gained from the Report of the Royal Commission on Population which estimated that in 1947 83·5 per cent of all women aged 45–54 in Great Britain were, or had been, married.

Starting their adult lives on the labour market the majority retire from it to set up a family. The contemporary feminine problem is not—as it is sometimes represented—that married women want to break loose in order to have a career; the question is rather whether or not working women are to abandon their employment for work in the home. This situation has led Swedish feminists to turn the age-worn campaign slogan about 'married women's right to work' into 'working women's right to marry'.

Nobody will dispute them this right. Nor their right—which

some people even regard as a duty to society—to set up, and look after, a family.

The point seriously to be considered, however, is the question: for how long, out of the 50 years of an average married life, are domestic responsibilities a full-time occupation?

It is of course true that most women, once they are married, regard home as their job, and take on themselves all of it, from the drudgery to the more or less necessary embellishments.

Those who see home-making as their career, in the traditional manner, are unlikely to agree that it is only the period of 'active motherhood' which calls for their presence in the home. What are the facts, as far as they can be measured, concerning the time consumed by housework?

Working Hours of Housewives

A leading Swedish expert on the rationalization of management, Tarras Saellfors, made the rather horrifying calculation that 2,340 million working hours are spent annually in Sweden on shopping, cooking and washing-up, while, by comparison, Swedish industry uses only 1,290 million hours. On washing-up alone, one of the least edifying or productive domestic activities, one and a half million hours are spent per day. On this scale, it is easy to see the enormous effect rationalization of housework would achieve.

Among the many studies that exist on the working hours of housewives, most, unfortunately, do not distinguish between the 'active motherhood period' and the other years. Still less do they discriminate between really necessary work and work that is less so; this, of course, is a very difficult distinction to make. It could be argued, too, that since the housewife would not be using on other productive work any time saved in the home, many labour-consuming jobs might as well be done there, although they could be done more economically, and at least as satisfactorily, elsewhere.

The most interesting investigation, from our point of view, of the working hours of housewives was carried out by the French 'Institut national d'études démographiques' in 1947.[1] It was made with the intention of finding out the cost to mothers, in terms of women-hours, of rearing a family. It is of special interest to us, firstly, because it differentiates between the working week of child-

---

[1] Jean Stoetzel; 'Une étude du budget-temps de la femme dans les agglomérations urbaines,' in *Population*, Paris, 1948, No. 1.

less married women and that of mothers of one, two, three or more children and, secondly, because it compares the hours spent on housework by full-time housewives with those of married women who go out to work. The research involved 1795 married women below the age of 47 in French towns of over 5,000 inhabitants.

According to this study the working week of married women varied from 47 to 74 hours depending on the number of children. The average number of hours spent on household activities, including also the time contributed by paid domestic helpers and members of the family, where available, was 61 hours in childless homes. One child adds 18 hours to this total, two children add 28 hours, three or more children mean 39 additional hours per week.

Married women who go out to work reduce their domestic activities by 10 hours per week if they are childless, and by up to 30 hours per week if they have children, compared with full-time housewives in the corresponding categories. M. Stoetzel compares the working hours of full-time housewives and of married women in employment in the following table:

Table 5

WORKING WEEK OF MARRIED WOMEN WITH AND WITHOUT OUTSIDE
EMPLOYMENT IN FRENCH CITIES

| | | Hours per week | | |
		spent in housework	spent in job	Total
0 child	full-time housewives	56·0		56·0
	married women with jobs	45·5	39·1	84·6
1 child	full-time housewives	73·5		73·5
	married women with jobs	44·1	38·0	82·1
2 children	full-time housewives	72·8		72·8
	married women with jobs	46·2	35·2	81·4
3 and more children	full-time housewives	77·7		77·7
	married women with jobs	48·3	35·2	83·5

Source: *Population*, 1948, No. 1.

The most interesting deduction from this table is that the more than 80-hour week of the married women in employment exceeds the working week of a full-time housewife with children by only 6 to 8 hours per week, i.e. by roughly one hour per day. In terms of productivity this daily extra hour achieves results which are out of proportion to the exertions it involves.

Among authoritative investigations in the United States one of the better known studies is the Bryn Mawr report: *Women during the War and After* (1945).

Dividing families into four typical groups this study records that housekeeping activities consumed, per household:

60·55 hours per week in farm families,
64·09 hours in non-farm rural households,
78·35 in urban households of cities under 100,000 inhabitants,
and 80·57 in households in cities of over 100,000 inhabitants.

Contrary to common-sense expectations, the time spent on domestic activities is considerably larger in city households than in the country, in spite of the far greater amenities available to the urban housewife. This is partly accounted for by the fact that cities are dirtier, and more time is therefore consumed in cleaning and laundering, and partly because more rooms are normally used. More time is also spent on shopping and looking after children. Significantly, the report observes: 'As living standards grow higher and more appliances and services enter the home, women tend to spend more time on home activity.'

According to a British Mass Observation survey (1951) suburban working-class housewives in London spend an average of 71 hours a week on domestic activities, the largest share of which is taken up in connexion with meals, which absorb one quarter of their working day. This estimate is rather generous in that it includes, under the general heading 'meal-time activities', time spent on consuming as well as on preparing meals, and it also counts time spent on personal toilet among 'domestic activities'; neither of these would be included in a similar record of a man's, or an office girl's, working day. Nevertheless, it is still true to say that the housewife's job—though proceeding at a more leisurely pace— is more time-consuming than most other work and that, as the report says, 'by comparison, the rigours of office or factory life provide escape into and contact with an outside world which, because it is largely denied the woman in the home, possesses for her all the charm and mystery of the unattainable'.

Be it then accepted as a fact that housewives with children spend an average of at least 60 hours, often more, per week on domestic chores of various kinds. The question still remains whether all this amount of work is really necessary or whether, given better planning, both on the individual and on the social level, the number of hours could not be considerably reduced without damage to the home.

Though lamenting it, most housewives are, fundamentally, proud to say that 'a woman's work is never done'. But most work is 'never done'—unless one puts a full stop to it at some point. The clerk who leaves his desk, the shopkeeper who pulls down his shutters, the worker who downs his tools at the end of an eight-hour day have, as a rule, also not completed their work. They break off and adjourn for the next day. This discipline is, of course, much easier to maintain if home and workplace are separated and the unfinished work is not kept under one's eyes. The claim for an eight-hour day only arose after the Industrial Revolution and could not have occurred under a system in which workshop and home were one. It still does not apply to free-lance workers, artists, doctors, and many one-man businesses.

Housewives, whose home is identical with their workshop, are in this as in many other respects still in the pre-industrial phase. The situation is, however, complicated by the fact that they live in a world in which most other work is done in eight-hour shifts and in a five to five-and-a-half day working week, and where leisure activities are organized on that basis. No wonder therefore that they have a sense of grievance, particularly as some of the top-load of their work falls into periods which are the leisure time of people with more regulated working hours.

The fact that modern labour saving devices have tended to raise the standards of housekeeping rather than to reduce the time spent on it seems to support the view that the problem of 'household drudgery' is a psychological one, at least in part. Domestic work is expandable to an almost unlimited degree and there is sufficient evidence to justify the suspicion that housewives often unconsciously expand it in order to allay their feelings of frustration by providing evidence that they are fully occupied and indispensable.

(c) THIRD PHASE OF ADULTHOOD. Psychologically, as well as economically, the most important question is: what happens when women in their forties reach the stage which, to most of them, means 'retirement' from active motherhood? By that time their children will have grown up sufficiently not to need their full attention any longer and will in many cases have left home.

Perhaps only the statistically minded have noted the paradox that in an era when women have managed to preserve their youth and health longer than ever before, they should at the same time expect to 'retire' so much earlier.

The state of reduced participation is normally not felt as retirement by the women themselves. There is no abrupt break of habit, no discontinuity of occupation, only a generally reduced pressure of work, a barely perceptible shift of emphasis from one kind of domestic activity to another—less darning and cooking but more knitting, as it were.

Nevertheless, many women pass through a phase of acute emotional crisis when they reach the point at which their children have become independent. Their husbands, after long years of marriage, and used to a mere share of their wives' attention, are no longer fit to hold the stage single-handed in the full lime-light of wifely devotion. Margaret Mead has given a lurid description of this situation:[1] 'Some day, while she is still a young woman, she will have to face a breakfast table with only one face across it, her husband's, and she will be alone, quite alone, in a home of their own. She is out of a job; her main justification, the work for which she "gave up everything", is gone, and yet there are still two, possibly three, meals a day to get, the door to be answered, the house to be cleaned. But there are only dishes for two and floors do not need to be polished so often when there are no children's feet to track them up. She isn't completely out of a job, but she is on the shelf, kicked upstairs, given one of the placebos by which large organizations, whose employees have tenure, try to disguise from the employee who is still too young to be retired the fact that he ought to be.'

Under such circumstances not a few women are seized by a feeling of emptiness and lack of purpose, to which they react in different ways according to temperament and disposition. Whether they become nagging and discontented, whether they have a nervous breakdown, or whether they find an outlet in playing bridge or golf, in 'visiting' and shopping, or in devoting their energies to local charities or, in rare cases, to politics or artistic creation—the basic motive underlying these and other variations is that, in the middle of their lives, in full possession of their powers, they have come to the end of their chosen career.

[1] Margaret Mead, *Male and Female*, London and New York, 1949, pp. 332–8.

THE PHASES OF A LIFE-SPAN

Starting afresh at Forty

For a fresh start at 40 many women think themselves too old. Several social factors militate against the idea of beginning a new career at that stage of life. Foremost among them are lack of adequate opportunities, or want of suitable professional training, and of facilities for 're-training ex-service mothers', as Margaret Cole has called it. In addition, there still exists a social prejudice, particularly in smaller communities, which inflicts a loss of caste on the working woman and her family. Finally, the traditional stereotype is still at work in the minds of women themselves, making them believe that they are much older and much less capable than they in fact are.

Personal or national emergencies, however, tend to overrule all these factors. The loss of their husbands, economic crises, pressure of manpower shortage, or political upheavals have turned innumerable 'middle-aged' married women, with or without previous training, into breadwinners during what we have called their 'third phase' of adulthood.

Women who had long ago given up their jobs, felt, under the compulsion of war, that they ought to place their past experience at the service of their country. Others who had never received a professional training felt nevertheless that their energy and intelligence could be put to use in the war effort. Among the many thousands of refugees whom Nazi persecution scattered all over the world it was usually the women who proved more adaptable to the new situation than the men. Many a middle-class woman of over 40 who had never in her life done any outside work learned a new trade or skill and good-humouredly supported not only herself but also her husband who, uprooted from his career and milieu, could not so easily find his feet again under the changed conditions.

Employment statistics show that the percentage of widows and divorced women in the labour force is substantially higher than that of married women in employment. This fact alone is sufficient evidence to show that, national calamities apart, many women have to start earning their living later in life driven by circumstances beyond their control and contrary to their expectations.

As can be seen from all these examples, the return of married women to the labour market later in life has been possible under

abnormal circumstances. It has occurred frequently and successfully in spite of haphazard improvisations.

If it can be done in case of emergency why, it may well be asked,
not prepare for it? Why do we have to wait until Fate catches us
unawares?

These and similar practical considerations have in recent years
begun to carry increasing weight with the younger generation of
women—even if the majority still tends to think in terms of current
prospects rather than long-term plans.

However, some important new factors have entered the situation. First and foremost among these are (1) shortages in all industrial countries of highly-trained personnel, especially in service
occupations; and (2) the fact that acquiring a skill brings immediate rewards in the shape of higher income, increased status and
better chances of upward mobility.

Consequently—and because of a growing general belief in
'equality of educational opportunity'—increasing numbers of
young women train for professional and semi-professional occupations, irrespective of whether or not they think of adopting a
'career'.

Their training not only provides them with a better chance of
finding a suitable and interesting employment in later years if they
so wish (unpremeditated though these results may be), it also
creates in very many of them the urge not to let their acquired
skills go to waste.

The last decade has therefore been characterized by the ever-
increasing return to employment of married women aged forty
and over, especially in 'white-collar' occupations. This development is likely to continue and to be cumulative as larger generations of trained women mature and traditional prejudices—already
on the wane—eventually break down.

CHAPTER FOUR

WOMEN IN THE LABOUR FORCE TO-DAY

If the moral we were trying to point in Chapter 2 may briefly be summarized in the one sentence, 'Women are wanted', the moral of Chapter 3, correspondingly, is 'Women are available'. But, of course, a good many of them are already at work and have been so for a long time.

The industrial employment of women, including married women, was a fairly widespread phenomenon in the nineteenth century. To-day, with rising wages and standards of living, fewer working-class women have to go out to work after marriage merely to earn a subsistence minimum for themselves and their families. Yet the number of women in skilled occupations, and of married women staying on in their jobs without being forced to do so by economic necessity, is increasing. Jointly, these two processes have tended to keep the actual proportion of women in the labour force more nearly constant than might have been expected. However, the latter development is of fairly recent growth and can be taken to indicate the direction in which the employment of women is likely to move.

What is the present situation in the field of feminine employment? Even in baldly quantitative terms, a survey of social developments in a few Western countries reveals significant national differences from which useful lessons can be drawn.

Readers who are bored by statistics would do best to skip this chapter. However, those who want to look at facts dispassionately may find both the similarities and the differences in the development and structure of female employment in the various countries to be worth closer scrutiny.

The Hazard of International Comparisons

The attempt to compare social data from different countries is beset with a number of difficulties. Each country has a different method of compiling statistics and, moreover, the latest dates for

WOMEN'S TWO ROLES

COMPOSITION OF THE FEMALE LABOUR FORCE BY MARITAL STATUS
IN FOUR COUNTRIES

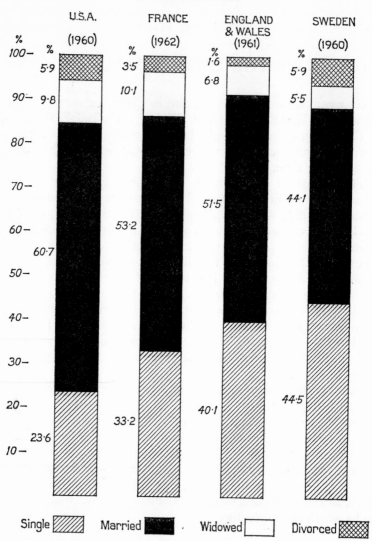

Source: *U.N. Demographic Yearbook,* 1964.

which figures are available vary considerably from one country to another. In these times of rapid change data compiled at four or five years' interval are not strictly speaking comparable, but such figures often have to be put side by side for lack of more closely corresponding ones.

A few examples may serve to illustrate various difficulties in finding common denominators:

British and American data count, under the heading 'percentage of women in employment' only those of working age, which is 15–60 and 15–65, respectively. French returns usually give the employment rate of women either as percentage of women of *all* ages from birth to death—in which case the proportion working is incomparably low (22 per cent)—or else as a percentage of all women from 14 years upwards without upper age limit.

A fairer picture of the proportion of women employed in France is obtained by comparing the number of working women with the total *working* population instead of the total *female* population. Then the participation of women will be found to be very much higher, namely as much as 35 per cent of the working population.

This figure, however, is again not comparable with American, British, or Swedish data since it does not include the relatively high percentage of women in French agriculture. While other countries do not, normally, discriminate between agricultural and other work in their total employment records, such discrimination has become necessary in France because all farmers' wives are automatically counted as employed under the heading of 'chefs d'établissements'. Though a very large proportion of them do, of course, actually work on the land, it has been thought fairer to treat them as a category apart and to include in the labour returns only the women in non-agricultural occupations actually registered as employed.

However, keeping all these reservations in mind, it is nevertheless possible to make cautious comparisons of the employment situation in various countries based on their census and labour returns.

Contrasting Developments

The present employment position of women is not very different in the four countries we are dealing with. With minor variations women to-day form roughly one third of the total labour force in each of them. The historical development and traditions, however, are different in each country. This can be seen from the following graph which shows the long-term trend at ten-year intervals from the turn of the century onward.

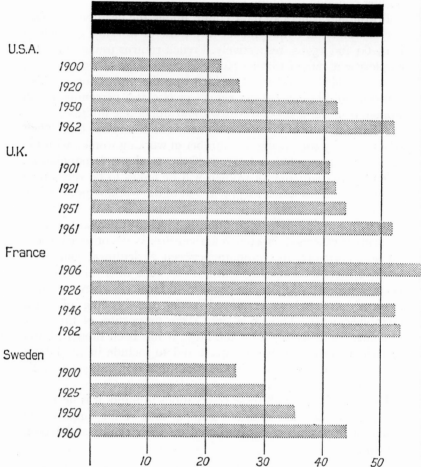

Women in the Labour Force
per 100 working men

The two extreme examples are France on the one hand, and the United States on the other hand. Whereas in France women have continuously formed just over one-third of the working population ever since the first census was taken, in the United States there has been a steady rise (disregarding temporary fluctuations) in the proportion of women in the labour force, albeit starting at a much lower point (15 per cent in 1870 rising to 32 per cent in 1960). The development in Sweden is similar, where, with the exception of a decline during the war and immediate post-war years, the proportion of women in the labour force rose from 27·4 per cent in 1930 to 30·2 per cent in 1960, and, according to the latest labour statistics, was as high as 38 per cent in 1965.

The long tradition of gainful employment among French women is a well-known fact, and we expect to see that the proportion of women in the French labour force has been high and stable for many decades. It will, however, surprise many people to see that in Britain, too, female employment has been fairly constant, though at a somewhat lower level than in France. Here the constant and fairly high employment rate of women seems to be due to the early industrialization which drew large numbers of women into the mills and factories. It is generally assumed that many more women are working in Britain to-day than did in the past chiefly because the phenomenon of the unmarried daughter sitting at home waiting for a husband has disappeared.

But this particular change applies to the middle classes, and though the middle-class girls of the nineteenth century form the subject of many novels, their number in the whole population was relatively small. Since their modern counterparts are employed (often in highly skilled and responsible jobs) one might expect a steep rise in the proportion of women at work to-day. That this proportion has, in fact, not greatly increased is clearly shown in the above graph. The false impression is due to the growth of the middle classes, which now include large strata of society that previously did not belong to them.

France

STRUCTURE AND COMPOSITION OF THE FEMALE LABOUR FORCE. As mentioned before, women in France have at all times formed a considerable proportion of the labour force. With only minor variations, every census return since 1866 showed women forming somewhat over one-third of the working population. During this century, figures were as shown in Table 6 on the following page.

45

Table 6

WOMEN AS PROPORTION OF THE LABOUR FORCE IN FRANCE, 1906–62

1906	37·1 per cent
1926	36·6
1946	37·9
1962	33·4

The reduction between 1946 and 1962 is due to a decline of female employment in the agricultural sector. The activity rate of women in non-agricultural employment has remained more or less constant since 1906.

The structure and composition of the female labour force in France has, of course, changed in these decades despite the relative quantitative stability.

The employment rate of *all* women (i.e. the proportion of all women working) in non-agricultural occupations was 22 per cent in 1906, 21·9 per cent in 1946 and 22·1 per cent in 1962. (The comparable employment rates of women over the age of 14 was 22·1, 28·4 and 29·3, respectively.) There has, however, been a very marked decline of women working on the land, both in absolute figures and in relation to all persons in agricultural employment. This, together with the difficulties of enumerating the agricultural population, mentioned on page 43, has led to a reduction of the *overall* employment rate of women over the age of 14 from 39 per cent in 1906 to 36·3 per cent in 1962, with various fluctuations in the intervening years. Since agriculture is a field which still employs a substantial number of women in France, who are excluded from the above figures, it is clear that the participation of women in the economic life of the country is larger in France than in any other Western country.

Women engaged in agricultural occupations are, however, not afflicted in the same way by the problems typical of our industrial society and which result from the separation of home from workplace. This sector of the female working population can therefore safely be left out of account for the purposes of our study without affecting the main line of our argument.

In France, as elsewhere, there has been a steady increase in the employment of married women since World War II.

Table 7

DISTRIBUTION OF THE FEMALE LABOUR FORCE IN FRANCE BY MARITAL
STATUS, 1946, 1949 AND 1962

Per 100 working women	All occupations		
	1946	1949	1962
Single	36·8	35·7	33·2
Married	47·8	49·0	53·2
Widowed and Divorced	15·4	15·3	13·6
	100·0	100·0	100·0

Considering different age groups separately, married women
are nearly one-half of the women in employment between the ages
of 20 and 29, more than 60 per cent of all women in employment
between 30 and 39, and over one half of the women in employment
between the ages of 40 and 49.

It is an interesting fact that the proportion of married women
in employment varies only little from one social class to another.
This is shown in the following table, based on employment figures
for December 1951,[1] in which married women are classified according to their husbands' type of occupation and the number of
their children.

Table 8

PERCENTAGE OF MARRIED WOMEN EMPLOYED IN FRANCE IN 1951,
ACCORDING TO SOCIAL CLASS AND SIZE OF FAMILIES

Husband's type of work	Childless	1 child	2 children	3 or more children
	%	%	%	%
Liberal professions	33	30	20	26
Employees	31	29	17	2
Industrial workers	38	30	19	12

It may be assumed that the wives of professional men who are
employed are themselves largely professional women and it is

[1] Quoted from: M. Guilbert and V. Isambert-Jamati, 'Statut professionel et rôle
traditionnel des femmes', *Cahiers Internationaux de Sociologie*, Nouv. Série, Vol. XVII,
Paris, 1954.

remarkable to what a small extent they are influenced by the size of their families in the pursuit of their careers.

There is, in fact, a correlation between the level of education and the employment rate of women which may have a bearing on this point. In 1954, 41·4 per cent of all women between the ages of 15 and 65 with elementary education were economically active; the proportion of those who had passed the *baccalauréat*, however, (roughly comparable to an 'A Level' Certificate) was 64·6 per cent. Among university graduates, the activity rates were 77·4 per cent of those with arts degrees and 75 per cent of those with degrees in sciences and engineering; yet among women with a diploma as medical auxiliaries and social workers the proportion in employment was as high as 82·4 per cent.[1]

Table 9

CHANGES IN THE OCCUPATIONAL DISTRIBUTION OF WORKING WOMEN IN FRANCE, 1906, 1946 AND 1954

(*of 100 Women employed in Non-agricultural Occupations*)

Branch of employment	1906	1946	1954
Industry	57·7	42·3	39·4
Commerce	17·9	25·8	27·8
Liberal professions and public service	6·7	17·6	21·1
Domestic services	17·7	14·3	11·7
	100	100	100

STRUCTURAL CHANGES. Very remarkable structural changes have taken place within the non-agricultural labour force. There has been a movement away from industry and domestic service towards increased employment in commerce and the liberal professions. Whereas the proportion of women in the professions has more than doubled since 1906, and that of women in commercial occupations has, during the same period, increased by nearly one half, the proportion of women in industry has in the meantime decreased by well over one quarter, as can be seen from Table 9.

[1] Quoted from Françoise Guelaud-Leridon, *Le Travail des Femmes en France*, Institut national d'études démographiques & Commissariat général du Plan d'équipement et de la productivité, Presses Universitaires de France, 1964.—Cf. also pp. 64–5 and 74 below.

Though similar trends were noticeable during the same period in the male working population as well, the shift was much more pronounced among women. While, for instance, the proportion of women to men in industry was one to two in 1906, it was one to $3\frac{1}{2}$ in 1954. In commerce, on the other hand, the ratio of women to men has changed during the same time from roughly 1:2 to nearly equal numbers; in the liberal professions and public services the proportion of women has increased from 1:4 to 1:1·7.

Though the proportion of married women increased slightly among all categories of women in employment, the increase was most spectacular among the liberal professions and public services. They formed 22·5 per cent of all women employed in this category in 1906, 30·4 per cent in 1936, and roughly 32·5 per cent in 1946. The actual number of married women in the professions and public services has trebled since 1906.

Of 20 gainfully occupied women in France

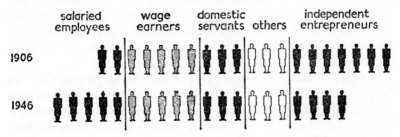

A related fact becomes evident if the employment data are grouped not according to broad professional categories but according to social status within them. Between 1906 and 1962 the number of wage-earners (*ouvrières*) was halved (from over 3 millions to $1\frac{1}{2}$ million)[1], while the number of employees rose from 344,000 to 1,403,000. The former were reduced from 35·6 per cent of all working women in 1906 to 23 per cent in 1962, while the latter rose from 3·7 per cent to 21·3 per cent. In the liberal professions no women were enumerated in 1906; now they absorb 14 per cent of the (non-agricultural) female labour force.

The increase in the salariat was effected chiefly at the expense of

---

[1] The 1906 figures apply to workers in all sectors of the economy; the 1962 figures exclude workers in agriculture.

the small independent entrepreneurs and to a certain extent also of domestic workers. The former suffered a reduction from 1,560,000 to 830,000 (or from 35·9 per cent of all working women to only 19 per cent), the latter from 759,000 to 628,000 (or from 17·4 per cent to 14·3 per cent of all working women) between 1906 and 1946[1]. Since then, the development has continued in the same direction, but owing to a new method of classifying occupational groups it is impossible to give comparable data for the period since 1946. The reduction in the number of small independent businessmen or domestic manufacturers is, of course, a feature not particularly characteristic of female work but typical of increasing industrialization.

These figures give no more than the barest outline. The main fact which emerges from them is that the gainful employment of women, regardless of structural changes in the composition of the female labour force, has a longer tradition in France than in most other Western countries, longer, in fact, than in the rest of the world. Without causing much concern, or even discussion, feminine employment in France was on a level which other countries achieved only under the stress of rearmament and labour shortages and when the emancipation of women had become an accepted fact.

To gain a fuller and more three-dimensional picture than an accumulation of statistics can provide, we must study the above data in relation to a number of sociological factors. For instance, it might well be possible to establish a connexion between the long tradition of female work in France and the special nature of the French economy in which, to this day, the small family enterprise plays a considerable part. It is, doubtless, easier for women and workplaces to adjust themselves to each other in small-scale businesses than in large, impersonal commercial or industrial enterprises.

A significant section of French industry and trade, moreover, not only employs but chiefly caters for women, or else is based on skills that are traditionally feminine. Between this fact and the large participation of women in the French economy there is cer-

---

[1] The figures quoted in this section are taken from *L'activité professionelle des femmes en France*, by Jean Daric (Paris 1947) and from 'Aperçu général de l'évolution du travail féminin en France' by the same author, published in *Avenirs*, Nos. 35-36, Paris 1951. They have been brought up to date with M. Daric's kind assistance.

tainly a causal relation, though it is by no means clear what is the cause and what is the effect.

A correlation which would also be worth detailed study is that between the high incidence of employment among women in the child-bearing age-group of 20–39 and the more closely-knit unit of the French family. Has the employment of young mothers been possible in France because they are more able than women in other countries to devolve some of their domestic and maternal duties upon their mothers and mothers-in-law? The investigation carried out by the 'Institut national d'études démographiques' from which we have quoted before (pp. 34–35) found that three-quarters of the families studied consisted of parents and children only. The remaining quarter included in-laws; and particularly in families of more children or where the mother went out to work, the grandmother was usually a very active home help.

If this is the case in towns with their necessarily restricted accommodation the proportion of families with three generations living under one roof will be considerably higher in rural areas. It is said that in Soviet Russia, too, with its very high incidence of married women in employment, grandmothers have enormously gained in importance as guardians of the domestic hearth. But in France there seems to be an unbroken line between the old type of family as an economic unit and its contemporary smaller counterpart.

The study of these and other related questions, important and fascinating as it might be, is outside the scope of this book. The problems can here only be indicated and recommended for more detailed observation to students of the family who are prepared to undertake comparative research on this institution not only in primitive societies but also in the Western world.

Great Britain

WAR-TIME EXPERIENCE. The proportion of women in employment in Britain reached its highest peak during the second world war. Out of a total of 17·25 million women between the ages of 14 and 64, about 7·3 million worked either in paid employment or were drafted into auxiliary military services. Of the 4 million women insured under the Unemployment Insurance Act, 2·2 million were married. Many mothers of young children, to the surprise of many, became part and parcel of the war effort. Nine hundred thousand women with domestic ties did part-time work and 1,000,000 women, not counted in the above total, were engaged in unpaid voluntary war work.

Mobilization in Great Britain was probably more comprehensive and thorough than in any other belligerent country, with the possible exception of Soviet Russia. In the tremendous effort to win the war every nerve was strained. Sex discrimination in

Table 10

WAR-TIME DISTRIBUTION OF MANPOWER, GREAT BRITAIN

(*Men aged 14-64, women aged 14-59, including employers, self-employed persons and employees, but excluding indoor private domestic service. Women in part-time paid employment are included, two being counted as one unit.*)

(*in thousands*)

		1939	1940	1941	1942	1943	1944	1945
Total working population		19,750	20,676	21,332	22,056	22,285	22,008	21,649
	M	14,656	15,104	15,222	15,141	15,032	14,901	14,881
	F	5,094	5,572	5,110	6,915	7,253	7,107	6,768
Civil	M	13,163	12,452	11,844	11,296	10,675	10,347	10,133
Employment	F	4,837	5,306	5,907	6,582	6,769	6,620	6,283
Armed Forces and	M	480	2,218	3,278	3,784	4,300	4,500	4,653
Auxil. Services	F	—	55	105	307	461	467	437
Unemployed	M	1,013	434	100	61	44	40	68
(Registered)	F	257	211	98	26	16	14	35

Source: *Statistical Digest of the War*, Central Statistical Office, London, 1951.

matters of employment almost disappeared. Of the single women between the ages of 18 and 40, 91 per cent were either in auxiliary war services or employed in the civilian labour force. Taking into account invalids and disabled and those with special family responsibilities, this means that the employment of unmarried able-bodied women was universal. It still is so.

Of the married women without young children, 80 per cent in the age group 18 to 40 were actively engaged in the war effort.

To set this all-out effort going, the Government went out of its way to provide amenities, to reorganize social services and to over-come traditional prejudices. The compulsory registration of women between the ages of 18 and 50 and their direction into at least part-time work was only one side of the picture. The other, more positive, side was a constructive effort to create conditions which made the mobilization of married women practicable on a national scale. War factories were moved into areas where labour reserves were available; day nurseries were set up and canteen services were organized; the provision of part-time jobs was en-couraged; the marriage-bar for women in non-industrial occu-pations, such as the civil service, the teaching profession (Educa-tion Act, 1944), the police, the London County Council, the Metro-politan Water Board, the British Broadcasting Corporation, and others, was removed.

This reorganization of working conditions to meet the needs of women workers assumed such dimensions that it may well be called a social revolution—provided that its effect was more than a temporary adjustment to an emergency. The question arose in many people's minds at the time: Will it be possible to retrace our steps, or are we in face of a new departure in our social organ-ization? Will the end of hostilities bring a reversal to the old order, or will the measures adopted at the time of national danger outlast the emergency? Opinions were divided between the hope for a re-turn to pre-war conditions and a preference for social ideals that involved a development in the opposite direction.

The decision lay, to a large extent, with the women themselves. Investigations were carried out from time to time to probe the post-war intentions of women workers. The proportion of those who wished to stay at work, particularly among the older women, was astonishingly high. An analysis of a survey carried out by the Amalgamated Engineering Union in 228 factories in the spring of 1945 showed that about two-thirds of the 2,000 women inter-viewed expressed their desire to go on working. Broken down into age groups, 86 per cent of the women between 41 and 50 wanted to remain in the industry, and 89 per cent of those over 50, com-pared with 66 per cent of those between 26 and 35, 57 per cent of those between 21 and 25, and 63 per cent of the 18- and 20-year-olds.

But with the end of the war most of the married women returned home. The reason was not only that the conscription of labour was first relaxed and then came to an end. This would still have left in employment the large number of women who had wanted to keep their jobs. But when the hostilities ceased and the men came back from the war there arose, as a general reaction, the feeling that the jobs ought to be 'kept for the boys' and that women should make way. Firms showed themselves less prepared than during the war to organize shifts for part-time workers. Many war-time nurseries were closed down. In short, there was a marked tendency to go 'back to normal'.

By 1947 the number of married women in gainful employment had shrunk to 18 per cent of all married women living with their husbands. The proportion of single women at work remained unchanged at 92 per cent, though their absolute number was reduced, partly owing to the raising of the school-leaving age from 14 to 15, partly as a consequence of the increased marriage rate at the end of the war, and partly because of a general fall in the number of women of working age. This decline in numbers is due to continue for some time to come. It has been estimated that in the fifteen years between 1944 and 1959 the decrease in the number of women between the ages of 15 and 45 will be as much as 1,150,000, with a corresponding reduction of the total labour force unless older people or married women are employed to a greater extent than before.

The post-war spell of relaxation was, however, short-lived. Shortage of labour, the Government-sponsored export drive, the outbreak of the war in Korea and renewed rearmament, all contributed to bring more and more women back into industry, this time without conscription.

The number of women in employment rose from 6,620,000 in 1947 to 7,650,000 in 1957 and to 8,400 in 1965. This increase in the female labour force is very largely due to the growing practice of married women to seek employment. Between the two census periods of 1951 and 1961 the proportion working outside their homes rose from 1 in 4 to 1 in 3. While married women were 41 per cent of the female labour force in 1950, they were 54 per cent in 1965.

Over the last fifteen years the annual increase in the number of women working has consistently outstripped the growth in the male labour force. Well over one-third of Britain's working population (34·6 per cent in 1965) is female.

OCCUPATIONAL DISTRIBUTION. How this labour force is distributed over the various industries is shown in Table 11 below.

Table 11

ESTIMATED NUMBERS OF WOMEN EMPLOYEES IN GREAT BRITAIN,
JUNE 1964

Industry	Number of women in thousands	Percentage of all employees
Agriculture, forestry, fishing	88	16·5
Mining and quarrying	23	3·6
Food, drink and tobacco	347	42·7
Chemicals and allied industries	142	27·7
Metal manufacture	76	12·1
Engineering and electrical goods	604	27·5
Shipbuilding and marine engineering	11	5·1
Vehicles	118	13·5
Metal goods n.e. specified	198	34·6
Textiles	415	52·8
Leather, leathergoods and furs	26	41·3
Clothing and footwear	397	73·4
Bricks, pottery, glass, cement, etc.	79	22·3
Timber, furniture, etc.	58	19·9
Paper, printing and publishing	215	34·4
Other manufacturing industries	126	38·9
Construction	81	4·9
Transport and communications	251	15·1
Distributive trades	1,559	52·6
Insurance, banking and finance	281	44·8
Professional and scientific services	1,530	66·2
Miscellaneous services	1,243	56·9
Public administration	369	28·6

Source: Ministry of Labour.

The manufacturing industries together absorb slightly more than one-third of all employed women; nearly one-fifth each work in the distributive trades and in professional and scientific services.

The occupational structure of the male and female labour force differs sharply on a number of points (see Table 12): a smaller proportion of women than men is employed in manufacturing and other industries and considerably higher proportions are engaged in trade, professional and scientific as well as other services.

Table 12

PERCENTAGE DISTRIBUTION OF THE MALE AND FEMALE LABOUR
FORCE IN BRITAIN

Occupational sector	Men	Women
Agriculture, forestry, fishing, mining and quarrying	7·5	1·3
Manufacturing industries	41·3	34·1
Construction	10·9	1·0
Transport and communications	9·9	3·1
Distributive trades	9·7	18·9
Insurance, banking, finance	2·4	3·4
Professional and scientific services	5·4	18·6
Miscellaneous services	6·5	15·1
Public administration	6·4	4·5
	100·0	100·0

Based on the figures for June, 1964, published by the Ministry of Labour.

If, on the face of it, these figures appear to indicate that a very high percentage of women is in 'middle-class' occupations, it has to be borne in mind that the data published by the Ministry of Labour are classified into 'industrial groups' and do not distinguish between operatives and clerical or other employees. In this way, over one-and-a-half million women are classified as being in the professional and scientific services, out of a female working population of eight-and-a-quarter million. However, the figure includes not only members of the professions (education, law, accountancy, etc.) but also those serving them; that is to say, the medical profession, e.g. embraces receptionists, hospital staff—including domestic and clerical workers—as well as doctors and dentists.

The Occupation Tables of the 1961 Census (based on a 10 per cent sample) which adopt a different method of classification show that female clerks, typists, shorthand writers, secretaries, etc., in England and Wales (including the lower grades of the civil and local authority service) formed an army of 1,796,000, that is, more than a quarter of all working women[1] (in 1951 they were

---

[1] The Census figures differ from those quoted earlier from the Ministry of Labour not only because of their different basis of classification and the different years of enumeration but also because they apply to England and Wales while the MoL data are given for Great Britain as a whole.

only just over one-fifth). Women are nearly two-thirds of all clerical personnel.

A somewhat smaller number of women (1,512,720) were employed in the service industries (including domestic services, catering and hotel-keeping, hairdressers, launderers, dry-cleaners, etc.); together they employed more than one-fifth of all working women.

One in eight of the female labour force in 1961 were sales personnel, and one in ten in the category which the Census groups under the heading of 'professional, technical workers, artists'—i.e. the occupations listed in Table 13 overleaf.

WOMEN IN THE PROFESSIONS. Table 13 gives a rough picture of the number of women in the professions and the proportion they form of the total manpower in each occupational category. The latter serves to show how 'sex-typed' some of the professions are: Nursing and radiography, for instance, are preponderantly feminine occupations, while all varieties of engineering, surveying and architecture, law and the sciences are overwhelmingly masculine domains. Higher civil servants, senior local authority officials and other administrators and managers (together 0·5 per cent of the female labour force) are classified by the Census under a separate heading and are therefore not included in Table 13.

Comparisons between this and a similar Table published in earlier editions of this book are, unfortunately, not possible because of a reclassification of various occupations between the two Census enumerations. Some professions listed in 1951 have disappeared in 1961 under a more general heading, others have been re-defined. Librarians, for instance, are among those no longer in evidence; while the social welfare workers of 1951 have become 'social welfare and related workers' in 1961—a change of shift which has altered the sex balance in this category. Attempts to trace developments in the professions during the ten-year period are therefore futile.

The 1961 Census allows, on the other hand, a breakdown of occupations by marital status which shows that the professions with the highest proportion of married women among its members —nearly two out of three—are medical and dental practitioners and company secretaries, while among the relatively few lawyers only a small minority (29 per cent) are married. The fact that 35

Table 13

PROFESSIONAL, TECHNICAL WORKERS AND ARTISTS IN ENGLAND AND WALES, 1961

Professions	Number of Women	Women as Percentage of profession
Medical practitioners (qualified)	8,340	15·9
Dental practitioners	880	6·8
Nurses	262,740	90·2
Pharmacists, dispensers	8,650	31·1
Radiographers	4,590	72·6
Medical workers n.e.c.	15,950	46·6
University teachers	1,430	12·5
Teachers	261,660	58·8
Civil, structural and municipal engineers	20 ⎫	—
Mechanical engineers	110 ⎬	2·3
Electrical engineers	140 ⎭	
Technologists n.e.c.	860	10·3
Chemists, physical and biology scientists	3,320	6·8
Authors, journalists and related workers	7,600	20·3
Stage managers, actors, entertainers, musicians	8,890	33·9
Painters, sculptors and related creative artists	12,560	35·7
Accountants (prof.), company secretaries and registrars	13,320	13·8
Surveyors and architects	1,580	2·3
Clergy, ministers, members of religious orders	13,600	25·0
Judges, barristers, advocates, solicitors	1,030	3·5
Social welfare and related workers	18,100	47·5
Professional workers n.e.c.	13,640	36·7
Draughtsmen	16,710	10·0
Laboratory assistants, technicians	28,360	32·2
Technical and related workers n.e.c.	3,240	4·5
Total	707,320	37·6

Source: Occupation Tables, Ten-Percent Sample, Census, 1961.

per cent of all practicing nurses are married indicates a major breakthrough in a profession formerly confined to spinsters.

Similarly, there has been a significant re-adjustment in the teaching profession which, on the face of it, is almost evenly divided between married and single women. However, these data do not discriminate between full-time and part-time employees, and since part-time work is almost exclusively done by married women, the main teaching load in terms of women-hours still rests on the unmarried teacher.

AGE DISTRIBUTION. Thanks to the increasing return in recent years of married women to the labour market after having raised their families, the average age of working women has been moving up. The largest proportion of the female labour force is no longer in what we have called the 'family phase', as it was in 1951, (namely, between the ages of 20 and 39) but is between 40 and 59 years old. The age distribution of the female working population is now as follows:

> 17 per cent under 20
> 36 per cent aged 20–39
> 40 per cent aged 40–59
> 9 per cent aged 60 and over.

The number of women in employment which declines rather steeply between the ages of 20 and 34, rises once again from the age of 35 upwards. In Britain, as in the other three countries, the characteristic graph of female employment by age is a two-humped curve, with a first high peak around the age of 19 and a second, somewhat lower and flatter peak at the ages of 40–44.

Of 20 gainfully occupied women in Great Britain. 1951-1964*

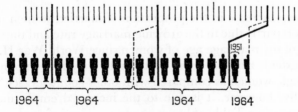

| under 20 years | 20-39 years | 40-59 years | 60 years and over |
| WORK PHASE | FAMILY PHASE | POST-FAMILY PHASE | |

1964   1964   1964   1964

*——1951 distribution   - - - -1964 distribution.

The United States

From each census period to the next the number of women gainfully employed in the United States has been rising. Between March 1940 and April 1950, there was an increase of over five-and-a-quarter million women in employment, and a further steep increase—by 615,000 or 3·3 per cent—took place during the following year owing to the war in Korea, bringing the total number of women in the labour force to nearly twenty million in 1951. By 1962 the number of women working was around 23 million and is expected to rise to 30 million by 1970. As in Britain and France, women are just over one-third of the working population (34 per cent in 1963).

HIGH EMPLOYMENT RATE OF MARRIED WOMEN. The outstanding feature of this rising tide has been the growing number of married women working outside their homes. While in 1930 11·5 per cent of all married women were gainfully employed, in 1940 the percentage was 17, in 1950 it was 24, and in 1962 one-third of all white married women—and nearly one-half of the non-white married women—were in employment. More than one-half of the female labour force in 1950, and over 60 per cent in 1962, were married.

Table 14

WOMEN IN THE U.S. LABOUR FORCE, 1940–60, BY MARITAL STATUS

Status	Percentage of the female labour force		
	1940	1950	1960
Single	48·5	32	23·6
Married	36·5	52	60·7
Widowed and divorced	15	15	15·7
	100·0	100·0	100·0

The steep increase in the proportion of married women in employment is partly due to the growing marriage rate and the steady lowering of the marriage age of women since World War II. It is, to some extent, also the result of the relatively low employment rate of single women as compared with other countries (see Table 15); chiefly, however, it is due to the increased employment of older women (see Table 16).

The disproportionately low employment rate of single women in the United States is due to the concurrence of two factors, namely, the lower average age of marriage and the widespread practice of high-school education. More than two-thirds of American girls between the ages of 15 and 19 are attending school; over one-third of American brides are no more than 19 on their wedding-day.

Against this background it is easy to understand that working

Table 15

ACTIVITY RATES OF WOMEN BY MARITAL STATUS IN FOUR COUNTRIES*

	England and Wales (1961)	United States (1960)	France (1962)	Sweden (1960)
	%	%	%	%
Single	69·4	44·1	54·6	60·3
Married	31·5 (37·7)†	30·5	32·4	26·3 (31·5)†
Widowed and divorced	22·8	40·0	26·9	57·5
All women	37·7	34·8	36·2	37·9

Source: Census Reports of each country.

* U.S.A. data apply to women aged 14 and over; those for U.K. and France to women aged 15 and over; those for Sweden to ages 15–64.

† Both in England and Wales and in Sweden the Census appears to underrate the employment figures for married women as compared with the data collected in the official labour statistics. Percentages based on the latter have therefore been added in brackets.

Of 20 gainfully occupied women in U.S.A.

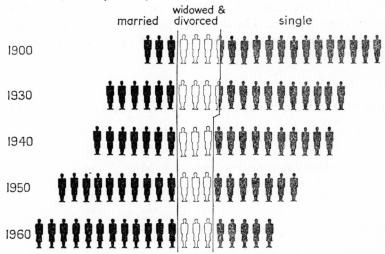

wives form the vast majority of recruits to the female labour force (9·2 million married to 5·5 million single women in 1952, 12·3 million married to 5·4 million single women in 1962), even if the activity rate of married women is lower than that of any other group (see Table 15).

There is, of course, a significant difference between rural and urban areas which must not be overlooked when average figures are quoted for a country as vast and varied as the United States. The relative lack of opportunities for employment in rural areas affects both married and single women, but the disparity between country and town is more marked in the case of single girls. In 1950, only 25 per cent of the single women living on farms were employed compared with 58 per cent of those living in urban areas. For married women the percentages were 17 in rural and 26 in urban areas. This does not mean that women in rural areas are more given to idleness than townswomen, but that much of the work done in family businesses and farms does not count as employment because it is unpaid.

AGE DISTRIBUTION. The large increase in the female labour force between 1940 and 1960 was mainly achieved by the growing participation of women in the middle and older age groups. As in other countries, there has been a steadily rising employment of women over 35, and especially of those aged 45 and over. Nearly two out of every five working women in the United States belong to this age bracket. The average age of the American woman worker in 1960 was 41, compared with 26 at the turn of the century and 37 in 1950.

Table 16

THE FEMALE LABOUR FORCE OF THE UNITED STATES BY AGE GROUPS

Age	1940 %	1950 %	1960 %
Under 25	30	23	19
25–44	48	46	42
45 and over	22	31	39
	100	100	100

Source: U.S. Bureau of the Census.

It became obvious in the 1950s that the rapid increase in the number of married women at work, particularly in the older age groups, represented a long-term social change of some magnitude. This realization led to a large number of investigations, resulting in a wealth of literature on the subject of American women.[1] It also prompted President Kennedy in 1961 to set up a Presidential Commission on the Status of Women under the chairmanship of the late Eleanor Roosevelt. The Commission and its seven sub-committees (on Civil and Political Rights, Education, Federal Employment, Home and Community, Private Employment, Protective Labour Legislation, Social Insurance and Taxes) reported

Table 17

EMPLOYED WOMEN IN THE UNITED STATES—SELECTED OCCUPATIONAL GROUPS 1940, 1950, 1960

Occupational group	Number of women in thousands	Per cent distribution		
	April 1962	1962	1950	1940
Professional workers	2,941	13	11	13
Clerical workers	6,948	31	26	21
Sales workers	1,685	7	9	7
Service (except households)	3,364	15	13	11
Private-household workers	2,275	10	10	18
Operatives	3,290	15	19	18
Miscell. other occupations	2,138	9	12	12
All employed women	22,641	100	100	100

Source: 1962 *Handbook for Women Workers*, U.S. Department of Labor, Women's Bureau, Bulletin 285 (1963).

in 1963[2] and submitted a large number of recommendations some of which have since been embodied in Federal legislation. It is perhaps significant of the current situation that the Committee on Education opened its report with a chapter on 'The Mature Years', beginning with the sentence, 'Vitality and relative freedom from the concentrated demands of the home mark today's mature woman.' . . .

TYPES OF WORK. In the United States, as elsewhere, the most conspicuous increase in the number of women employed in any occupational group took place among clerical and kindred

[1] Some of the titles will be found in the bibliography at the end of this book.

[2] *American Women*, Report of the President's Commission on the Status of Women, U.S. Government Printing Office, 1963.

workers. They are nearly one-third of all working women. Between the two census periods of 1940 and 1950 their number rose from 2·5 millions to 4·5 millions; by 1962 it had grown to almost seven millions.

Nearly as striking as the increase in clerical personnel is the decline (in absolute numbers as well as in relative proportions) in production workers. This feature, which is the result of increasing automation, is not confined to women but is characteristic of the American economy as a whole. There is a growing demand for clerical, professional and technical workers and an expansion of the service sector at the expense of unskilled and semi-skilled occupations.

PART-TIME WORK. A relatively new phenomenon has been the expansion of part-time employment. One-third of all employed women worked less than 35 hours a week in 1960 (compared with one-fourth in 1950), mostly in trades or service industries. Slightly over one-fifth of these part-time workers are teenagers working their way through school or college; more than one-half are women between the ages of 25 and 54.

EMPLOYMENT AND EDUCATIONAL LEVEL. What has been said about the correlation between the employment rate of women and their level of education in France (see page 48) holds true also of the United States. As can be seen from Table 18, the more highly

Table 18

EMPLOYMENT OF AMERICAN WOMEN, AGED 18 AND OVER, BY EDUCATIONAL LEVEL, MARCH 1962

College education	Employed		Not employed		All women	
	(1000s)	%	(1000s)	%	(1000s)	%
1–3 years	2,573	41·8	3,584	58·2	6,157	100
4 years	1,585	53·4	1,381	46·6	2,966	100
5 years	597	69·6	261	30·4	858	100
No college education	18,222	36·2	32,110	63·8	50,332	100
Totals	22,977	38·1	37,336	61·9	60,313	100

Based on figures published in Dennis F. Johnston, *Educational Attainment of Workers*, March 1962, U.S. Department of Labor, Bureau of Labor Statistics, Special Labor Force Report No. 30.

educated a woman is, the more likely she is to be economically active.

If this is true of the overall picture, a break-down by age groups shows that the difference in employment rate between those with and without higher education is increasingly marked with growing age; but it also reveals (see Table 19) that the correlation does not universally apply: Women aged 35–44 with a college education lasting 1–3 years form an exception to the rule. Their rate of employment is lower than that of any other group of their contemporaries, including those who have never been at college.

Table 19

PROPORTION OF AMERICAN WOMEN IN THE LABOUR FORCE BY
EDUCATIONAL ATTAINMENT—SELECTED AGE GROUPS, MARCH 1962

Educational level	Age: 25–34		35–44		45–54		Total number working	
	(1000s)	% of group working	(1000s)	% of group working	(1000s)	% of group working	(1000s)	% of group working
1–3 years college	481	38·6	552	42·0	541	54·7	1,575	44·3
4 years college	382	46·6	361	52·5	371	67·8	1,114	54·3
5 years college	116	59·5	159	74·3	170	79·8	445	71·6
No college education	3,171	35·0	4,397	43·2	4,225	47·4	11,790	42·0
Total in labour force	4,150	36·7	5,466	44·1	5,307	49·9	14,923	43·5
Not in labour force	7,160	63·3	6,927	55·9	5,328	50·1	19,415	56·5
Total	11,310	100·0	12,393	100·0	10,635	100·0	34,338	100·0

Source as in Table 18.

Without a great deal more detailed information than is at present available—for instance, on the size of families of women with different levels of education and of different social backgrounds— it would be rash indeed to offer any explanation either of the very high incidence of employment among women with superior educational attainments or of the relatively low employment rate of college-educated women in their late thirties and early forties.

WOMEN IN THE PROFESSIONS. Two-thirds of all professional women in the United States are either teachers or nurses (43 per cent are teachers, 23 per cent nurses). In some other professions women are a majority of persons engaged in them, for instance, as

librarians, social workers, dietitians, medical and dental technic-
ians. They are a substantial proportion of journalists, authors and
editors (35 per cent); but they have made remarkably little impact
on the older professions. No more than 6 per cent of medical
practitioners, 4 per cent of lawyers and 8 per cent of pharmacists
are women. As John P. Parrish has shown in a number of articles,[1]
there has, in fact, been a relative decline in all high-level occupations requiring a long training. Not only has the proportion of
Ph.D. degrees conferred on women been reduced from 17 per cent
of all doctorates awarded in 1932 to 10 per cent in 1955-60, the
proportion of first professional degrees in law has declined from 6
per cent in the 1930s to 3 per cent in 1959, and the percentage of
women taking medical degrees has remained static at 5 per cent
since the 1920s. There has been a corresponding decline in high-
level teaching and research: women were 30 per cent of university
staff in 1930 and 22 per cent in 1960. This is still a respectable proportion compared with most other countries, but is a 'come-down'
by previous American standards. Similarly, the 1902 edition of
Who's Who in America included 8·5 per cent women; in the 1958
edition they were no more than 4 per cent of the eminent people
listed. The answer, Professor Parrish points out, appears to lie in a
voluntary shift in the preferences of women. High-level intellectual
activity has suffered under the impact of earlier marriage, a rising
rate of marriage and earlier family formation. The ever-increasing
participation of women in the labour force is achieved, it seems,
through their willingness to accept low and medium-skilled
occupations—either short-term or long-term—in preference to
more ambitious career plans which might in the long run conflict
with their family role.

Sweden

In many respects the Swedish situation resembles that of the
larger industrial countries. There are, however, some features of
particular interest. Thus, Sweden has gone through industrialization at a much later period in history, but also at a more rapid
pace, than the other countries we have been dealing with. Patterns

---

[1] 'Professional Womanpower as a National Resource', *The Quarterly Review of
Economics & Business*, vol. 1, Feb. 1961, University of Illinois; 'Top Level Training of
Women in the United States, 1900-1960', *Jrl. of the National Association of Women Deans
and Counselors*, vol. XXV, January 1962, 'Women in Top Level Teaching and Research', *Jrl. of the Amer. Association of University Women*, January 1962.

of life and public attitudes have shifted unusually swiftly. The real increase in the employment of women has occurred during the last decade. The debate about the respective 'roles' of men and women to-day has its most markedly 'radical' slant in Sweden.

AGRICULTURE. Sweden remained for long an agrarian community. The farm population, which has never been subject to feudalism, has been distributed over a large number of small or medium-sized farms of an independent type, more often than not with an isolated homestead rather than part of a village. This has had considerable effects on the status of women. Most married women lived a life marked by hard work but also characterized by a position of respect and authority.

This population of working farmers, which constituted some 75 per cent in 1870, about 55 per cent in 1900, 40 per cent in 1925, and about 24 per cent in 1950, has largely influenced the pattern of life of the whole country. It left less room for the leisured lady of aristocratic society or Victorian middle-class than the other countries we have discussed, but also very little room for a female industrial proletariat.

As may be expected under these circumstances, the gainful employment of women had a late start. The steep decline in the farming population which has occurred after the second world war (in 1960 it accounted for only 16 per cent of the labour force and in 1965 for about 10 per cent) went hand in hand with an increase in women's employment. The common factor is the general shift to non-agricultural, largely urban, occupations.

For a historical comparison it is difficult, in Sweden as in France, to define clearly the term 'employment' in relation to women, owing to the nature and social organization of work in a large agricultural population. In 1890, when the proportion of 'income-earners', according to the Census returns, was as low as 6 per cent of women above the age of 15, the corresponding proportion among men was 59 per cent. To this should be added 11 per cent of adult women and 5 per cent of the men who were classified as servants. In 1930 this category had already shrunk to 9 per cent of women and 2 per cent of men; later, men have practically disappeared from the servant category and only a fraction of one per cent of adult women now remain classified as domestic workers.

The employment rate of persons aged 15–64, has remained well above 90 per cent for men and 40–50 per cent for women since

1930. (1930, men 94 per cent, women 49 per cent; 1940, men 93 per cent, women 45 per cent; 1950, men 93 per cent, women 41 per cent). In 1960, there was a considerable drop in the male employment rate, down to 87 per cent, while the female employment rate at the same time slightly rose to 42 per cent. The drop in the employment rate of men is largely due to the prolongation of studies; a corresponding decrease is found among young women but it is more than offset by the greater participation of older, mostly married, women.

According to the Census returns, women formed 35 per cent of the labour force in 1930, 32 per cent in 1940, 31 per cent in 1950 and 32 per cent in 1960. The labour market statistics show somewhat higher returns, including as they do everyone who has worked at least one hour in the week of the survey. (The Census includes as 'economically active persons' all those who have worked at least half the normal working time during the week of enumeration.)[1] According to the Labour Market Statistics, women were nearly 36 per cent of the labour force in 1960 (compared with the 32 per cent of the Census); since then they rose to 36·5 per cent in 1962 and 37·5 per cent in 1965.

It is generally accepted that, by either standard, the number of married women, economically active, is underrated, especially with regard to those working in agriculture. The National Statistical Bureau estimated this underenumeration to be as high as 31·4 per cent, according to a special check made after the Census of 1960. (The data given above are adjusted to correct this underestimation.)[2]

GENERAL TREND. The most noteworthy change, in Sweden as in the other countries surveyed, is the highly increased marriage rate and the lower marriage age. This means that, even if it were 'just the same women' who worked, there would be a reduction of single women, and a corresponding increase in the proportion of married women, in the labour force. In fact, however, the employment rate of married women has risen far beyond this.

---

[1] Census data are published annually in *Statistisk Årsbok* with table texts and summaries in English. Labour Market Statistics, based on sample surveys, are included in the *Manpower Statistics* of the O.E.C.D.—In the above text the Census figures have been corrected for comparability by including men in military service and women working in employers' households.

[2] The statistical information in this section is based on *The Women in the Labour Force I*, Statistiska Centralbyran, Stockholm, 1965: 5. (Summaries in English.)

To illustrate this change: in 1930, the proportions of single and married women in the female population aged 15–64 were nearly equal (45·9 per cent single, 48·5 per cent married, and 5·6 per cent previously married). In 1960, the respective ratios were 27·7 per cent single, 65·2 per cent married and 7·1 per cent widowed and divorced. The female *working* population in 1930 included 79·4 per cent single, 12·8 per cent married and 7·8 per cent previously married women; in 1960 the three categories were 44·0, 45·2 and 10·8 per cent, respectively.

The employment rate shows a corresponding increase in the latter two categories. While in 1930 only 8·8 per cent and in 1940 only 10·1 per cent of the married women were returned by the Census as employed, the percentage rose to 15·6 in 1950 and, steeply, to 26·3 per cent in 1960.[1]

The employment rate of unmarried women shows no such drastic developments. From 59·1 per cent in 1930 it rose gradually to 67·0 per cent in 1950, and dropped to 60·3 per cent in 1960,[2] reflecting without doubt the greater prevalence of students among single women who, as a group, are now much younger than in earlier decades.

The high and growing employment rates of married women, especially within the last ten years, is a phenomenon not confined to Sweden, as we have seen. As in Britain and the United States, the ratio of married women gainfully occupied in Sweden rose from one in four to one in three during the last decade. This change is most striking in the higher age groups, showing that Swedish women have begun to accept their 'double role' and return to employment after some years spent at home. This feature, which is so germane to the thesis of the present book, is presented in the graph overleaf.

The increase in gainful employment is taking place not only among the married women who have completed the child-raising phase of their lives but also among mothers of young children. As Table 20 shows, the presence of children at home is characteristic for a majority of married women who work.

[1] With corrections of the underestimation of economically active women in employers' households this series is: 24·5 per cent in 1930, 23·0 per cent in 1940, 25·4 per cent in 1950, and 31·5 per cent in 1960.

[2] After correction for underestimation this series is: 76 per cent in 1930, 74·6 per cent in 1940, 72·5 per cent in 1950, and 63·1 per cent in 1960.

EMPLOYMENT RATES OF MARRIED WOMEN IN SWEDEN BY AGE GROUPS AT THE CENSUS PERIODS OF 1930, 1940, 1950 and 1960

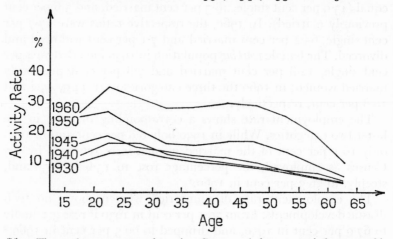

(Note: The employment rates at the various Census periods are not strictly comparable because of a variable underestimation of the economic activity of women in employers households, at least during the post-war period. In general terms, however, the graph gives a true indication of prevailing trends.)

While for childless women the most active age group is 25–29, for women with one child it is 30–34; for women with two children it is 35–39 and for women with three children 40–44. That is to say, as children grow older, many women respond to the reduction of family responsibilities by returning to gainful occupations, and their ability to do so is directly related to the age of the youngest child.

The female labour reserve is, however, by no means exhausted. At the time to which the above statistics refer, there were in Sweden half-a-million married women with no children under 16 who were not employed.

TYPES OF OCCUPATION. While during the last century women were still practically excluded from employment in the crafts, and also largely in commerce, by the traditional regulations inherited from the guilds, they early entered the manufacturing industries which were few in number but free from restrictions. Between 1800 and 1850 women formed nearly 10 per cent of the industrial labour force, and this proportion increased to about 20 per cent at the end of the century. With the exception of the nineteen-thirties and

Table 20

EMPLOYMENT RATE OF MARRIED WOMEN AGED 15–64 BY AGE GROUP
AND NUMBER OF CHILDREN UNDER 16 IN SWEDEN, 1960

| Age | Percentage of women employed having | | | | Employment rate of | |
	0 child	1 child	2 children	3 or more children	all women with children under 16	all married women
15–19	54·3	16·4	—	—	14·3	23·9
20–24	71·4	21·4	8·8	—	17·1	34·2
25–29	73·4	27·1	11·9	6·5	18·0	29·0
30–34	64·7	32·8	17·8	11·1	21·1	26·6
35–39	53·3	32·5	21·3	13·3	23·0	27·1
40–44	45·1	28·0	19·4	13·9	22·4	28·2
45–49	34·8	23·2	17·9	12·8	20·8	27·1
50–54	27·0	18·6	14·8	—	17·8	24·0
55–59	19·8	10·9	—	—	10·3	18·7
60–64	9·8	—	—	—	—	9·9
Total	32·0	25·2	17·3	11·9	20·5	25·2

Source: *The Women in the Labour Force I*, Statistiska Centralbyran, Stockholm, 1965: 5.

forties the proportion increased and is now roughly 26 per cent of all persons employed in manufacturing industries. As in other countries, women are very unevenly distributed in the different branches of industry, the proportions varying from 7 per cent in timber to 68 per cent in the clothing industry.

Nothing is more typical of a country's change-over from a subsistence economy to a developed money economy than the increase in the number of people engaged in the process of distributing goods. Sweden passed through this phase within this century, and, as at this time new groups of women were willing to accept employment outside their homes, while men were already more fixed in traditional jobs, it is not surprising that this field has absorbed a considerable proportion of women. Of the main occupational groups concerned with the distribution of goods, namely, commerce, catering and transport, the first two take most women. In 1965 women formed 52 per cent of all persons employed in commerce,

77 per cent in catering and 18 per cent in transport; among executives in hotels and restaurants women were roughly 65 per cent.

The Civil Service in Sweden has not grown in any way which might either alarm the conservatives or encourage the planners, as for about two centuries it has occupied no more than 5–10 per cent of all gainfully employed people. While the number of women in the Civil Service was nil up to 1870, the proportion increased from decade to decade, being 4 per cent at the turn of the century, 8 per cent in 1910, 22 per cent in 1920, 25 per cent in 1930, 49 per cent in 1940, 57 per cent in 1950 and 64 per cent in 1960. A breakdown of these totals would, however, show, as usual, that women are very rare at the top of the ladder of influence and income.

More marked was women's advance in the field of education, where they already in 1890 outnumbered men. They do not dominate the field of school education as much as, for instance, in the U.S.A., but they have a practical monopoly with regard to children up to the age of 9. Figures published by the Swedish Ministry of Education show that for every 100 men teachers, including both elementary and secondary schools, there were 188 women teachers in 1930, 160 in 1940, 156 in 1950 and 142 in 1960. This gradual decline in the proportion of women in the teaching profession over the last twenty years is due to the fact that for the young adolescent years, when most Swedish children are in the public elementary schools, the State regulates the intake of men and women candidates to the training colleges so as to produce 55 per cent male teachers and 45 per cent female teachers. This profession remains one of the few without equal right to free competition, and it is common knowledge that women would gain considerably if the career were opened without this quota, as more highly qualified women candidates present themselves every year for the entrance examinations to the training colleges. In secondary schools or at university level, where there is no quota system, the number of women has considerably increased in recent years. They tend, however, to specialize in languages and the humanities, while the natural sciences are starved of teachers because qualified scientists —in Sweden no less than in other countries—are usually more attracted by the vastly more profitable prospects of technological jobs in industry.

WOMEN IN THE LABOUR FORCE TO-DAY

It has already become a tradition in Sweden that the more alert and ambitious girls go into the professions. For purposes of comparison with the data we have given on the participation of women in the professions in Britain and the United States we have set out the following table based on the Census figures of 1945 and 1960.

As can be seen from this table women have made a real impact on certain professions, particularly in the field of social work (in the wider sense of the term), and it is difficult to see how the highly developed social services in Sweden could be run without their very active participation.

Table 21

WOMEN IN THE PROFESSIONS IN SWEDEN, 1945 and 1960

	Per cent of women among persons in each profession	
	1945	1960
Teachers	60	55
Nurses	99	100
Social and welfare workers	80	67
Librarians and museum keepers	42	54
Musicians	23	11
Authors	27	20
Journalists, editors, reporters	12	19
Physicians and surgeons	7	13
Dentists	23	24
Pharmacists	30	67
Lawyers	4	5
Dramatic profession	37	51
Preachers	17	17

It will be seen that there have been some marked changes since 1945: shortages of teachers and social workers have—as in the other countries—led to a greater influx of men into these previously feminine domains so that, even if the absolute number of women in these professions has been increasing, in relative terms their participation has declined; at the same time women have made substantial inroads in some other professions, for instance, as doctors, pharmacists and librarians.

A question of great social importance is that of the extent to which women 'waste' higher training—or, to put it differently, of the potential reserve which may exist among women for filling the vacancies in schools, hospitals, pharmacies, etc.

To throw light on this problem a special investigation was carried out by the National Central Bureau of Statistics.[1] The most conspicuous feature of its findings is that women graduates with a long training, particularly doctors and dentists, are apt to retain very high employment rates. Among married women with a medical training 78·7 per cent of those in the age group 25–29, 82·0 per cent of those aged 30–39 and 90·1 per cent of those aged 40–59 were working professionally in 1960. The corresponding figures for dentists were 83·7, 91·1 and 85·5 per cent, respectively. The rates were considerably lower for pharmacists, social workers, nurses and engineers.[2]

The fact that not only the length of training but also more or less convenient working hours play an important part in making it possible for married women to work is illustrated by the high employment rate of school teachers, varying between 82·6 per cent in the age group 25–29, 75·1 per cent in the age group 30–39 and 84·4 per cent in the age group 40–59. These high employment rates are, to some extent at least, also the result of widespread appeals by the authorities, publicizing staff shortages in schools, hospitals, etc. Nurses show the most remarkable increase in employment at a later age, raising their activity rate from 44.2 per cent in the age group 30–39 to 77·1 per cent between the ages of 40 and 59. The general public, and not least the married women, are increasingly being made aware of their social obligation to give service in return for their training.

In mentioning this fact it is not asserted that a sense of duty is the only, or main, motivation underlying the high employment rates of professional women. It combines with other factors, such as a psychological need for achievement, the financial rewards of the job, and the relative tediousness of household routine.[3] Together, they have produced, in Sweden as elsewhere, the growth

---

[1] Published as *The Women in the Labour Force II*, Stockholm, 1965:7 (Summaries in English).

[2] Compare corresponding data for France (p. 48) and the U.S.A. (pp. 64–5).

[3] An interesting calculation, made by the Swedish National Central Bureau of Statistics, established that an increase of one year in the length of training raised the employment rate by 7 per cent, and that an increase of income by 1000 s.Kr. annually raised the employment rate by 1·7 per cent.

of a fairly recent phenomenon: the 'career woman' with family ties.

The General Picture

The above data will suffice to show that the employment of women has become an important feature of the social structure in industrial countries, and further, that large and increasing numbers of married women are part of the labour force in all of them. This phenomenon has grown in importance during recent years irrespective of the rising living standards. Economic fluctuations have, in fact, influenced it only little; it is now integral to the pattern of Western civilization, notwithstanding national and regional differences which spring from varying social traditions and historical developments.

The common factors can be summarized as follows.

In all the countries under consideration women form roughly one third of the labour force. Everywhere the development in recent times has been characterized by a reduction in domestic service, a relative decrease also in industrial work (relative, that is, to the total number of women working), and an increase in the number of women in clerical, distributive and professional services. The proportion of women in employment rose more significantly among the salaried employees than among the manual workers, and a general tendency can be observed towards 'white-collar jobs' and sedentary occupations.

It is worth noting, too, that there is a correlation between the development of the social services in modern countries and the participation of women. This correlation is twofold: while the growing social services require large numbers of skilled workers, and have to a considerable extent recruited women for this purpose, women, both politically and professionally, have had their fair share of responsibility in calling forth these services.[1]

The second most definite feature is the general trend towards greater employment of married women in all classes of society.

The simultaneous decline in domestic services has created a host of new problems. On the one hand, the absence of reliable home-help prevents many able women from accepting jobs; on the other hand, the increasing number of married women wishing to take up

[1] Maurice Duverger, *The Political Role of Women*, publ. UNESCO, 1955.

employment outside their homes creates a growing demand for domestic services of some kind, be it in the shape of organized home-help, commercial services, or the reorganization of existing housing, shopping and nursery arrangements, etc. It is increasingly difficult to meet this demand within the traditional framework; social re-adjustments, which make it possible to dispense with domestic service of the old style and yet free married women from a great deal of domestic drudgery, have nowhere kept in step with the growing need for them.

The withdrawal of women from domestic service, and, to a minor extent, also from industry, may give the impression of a movement away from unskilled occupations. This, however, is not entirely true. A closer examination of the jobs held by men and women in each branch of employment shows that women continue to occupy the positions requiring less skill, training and responsibility. This is the price women pay for their uncertainty as regards their occupational future. Undoubtedly, this situation has nothing to do with their innate abilities or the psychological characteristics of their sex but with the fact that their fate is so closely linked with their role in the family.

A third remarkable feature of the situation which we have been surveying is that the average age of working women has increased. This is concomitant with the fact that the main body of new recruits to the female labour force are married women. Facts and figures prove more eloquently than any professions of opinion, that women increasingly refuse to retire into wholetime domesticity. Even more of them use their energies, in one way or another, for purposes which transcend the limits of their families, often at an age at which they are not encouraged by social tradition to do so.

Another observation, arising from the comparison of employment statistics of various countries, may appear rather unexpected. In the skilled and professional occupations a certain division of labour between the sexes seems to have developed, very much along the traditional lines. At the beginning of women's emancipation many men were haunted by the fear of having to compete with women for every job, or of being replaced by women in spheres of work which were considered masculine prerogatives. In practice, however, it appears that 'emancipation' has so far not greatly changed the traditional pattern. The statistics show that women still flock chiefly into a limited number of 'feminine' occupations such as teaching, and auxiliary medical services, apart from the vast army of shorthand typists and secretaries who are not replacing men in a traditional field but serving them in an occupation created by modern methods of business and administration. The effect of emancipation has been, it seems, to replace amateurs by professionals in the 'feminine' occupations rather than men by women in the 'masculine' spheres of work, though there is a fair sprinkling of women in most of the latter to-day.

In recording this fact we do not want to minimize the importance of the substitution of skilled, effectively trained, and salaried workers for amateurs. Enormous changes, particularly in mental outlook and attitudes, have resulted from this new development. There is all the difference—both in character traits and in social position, between a nurse parachuting behind a battlefield and an untrained woman applying traditional household remedies to the ailing members of her family. The replacement of superstition by scientific knowledge, of haphazard trial and error by rational organization, has produced a new woman, as it has produced a new society, although the occupation—tending the sick and wounded, in this particular example—is still fundamentally the same. Similarly with teaching, catering and a host of other occupations in which women play a prominent part.

The fact that, after several decades of emancipation and professed equality of education and opportunity, the traditional division of labour between the sexes still persists—even though in a revised version—may appear surprising, in particular to the extremists on both sides of the controversy about women's emancipation. Men's fear of being ousted from their jobs by aspiring women has not materialized and one argument against the employment of women has thereby lost much of its force.

On the other hand, the nature of the development, though contradicting the anti-feminist arguments, must also be disappointing to feminist hopes. For if women do not conquer the professions—also the highest professions—they will not develop enough leaders of their own, and will not sufficiently influence policy; they will not give encouraging examples, or stimulate a change in public opinion—in short they will not achieve complete equality.

The question remains open whether this new specialization along sex lines is characteristic only of our period of transition or whether it has come to stay. But even if it manifestly is the outcome of a change-over from the traditional role to a new role of women in society, there is doubtless a danger that the modern distribution of labour between the sexes may establish a pattern which isolates women in positions where their chances of independence and responsibility are low. The fact that so many educated intelligent women with executive ability fill secretarial posts to-day seems to be a portent of this development.

On the basis of the figures reproduced in this chapter this can be said, that the sex division in the professions, apart from teaching and nursing, which seem to be largely feminine domains everywhere, differs in several respects in the countries observed. In France and Sweden, for instance, pharmacology and dentistry are becoming feminine fields of work. While in the United States a relatively large number of women are employed in finance, insurance and real estate, in Great Britain they have hardly made any impact at all in this sphere.

It seems clear, therefore, that the division of labour between the sexes is the result of existing local conditions and traditions rather than of psychological sex differences. As newcomers women will naturally be attracted into the spheres of least resistance. These may differ from one country to another owing to the different systems of social organization. But in face of the evident national differences it can hardly be maintained that women's professional choices are the outcome of some innate sex characteristics. It would, otherwise, be difficult to understand why, for instance, British women should have less interest in finance than their American sisters, or why the medical profession should appeal so much more to women in Britain than to women in the United States.

Vocational choice is obviously the complex result of a great number of factors. Among these, opportunities and prevailing social customs are no doubt important elements. In the case of women this choice is also strongly influenced by the role they hope to play in a family; which after all is reasonable enough.

CHAPTER FIVE

WHY MARRIED WOMEN SEEK EMPLOYMENT

The movement which has brought ever-increasing numbers of married women of all social classes into the labour force has been speeded up in recent years. It has been in progress in all industrial countries and, by its extent, it amounts to a silent revolution.

This development has three main causes: Firstly, the vast majority of unmarried women are in gainful employment, unless they are either students or undergoing some other training.

Secondly, the number of marriages has risen and the average age at marriage has continually been reduced since the war. This means that many more women of 20 to 25 than ever before are married and many of them carry on in their jobs up to the first, and sometimes up to the second baby.

Thirdly, full employment and the exigencies of general re-armament have increased the demand for labour. Additions to the existing labour force can therefore only be achieved by enrolling more married women into full or part-time employment.

This fact may have been recognized a few years ago. Yet the speed and readiness with which married women came forward to fill the vacant jobs was entirely unforeseen. Only in 1947, for instance, the Social Survey of the Central Office of Information estimated after a sample inquiry that under peace-time conditions the number of additional women likely to be drawn into full-time employment in Britain would probably not exceed 200,000, with possibly another 250,000–500,000 part-time workers; but it was thought that only quite exceptionally energetic measures could secure anything like this addition to the then existing labour force. Since then events have moved so fast that reality has outstripped all prophecies. Between 31 December 1947 and June 1951, the number of women employed in Great Britain rose by some 710,000, despite the fact that in the meantime the school-leaving age was raised from 14 to 15 years, and by more than another million between 1951 and 1965. This addition to the female labour force is entirely due to the increased proportion of married women going out to work.

In Sweden, the total female labour force increased by 224,000 between 1945 and 1960; during the same period, the number of married women in employment rose by 273,000 (bringing the proportion of married women from 21 to 45 per cent).

Comparable figures for the United States tell a similar tale. Between 1940 and 1960 the number of women in the American labour force increased by round ten millions. During the same period (see Table 14) the proportion of single women was reduced from, roughly, 1 in 2 to 1 in 4 of all working women.

It is true that recent political and economic developments have reinforced existing tendencies and have speeded up a trend of long standing. But the circumstances, as far as the employment of women is concerned, can be called 'artificial' only in the sense that they have, within a relatively short time, created opportunities which otherwise might have taken much longer to develop. Wherever such opportunities existed women have been neither slow nor reluctant to make use of them.

This fact, that women are willing to be employed but that opportunities must be favourable actually to bring them into the labour market, is illustrated also by the very much larger incidence of wives in paid employment in big cities compared with country areas.

Opportunities: External and Internal

Opportunities can, roughly, be classified into two groups.

One type offers a sort of standing invitation to women from outside; the other acts in a more negative or indirect way from within. Opportunities of the first kind are the existence of a sufficiently wide range of suitable jobs within reasonably easy reach; good transport services; provision for the care of children; good training facilities; and the possibility of making arrangements for some of the more time-consuming household duties to be taken over by commercial services. The second kind of opportunity is created by the increased leisure women enjoy to-day as a result of their small families and by the invention of continually new and improved household conveniences. John D. Durand, in

80

his interesting analysis of the long-term trends in the field of female employment in the United States,[1] goes so far as to say that the final result of these technical developments 'might be virtually to eliminate the home as a place of work, and housewives as a functional group of the population'.

This may be an overstatement of the case. It is, at any rate, even as a distant possibility, very far removed from present-day realities. Recent developments have tended to bring more rather than less domestic functions back into the home, in spite of, or paradoxically even because of, the increasing use of modern gadgets. Many of these so-called labour-saving devices promote the decentralization of services which, in an earlier phase of industrialization, had moved from the home to the factory. (The example of this which most immediately comes to mind is washing of sheets at home instead of sending them to the laundry, which is the combined result of washing machines and high cost of labour having driven up the prices of laundries.) It looks as though the concentration of production, which was the governing principle of industrialization, had come to a standstill in the sphere of the home.

Whatever the eventual outcome of this development, at the moment it is only in its beginnings. Modern machinery has reached but a small minority of households. Even in the United States there are enormous differences in this respect between town and country, and between different social strata.

Nevertheless, leaving aside Mr. Durand's extreme formulation, all indications are that the general development is in the direction of increasing opportunities for married women to accept employment outside their homes. And with the probability of continued full employment these opportunities are bound to increase even without a further decline of the birth-rate.

But, Mr. Durand asks, will women's desire to work persist in an era of peace and ever rising standards of living? What are the incentives for women to work if neither national emergency nor personal need demand it? The answer was at the time difficult to see for, as the following table shows, the percentage of wives in employment was in inverse correlation to the income of their husbands.

[1] 'Married Women in the Labour Force', John D. Durand, *American Journal of Sociology*, November 1946.

Table 22

PERCENTAGE OF MARRIED WOMEN IN EMPLOYMENT IN U.S.A.,
GRADED BY THEIR HUSBANDS' INCOME, 1940

Dollars	Women with no children under 10 %	Women with one or more children under 10 %
1– 199	33·1	16·6
200– 399	28·5	13·9
400– 599	26·9	12·3
600– 999	24·8	12·1
1,000–1,499	21·5	8·9
1,500–1,999	14·0	5·6
2,000–2,999	12·1	3·3
3,000 and over	8·5	2·8

Source: J. D. Durand, op. cit.

This was true roughly up to the period of Mr. Durand's writing. However, a significant change took place between the 1940 and 1950 Census returns. An analysis of the 1950 data, carried out by the U.S. Bureau of the Census[1] shows that, where there were no children under 18, the women most likely to be employed were those whose husbands earned between $4,000–$5,000 a year, i.e. somewhat above the median male income of the time. Where children were between the ages of 6 to 17 only, the largest percentage of working wives was in the group whose husbands earned $2,000–$3,000; only among the mothers of pre-school children was the employment rate still inversely correlated with husbands' incomes.

Economic and Psychological Motives

The flow of women into the labour market can be seen as consisting of two streams. The one, particularly marked during the first phases of industrialization and connected with the generally low level of wages, consists of women who have to supplement the family income by accepting gainful employment. The relatively high proportion of working wives in textile districts compared to other parts of the same country is a case in point. This stream is likely to ebb when men's wages rise. It has, on the whole, gradually diminished its strength during the period of full employment.

[1] *Current Population Reports, Labor Force*, No. 87, Washington, 1957.

The other stream consists of women with specialized training or a higher education, and is far less directly related to their husbands' incomes. It seems to set in at a more advanced stage of economic development and to gain momentum with the increasing complexity of labour conditions in industrial society and with the accompanying higher living standards.

It would, of course, be mistaken to conceive these two streams as two separate entities; arising from different sources they intermingle sufficiently to lose their identity. The economic motive can no longer be separated from the ideological one; nor can the voluntary element be distinguished from the compulsory one. Does, for instance, the drive to improve one's standard of living—that is, to be able to afford luxuries—come under the same category as the need to make both ends meet? Is the choice of a career —as opposed to more leisure—still to be classed as 'voluntary' once it has become a universal practice which carries with it the approval of conformity? Does the woman who has been trained as a nurse when young in order to earn her living and who continues, or resumes, her job out of a sense of public duty, or the woman to whom unexpected opportunity has given a chance to develop hidden talents, belong to the one or the other 'stream'?

In an international survey of the conditions of working women with home and family responsibilities, carried out by the International Labour Office, only two motives were put forward as responsible for married women going out to work: the women's economic need on the one hand, and national necessity for increased production, supported by vigorous government efforts to recruit more women for industry, on the other.

A growing number of investigations, however, make it evident that other factors play an important part in influencing women to retain their jobs after marriage. Studies carried out independently of each other in Sheffield, York, and other industrial centres, have brought to light the fact that the social isolation of the modern housewife is a powerful motive for women to seek employment outside their homes.

For instance, Ferdinand Zweig, who has carried out a social investigation into the attitudes and habits of Lancashire working women,[1] estimates that 'among married wives no more than about one in three goes out to work under economic pressure either

[1] Dr. F. Zweig, *Women's Life and Labour*, London, 1952, p. 47.

83

because of inadequate housekeeping money or because she has to keep her husband. The rest go out in order to earn extras, to cover the educational expenses of their children, to buy things they want, or for other reasons, as they are used to going out to work and enjoy it.' Though he admits that the border-line between 'economic pressure' and the 'desire for improvement' is arbitrary and hard to define, he is quite emphatic that economic need is by no means the only or even the main motive for married women's work outside their homes. 'The social student often forgets that many women go out to work rather under the emotional pressure of loneliness than under the economic pressure of low wages.'[1]

Our disinclination to subscribe to the traditional explanation that married women go out to work because of economic necessity finds another very well-documented support in the findings of B. Seebohm Rowntree and G. R. Lavers.[2] Their social study of York in 1950 (which, incidentally, records that the increased employment of married women, as well as full employment, higher wages, and the various benefits of the Welfare State, is responsible for the virtual disappearance of poverty in the area of their investigation) notes that the practice of supplementing the family

---

[1] It is worth quoting some of Dr. Zweig's examples in this connexion: 'The typical answers one gets from the category of mothers who go out to work, so to speak, voluntarily, run like this: from a mother of a fifteen-months' baby, aged twenty-four: "I felt very bored at home", or from a mother of four children, fourteen, eleven and eight years and a fifteen-months' old baby: "I am more tired when I stay at home than when I am here"; from a mother of a fourteen-months' old baby, aged twenty: "I am working to help out in buying furniture"; from a mother of a baby of three years, aged twenty-three: "I want to help my husband to get on in his profession"; from a mother of three children, two grown up and one of fourteen years still at school, aged forty-nine: "I come out because I get bored at home, not because of money"; from a mother of a boy of three years, aged twenty-eight: "We have a lot of luxuries which otherwise we could not afford"; from a mother of two boys (seven and ten), aged thirty-one: "I would rather come to work. It is a change. The oldest boy has a key and a sister lives by"; from a mother of three children (twelve, nine and seven), aged thirty-eight: "Granny is like a mother. The work outside keeps you in touch with the world and makes you feel younger"; from a mother of a child of seven, aged thirty-three: "When the boy went to school, life became unbearable within four walls"; from a mother of two children (eight and four), aged thirty-four: "You don't get so morbid and you feel younger. When my husband and I have a bit of an argument, I can say to him: 'You don't keep me.' " Other motives stated were: "To help buying out a house", "a fridge", "a television set", to "Too small a house for two women"—her mother being at home.' (*Op. cit.*, p. 74).

[2] B. Seebohm Rowntree and G. R. Lavers, *Poverty and the Welfare State*, London, 1951.

income by paid full- or part-time work of married women 'appears to be especially prevalent among the best-off sections of the working class'. The authors explain this apparently paradoxical phenomenon by stating: 'The fact that, on the whole, the working class is more prosperous than it has ever been, has created a desire in many families for goods that would formerly have been rejected without consideration as being entirely beyond their means.' The investigation covered 12,708 families whose heads were men in full employment. In 1,278 (i.e. 10 per cent) of these households the wives were full or part-time employed (compared with only 3·2 per cent in 1936). Asked for their reasons for going out to work these women gave the following answers:

13 per cent—to buy furniture, etc., for their homes;
2 ,, ,, —to pay for children's education;
1·5 ,, ,, —'sense of duty' (most of whom were qualified nurses);
34·5 ,, ,, —to 'make ends meet';
27 ,, ,, —to buy luxuries;
21 ,, ,, —for the pleasure of meeting other people instead of being cooped up in their homes all day.

'Many women say frankly', so the report goes on, 'that they want a higher standard of living and are prepared to work to obtain it. Examples of the aims of these women are to buy a car, to have holidays away from York, to buy a radiogram, and to buy an electric washing machine for washing clothes or dishes.'

The process of democratization has brought with it not only a levelling of incomes but also an ever-increasing equalization of standards—such luxuries as travel abroad, higher education for the children, modern household equipment, and so on, are no longer considered prerogatives of a privileged class but are aims within the reach of large sections of the population to be had for an extra effort. And many women think them sufficiently worth while to be willing to make this extra effort themselves.

Not much attention has yet been paid to married middle-class women in employment; their number has seemed too insignificant to warrant close social investigation. A few small-scale studies are, however, at hand, and one, in particular, undertaken by Margot Jefferys among married women in the higher grades of the British

Civil Service and Government-sponsored research organizations,[1] is worth quoting in this context, though the 234 professional women who co-operated in this research may not be representative of the class as a whole. 'An examination of the individual replies of the group', she says, 'show that no single main reason for working predominated. Just over 1 in 5 were working because their income provided the sole or main source of family income. But among the rest, who were probably in a better position to choose whether they wished to work or not, interest in the work or failure to secure satisfaction from unrelieved domesticity, were given about as frequently as financial considerations as the *main* reason for working. In the majority of cases, however, while each individual has a predominant reason, other considerations also weighed. Thus, most of those who gave interest in their work as their main reason also mentioned the financial advantages, and vice versa.'— A somewhat surprising result of this inquiry is 'that financial considerations were given as the *main* reason for working more frequently by childless women than by those with children where the woman's salary was not the sole or main source of family income.' The author explains this seemingly strange phenomenon as follows: 'Women without children have, with few exceptions, smaller domestic ties and fewer reasons why they should not work. To many of them interest may be irrelevant in their decision to work though not, of course, irrelevant in their choice of job. The financial incentive, since it provides the means to satisfy demands for varied kinds of leisure activity, then becomes the dominant one, since giving up work would involve the curtailment of valued leisure pursuits. Women *with* young children, on the other hand, are faced with great difficulties if they are to work, not the least among them being the heavy cost of adequate domestic and child-minding arrangements. Their net financial gains is likely to be much less than that of the childless woman and it has to be set against the emotional strain involved in trying to do a job of work and raise a family at the same time. Only overwhelming interest or a positive dislike of domestic duties, or varying degrees of these two ingredients, are likely to weigh the balance in favour of working.'

Among middle-class as well as working-class wives, the financial

[1] Research Note published in the *British Journal of Sociology*, Vol. III, No. 4, December 1952, pp. 361-4.

incentive to seek work outside their homes is an important consideration, but in view of the experience gained in our period of full employment there are strong indications that economic necessity is no longer the prime motive. It has been replaced, at least to some extent, by a more complex psychological situation in which the desire for a higher standard of life, the need of company, the preference for more congenial types of work and the wish to be financially independent, are some of the constituent factors.

The fact that the proportion of married women in gainful employment has increased more in the United States than anywhere else, except perhaps Stockholm, also seems to show that personal economic necessity and the manpower need of the national economy—the two reasons analysed by the International Labour Office—are by no means the only factors influencing married women to go out to work. Both these countries have a high standard of living and, at least as far as the United States is concerned, there has been little encouragement on the part of the government.

It seems clear from these two instances that the employment of married women is the result of other factors besides material need, individual or national. On the one hand, it depends on the gap between real and desired family income—the latter, in its turn, being conditional on the things that the money could buy. It depends, on the other hand, on the existence of amenities which allow women to satisfy an urge which may be psychological as much as economic. It may have been created by a desire for more productive or more diversified work, by the wish to make better use of innate abilities or of acquired training, by wanting to 'keep up with the Joneses', or simply by sociability—most probably by a combination of some of these motives.

In cases of individual necessity, employment is sought even without relief from home duties, with great expenditure of nervous energy and at the cost of domestic comfort and happiness. In cases of national need, it has sometimes been found necessary to provide such relief, in the form of crèches, organized home-help, school meals, etc., in order to act as incentives for women to accept jobs. Where similar social services already exist, however, as the result of a high degree of industrialization combined with an effective social organization, the inducement from without—whether by the stick of material hardship or the carrot of government propaganda—need not be a decisive factor.

In discussions of the question why women go out to work, the economic motive has usually been in the foreground. Since in our society women are either paid at a lower rate than men for the same job, or else are confined to the more poorly paid grades, it is natural that the material hardships of women should have been stressed by those in favour of equal pay. Facts and figures have been produced to prove that a large number of women support children or other dependents, and that the argument put forward by some people in support of differential payment, namely, that women work only for pin-money, is a myth.

These facts have often been presented in such a way as to appeal for sympathy for the women who 'have to earn their own living'. Most women, it has been argued, would prefer *not* to work outside their homes; if they accept employment they only do so when driven by financial hardship. According to the American sociologist W. F. Ogburn, as many as 85 per cent of working women declared that they work not because they want to but because they have to.

A Question which is never asked

Put in this form, the question why women work appears both unfair and irrelevant. If men were asked why they work, the great majority would no doubt answer that they have to support themselves and their families. Nobody would pity them for it. It is taken for granted that this should be so. Only the lucky few can honestly claim to work for their own pleasure or to follow their interests. That they have to accept a job is a *conditio sine qua non* for the vast majority; if they can find an interest in it, all the better for them. But men are not asked such questions. Their choice is not between work or no work but between different kinds of jobs. Their personal problem is to adjust themselves as well as possible to this given situation.

The attitude adopted in the case of women is different. It is characteristic that the numerous investigations into the motives of married women in accepting gainful employment are not matched by other studies examining the question why married women, when they have no small children to look after, do *not* work outside their homes. This situation is so much taken as the natural order of things that it has caused no wonder, and hence no scientific inquiry. In spite of the marked social change, the idea still prevails that it is normal for women to be supported by their husbands under all circumstances. Many men, particularly in the middle classes, whose wives have jobs feel a sense of guilt for allowing them to do so and are apologetic about it. To some extent, to this day a married woman who has a career other than that of housewife is 'fallen from grace' and deserving of sympathy.

It is possible, of course, to describe this situation in different terms. *Life* magazine, for instance, published the results of a survey according to which there are twenty million 'idle women' in the United States. The term 'idle' was here applied to all women who are neither aged nor infirm, who have no jobs, and are not mothers of children under 18 years of age. If this interpretation became more widespread fewer men would feel they owe it to their ego to be the sole providers for their families, and more women would feel under a moral constraint to use their time and energies for more than domestic chores.

While men have no alternative but to work and are considered asocial if they refuse to do so, this same ethical rule has not been widely applied to women. The latter have, to a large extent, retained the privilege, typical for both men and women in the governing classes of former times, of not taking part in the social effort. They have surprisingly long been held all the more respectable for not doing so.

Equality or Privilege?

Here, obviously, is a gap in our democratic ideology; or, if one prefers to call it that, a 'time-lag' in the adjustment of our ideas to the changes in our conditions of life. Women should, in particular, be sensitive to it. They have for so long claimed equal rights, and have achieved equality in so many fields, that a re-assessment of their social contribution should now be made. In this assessment, all their productive efforts, whether paid or unpaid, whether inside or outside their homes, should be taken into account; whether they educate children or spin cotton is of minor concern in this connexion. But an account should be drawn up of what they do with their energy and their abilities and with the social investment that has gone into them. For in a democratic society no group has the right to claim exemption on account of birth from comparisons of their social contribution with that of others.

It would appear, too, that in the democratic competition between rival claims of the sexes, the time has come to put in a word for the equal rights of men. The egalitarian claims of women have been put forward so eloquently during the last century that one hardly dares to mention the privileges which women *qua* women enjoy. There are quite a number of them and we need not elaborate them here.

To-day, with the equality between the sexes so nearly achieved, it is only fair to admit that the disadvantages are not all on one side, and to demand that an equal measure be applied to both sexes. Equal rights should correspond to equal duties and responsibilities. Those, therefore, who demand equal pay should be the last to appeal for pity for the poor women who 'have to work' for their living. *Égalité oblige.*

It is, of course, a fact, and amply attested by the figures in the previous chapter, that opportunities for work and demands for labour are somewhat different for the two sexes under present market conditions. However, there is overwhelming objective evidence to refute the assertion that women, *per se*, whether married or unmarried, should have a different status. That mothers 'on active service' are in a special situation and deserve special consideration, is another matter. This is a point which will be more fully discussed in a later chapter. But to exempt all women, at all times, from general rules of conduct on the strength of their potential motherhood, or past achievement in that respect, is like exempting men from ordinary work because, one day, they may become heroes, or because they have fought valiantly in the past.

CHAPTER SIX

EMPLOYERS' PROBLEMS

Since we wish to advocate the more extensive employment of women it is important to analyse the resistance to this which undoubtedly exists among employers, fellow-workers, and the public generally. Objections are raised on a number of different grounds. Some of them are based on social prejudices or personal bias, others on verifiable facts and circumstances. Although it is difficult to argue rationally against emotional attitudes we must seriously consider the case against the greater employment of women —which chiefly means the employment of married women—advanced by disinterested bodies of opinion, such as psychologists, educationalists, social scientists, and so forth, and to study the evidence given by employers of female labour.

In order to gain as comprehensive and impartial a picture of our problem as possible, we shall have to scrutinize carefully the arguments brought forward by all interested parties. The employment of women has now had a sufficiently long history and wide application for the discussion to be taken out of the sphere of personal views into the more dispassionate atmosphere of practical experience and rational analysis.

To take the questions of economic efficiency first. Industrial machinery and organization—at least in the first phases of the Industrial Revolution which Western countries are only now outgrowing—was set up and run almost entirely by men. Looking back on the history of industrialization, it is quite clear why this was so. The steam engine, the invention of which initiated the Industrial Revolution, needed the strenuous physical labour of men to provide its main raw material, coal, as well as to serve the heavy machines in foundries and factories, and to build and operate the railways and canals. Moreover, the concentration of production, and of the growing administrative apparatus required by the new industrial development, took place at a distance from and quite independently of people's homes. The separation of home and workplace, of private and professional life, became as complete as possible. The same individual who is a member of a family with certain responsibilities, tasks and predilections in one place, assumes almost a different personality as a member of the personnel in office or factory. His loyalties, interests and aims differ between one place and the other.

The rift between the two sets of functions has been aggravated by the fact that the main burden of home duties could be taken over by women, who, more and more, became the centre of the family and the managers of the home. Some other functions, such as bringing up the sons in the craft of their fathers, either disappeared altogether or were taken over by educational and other institutions. Men's share in the life of the home and of the family shrank, while business and factory organizations could be built up as huge machines running on the assumption that human beings were cogs in the wheels. The fact that they had obligations and interests outside their jobs could be ignored.

When new industrial and administrative techniques brought women into this man-made organization, and when more and more of them were needed to keep the machines going, their efforts were, of course, measured by the established norms. How did their output, their attendance record, their perseverance, their interest in the job, compare with existing standards?

The achievements of women have been sufficiently praised elsewhere and are too familiar by now to need repetition. The fact that more and more women are not only accepted but wanted in industry, business, administration and public services of all kinds is in itself sufficient testimony to the value of their contribution.

This does not, however, answer the question whether adjustments in organization and techniques are not needed, or at least desirable, if women's services are to be used to best advantage, without causing conflicts in their lives and disorganization in their families. So far, the required adjustments have largely been one-sided, made by the women, and made often at great personal sacrifice. If the best use is to be made of labour, the more unwieldy apparatus of industrial and administrative organization will have to be re-adapted to the needs of the human beings who keep it going.

Concern for the welfare of the worker and his family is a fairly recent development, characteristic of the latest phase of industrialization. It seems not unlikely that the increasing share of women in hitherto masculine spheres of work may have contributed to the growing awareness that peoples' jobs are only one aspect of their lives.

This realization was given expression, for instance, in a pamphlet[1] published by the British Ministry of Labour and National Service in 1942, at a time of the most strenuous national effort: 'Home life has always been a person's very private business and has been the ultimate object and reward of his labour. Many government departments, societies and individuals deal with "Welfare". The matters dealt with under any "welfare effort" become very trivial when compared with a person's home life. . . .'

This publication, a model of official reasonableness, was dealing with the problem of absenteeism which was then particularly pressing. Married women, especially, were the worst offenders and the Ministry of Labour reminded employers: 'They are trying to do two full-time jobs. If they can carry on with a mere half-day per week off the ordinary factory hours, they are achieving something marvellous. It is time somebody said more about women's effort on these lines and more about the arrangements which ought to be made to enable them to carry on.'

The Ministry's recommendation was that these conditions should be taken into account and met by greater flexibility in the organization of industry. 'Adaptation of the industrial machine to meet the reasonable requirements of the human beings who operate that machine is essential if the optimum national output is to be maintained.'

This is, of course, no less true in times of peace than in times of war and must form the basis of any long-term policy of production. At this point we do not want to go into details of how such adaptation of the industrial machine, and of the social organization in general, is to be achieved; nor can we discuss the Ministry of Labour's specific recommendations to the employers. More will be said about these things later on.

Here we want to sketch the general background against which the disparities between men and women have to be seen. It is our

[1] *The Problem of Absenteeism*, Ministry of Labour and National Service, September 1942.

conviction that the only constructive approach to the problem of women in employment is to treat the organization of work, rather than of the women workers, as variable. The question to be asked, therefore, is not, 'What detrimental effects, if any, has the double function of the woman worker on the job, given existing standards and methods of industrial organization?' Instead, we have to ask, 'What are the working conditions most conducive to maximum efficiency, considering the fact that workers have home responsibilities as well as jobs and that married women, in particular, often have arduous as well as important responsibilities at home?'

If the ultimate aim is the adjustment of the industrial organization to the absorption of a new type of worker with different traditions and social habits, we must first see at what points friction has arisen from the meeting of the new worker and the old machine.

The shortcomings of women in comparison with men fall mainly under three headings: (1) absenteeism, (2) higher turnover and (3) connected with the latter, the higher relative cost and inconvenience of training people whose continuity in employment is precarious. The more highly skilled the job, and the longer and more expensive the training it requires, the more acute is this last problem.

Absenteeism

Absolute figures are difficult to obtain and do not convey a correct picture of the situation, since the rates of absenteeism differ not only from one branch of work to another, but from one workplace to another and from one location to another. They vary between married and single women, between skilled and unskilled workers, and between men and women in different age groups. They depend on such variable factors as the atmosphere of work in a firm, the method of selection of workers, the relationship between management and staff and, of course, on the general labour situation, such as the relative ease with which other jobs are available. For these reasons, all generalizations are bound to give a distorted picture. So much can, however, be said, generally speaking: absenteeism is considerably higher among women than among men—often twice, three or even more times as high. But there are offices and factories with particularly good conditions of work in which absences occur no more frequently among women than among men.

The U.S. Public Health Service has been collecting data on sick-absenteeism for some years from the records of mutual sick benefit associations, group health insurance plans, and company relief departments. The records cover only disabilities lasting for 8 consecutive days or longer, since most sickness benefits do not begin until after the first week of sickness. They are analysed periodically by Dr. W. M. Gafafer, in the U.S. Public Health Reports.

During 1950, these figures show men as having 116·8 such absences (per year per 1,000 workers) due to sickness and non-industrial injuries, while women had 258·4. The following table shows absences of men and women due to illness during the years 1949 and 1950 as well as the average figures for the preceding 10 years:

Table 23

ABSENCES OF WORKERS DUE TO NON-INDUSTRIAL ILLNESS, U.S.A.

Cause	Annual number of absences per 1,000 persons beginning in specified period					
	Males			Females		
	1950	1941–50 Average	1949	1950	1941–50 Average	1949
Sickness and non-industrial injuries	116·8	117·7	95·5	258·4	229·3	254·5
Percentage of female rate	45	51	38	—	—	—
Percentage of male rate	—	—	—	221	195	266
Non-industrial injuries (169–195)	13·7	12·1	10·9	19·3	16·2	18·5
Sickness	103·1	105·6	84·6	239·1	213·1	236·0

Source: W. M. Gafafer, D.Sc., *Industrial Sickness Absenteeism among Males and Females during 1950.* Public Health Reports, Vol. 66, No. 47, 23 November 1951, pp. 1550–51.

Another investigation[1] was made of over 300,000 workers employed in the U.S.A. and Canada by the General Motors Corporation who were enrolled in the company's 'group insurance programme' for hourly rated employees. It covered illnesses that began in the 12 months preceding 31 July 1950, and that lasted longer than seven days.

Men lost an average of 4·2 days a year because of temporary off-the-job illness, compared with 14·8 days for women workers, excluding obstetrical cases, or 17·2 days if such cases were included.

During the year studied, 87 out of every 1,000 hourly paid men workers had a non-occupational illness lasting more than 7 days. Such illness was nearly three times as frequent among insured men workers who were 50 years of age or older as among younger men —188 per 1,000 of the older men compared with 67 per 1,000 of the younger.

Women workers had a frequency rate of 239 per 1,000 (excluding obstetrical cases), i.e. nearly three times that of men. In the younger groups, the frequency rate for women was nearly four times as high as for men. According to the study, about 1 of every 4 insured women workers was absent because of off-the-job illness during the year; or 1 in 3 women under the age of 50, if sickness connected with pregnancy is included.

Hourly rated men workers lost an annual average of 48 days per claim for benefits during the year studied; women (excluding obstetrical cases) lost an average of 62 days per claim—2 weeks more than men. Young men lost 41 such days—20 fewer than the older men, whereas younger women lost 62 days—only 5 less than the average for the older group of women.

The basic findings of all these, and similar, studies show a common trend, in peace and wartime; women are absent more frequently than men, and their total time lost is greater; illness is the predominant reason for absence both for men and women and the incidence of illness resulting in absence from work is greater among women than among men.

The same trend is present in other countries. An interim report

---

[1] *Non-occupational Disability in General Motors*, by J. M. Gillen, Director, Personnel Research Section, General Motors Corp., Detroit, 1951. (Address before General Motors Medical Conference, Atlantic City, N.J. 23 April 1951.) (See Report in *Monthly Labor Review*, January 1952.)

on the working of the National Insurance system in Great Britain[1] shows that during the year 1950 sickness benefit was paid for an average of 1¾ weeks per man, and nearly 3 weeks per woman. These figures include all classes of employment except civil servants, who are covered by a separate scheme; but they do not include absences from work for which no insurance is paid, such as an odd day of sickness, or in certain circumstances the first three days of an illness.

The Industrial Health Research Board of the Medical Research Council[2] estimated that, under war conditions, 'lost time among men usually varies between 5 and 10 per cent of the possible hours of work; among women it is often between 8 and 20 per cent. In most factories, women lost about twice as much time as men; and married women may lose up to three times as much as single women.'

A Swedish committee of Trade Unions and Employers, set up in 1948 to investigate the problems of women's wages and of their position in industry generally, found that, disregarding special causes of absence such as holidays, military service, pregnancies and confinements, absenteeism is twice as great among women as among men in Swedish industry.[3]

Absenteeism in industry, as a rule, comes under two headings: absence through sickness and so-called 'voluntary absenteeism'. The second category includes any absence not justified either by illness or by injury. It may therefore have a variety of causes: fatigue due to long hours of work and travel, home and family responsibilities, housing shortage and resulting transport difficulties, shopping requirements, or it may have psychological reasons such as lack of incentive, lack of interest in the job, insufficient conviction of the importance of the work.

Though the sickness rate among women is itself higher than among men, the large difference in hours of work lost arises from other causes, chiefly connected with home responsibilities. Professor Zweig[4] says in this connexion: 'The point is that the

[1] The National Insurance Act, 1946, Second Interim Report by the Government Actuary for the year ended 31 March 1951, June 1952.

[2] *Absence from Work and Prevention of Fatigue. Conditions for Industrial Health and Efficiency*, Pamphlet 2, issued by the Industrial Health Research Board of the Medical Research Council, 1944.

[3] 'Enquiry on Equal Pay in Sweden', *International Labour Review*, July 1951.

[4] *Op. cit.*, p. 118.

concept of voluntary absenteeism has little meaning when one is judging a woman's behaviour. If her husband or her child or her parents or in-laws are sick, is she not justified to stay at home as much as if she herself were sick? If her children are running wild because the school holidays have started, is she not justified in making proper arrangements for them? Or if her husband is on night shift or evening shift this week, she cannot leave him all by himself in the house. The whole concept of voluntary absenteeism is a male's invention for judging males, but cannot be applied to women to the same degree.'

Since the incidence of illness among children is very much higher than among adults, and since children are as a rule their mother's charge, the rate of absenteeism among married women, especially those with children, is very much higher, not only than that of men but also compared with single women.

Table 24 shows figures for the different rates of sickness among single and married women. Considering these data, however, two factors have to be borne in mind. Firstly, they refer to the period of war when, partly for patriotic reasons and partly because of the direction of labour, large numbers of married women were drawn into the industrial effort who would otherwise not have worked outside their homes. The rate of absenteeism was for this and other reasons, e.g. bombing, nervous strain, home-leave of husbands and sweethearts, etc., considerably higher than in normal times.

Secondly, it is well to remember another point on which we may again quote Professor Zweig:[1] 'The difference between sickness absenteeism and voluntary absenteeism is all round marked in pencil rather than ink, but much more so for women than men. A woman, especially if she is a married mother, usually takes too much on herself, and her husband, who is generally speaking not very happy about her going out to work, will look at her in the morning and tell her: "You look tired to-day, you'd better take a day off"; he may even tell her straight away to stay home, and there are few doctors who would not give an appropriate certificate to a married woman with children who looks tired.'

The data presented in the study below are sufficiently broken down to reveal some interesting details: In the group of workers studied it was found that 16·3 per cent of the women were

[1] *Op. cit.*, p. 118.

EMPLOYERS' PROBLEMS

Table 24

ABSENTEEISM OF MARRIED AND SINGLE WOMEN IN INDUSTRY, GREAT BRITAIN

	Married	Single	Both
Average number of cases of sickness absence per 100 workers in period of six months	98·2	66·3	84·2
Average number of days of sickness per worker in period of six months	17·45	10·57	14·45
Average length of individual absences	17·8	15·9	17·1
Percentage who had absences of more than 28 days	17·9	9·9	14·4
Percentage discharged as medically unfit during period of six months	3·13	1·71	2·49

Average number of absences per worker in each age group—

	Average number of absences per worker:			Ratio:	
Age group	Married	Single	Both	Married	Single
15–19	1·03	0·52	0·57	1·98	1·00
20–24	1·06	0·70	0·82	1·51	1·00
25–29	1·07	0·75	0·95	1·43	1·00
30–34	1·04	0·70	0·94	1·49	1·00
35–39	0·95	0·86	0·89	1·40	1·00
40–49	0·86	0·49	0·81	1·76	1·00
50–59	0·61	0·32	0·54	1·91	1·00

Average number of days of sickness per worker in each group—

15–19	18·8	8·3	9·3	2·27	1·00
20–24	18·9	10·9	13·6	1·73	1·00
25–29	16·3	9·8	13·8	1·66	1·00
30–34	18·3	12·4	16·6	1·48	1·00
35–39	17·2	14·3	16·6	1·20	1·00
40–49	17·3	10·9	16·5	1·59	1·00
50–59	13·0	8·5	11·9	1·53	1·00

Source: *A Study of Certified Sickness Absence among Women in Industry*, Industrial Health Research Board Report No. 86, 1945.

responsible for approximately two-thirds of the time lost through sickness. Married women had 45 per cent more absences and lost 65 per cent more time on that account than single women. The percentage of women with no sickness absence during the six-month period covered by the Report was 45·3. (Married women 38·4 per cent and single women 54 per cent.) The figures were brought up to the very high total of 84·2 cases of sickness absence per hundred workers by the fact that some women were absent on several occasions.

Another very interesting fact revealed by the foregoing table is that women in the older age groups have fewer absences from work than younger ones in each category. Both the married and the single women between 50 and 59 come out specially well.

Since in recent years the increase in the female labour force has, to a large extent, been due to the return to work of women aged forty and over, it seems fair to assume that the overall attendance record of women will improve as a result.

Dr. Anna M. Baetjer, of Johns Hopkins University,[1] studying American data, analysed the reasons of women's absenteeism. She states that the greater sickness rate among women 'would not seem due to a difference in sex susceptibility to disease since the mortality rate for males exceeds that for females at all ages' and sick-absenteeism is 'not limited to those diseases which are associated with the sex functions of women but occurs for diseases common to both sexes'. She found that 'the chief causes of sick-absenteeism were respiratory diseases which accounted for about 50 per cent of the number of cases and also of the number of days lost annually, and digestive diseases, which were responsible for almost 20 per cent of the cases'.

Dr. Baetjer's findings that women are ill more frequently and lose more time from work because of it, but that their absences are shorter, corresponds to observations made among the general population and corroborated also by data collected for the Women's Army Corps.

'The frequency of short-term illnesses', according to Dr. Baetjer's findings, 'appeared to decrease with age, although the average number of days per illness increases. Since these two factors counterbalance each other, the annual number of days lost did not show any marked trend with age, except in the older age groups. This may be partly due to the fact that those women who are frequently ill are apt to stop working at younger ages, thus leaving a selected middle-age group. . . . The employment of middle-aged women, therefore, lowers the frequency and does not appreciably increase the annual lost time due to sickness.'

Length of employment also seems to act as a selective factor: 'The frequency of absences due to sickness was less in women who

[1] A. M. Baetjer, *Women in Industry*, London and Philadelphia, 1946.

had been employed longer, probably reflecting a selective process as well as age distribution.'

Among the various causes which Dr. Baetjer mentions to explain the greater sickness absenteeism of women, the following also deserves quotation: 'The excess frequency rate in sick-absenteeism among women as compared to men's may be due merely to the fact that women take their minor illnesses more seriously than men. This is supported by the fact that the average duration of sick-absences is shorter for women than men. Many persons believe that the excess sick-absenteeism among industrial women is due to the fact that they frequently attempt to do two jobs at once, their work in industry plus their duties at home. Part of the excess absenteeism among women may be due to a less serious attitude towards their work, so that they take time off for minor ailments or report unjustified absences as due to sickness more frequently than men. There is some evidence that women may have a higher incidence of nervous and mental disease than men, but how far a lack of emotional adjustment is responsible for the excess illness is not known. Some people have attributed the excess sick-absenteeism to poorer nutritional habits on the part of women, but there is little factual evidence to support this assumption at present.'

In view of the various causes of absence from work mentioned above, it is not surprising to find that the percentage of time lost is very considerably lower among part-time workers. The comparative figures published for one factory[1] were 1·83 per cent for part-timers compared with 3·3 per cent for married women on full-time work.

So far, we have quoted figures for industrial workers only, partly because of the abundance of sources on this subject, partly because in this field the conditions of employment for men and women are more comparable than in many other occupations. Moreover, as the large number of investigations itself indicates, absenteeism is a more serious concern in industry because of the large numbers of women involved and because of its higher incidence than in other occupations.

In non-industrial occupations, although the rate of absenteeism among women tends to be smaller on the whole, it is again higher than among men. Exact figures are often not available for a variety

[1] *Manchester Guardian*, 1942.

of reasons, and we can but quote a few random examples to indicate the general trend. It has, moreover, to be observed that absences through causes other than sickness are mostly not recorded; these would, in fact, be extremely difficult to ascertain. A civil servant, for instance, who wants a day off for shopping or for family reasons will take it at the expense of her annual leave and shorten her holiday period correspondingly. Since she may be entitled to four, five, or even six weeks' leave per year in the higher grades, she has quite a number of free days at her disposal. Her absences from work other than those for which she can produce a doctor's certificate will therefore not be shown in any statistics; they come under the heading of 'annual leave' and there are, of course, no data available to show how men or women civil servants distribute the periods of leisure to which they are legally entitled, that is, whether they take odd days off because they need them for shopping, or because a member of their family is ill, or because they attend a conference or watch a football match, or go to the seaside.

In some other services, employees are allowed a certain number of days per year as sick leave. This applies for instance, to all employees subject to civil service regulations in the United States. There, a maximum of 15 days per year is available as sick leave which is allowed to accumulate up to a total of 90 days. This system, too, gives a wide margin for irregular absences which do not have to be accounted for and obscures the issue of absenteeism among civil servants.

For the British Civil Service the following figures for the year 1943, taken in 63 departments, give an idea of the distribution of sickness absences between men and women:

Table 25

AVERAGE SICK ABSENCE IN DAYS PER YEAR (1943) OF ESTABLISHED
CIVIL SERVANTS, GREAT BRITAIN

Men			Women	
Above rank of Clerical Officer	Clerical Officer	Above rank of Clerical Officer	Clerical Officer	Clerical Assistant
(11,524)	(10,307)	(3,249)	(6,358)	(713)
11·6	15·39	15·8	17·8	22·2

Source: *Royal Commission on Equal Pay, 1944–46,* Appendix IV, 1946, Cmd. 6937.

Married women are not included in the above figures because before removal of the marriage bar in 1946 they were not eligible for employment in established posts in the Civil Service.

In Sweden, investigations were carried out on several occasions during the inter-war period into the problem of absenteeism in the Civil Service. On the basis of one of the earlier of these surveys, it was calculated that during a service period of 35 years, the excess absences of an average woman compared with a man would amount to about one year (860·85 days for men, 1,222·1 days for women). The later surveys, too, showed a conspicuous difference between the number of sick-leaves of men and women. Women exceed men, and married women exceed single women in the number of working days lost through sickness. When these matters were discussed by the Royal Commission on Women's Work, it was, however, pointed out that a higher relative proportion of women was in the lower grades of the Service and on that account entitled to shorter periods of annual leave than many men with equal length of service.

Relatively little information is available on absenteeism among school teachers, though in this field of employment comparisons between the sexes could well be made on an equal basis. A few cities made reports on this subject.

The town of Cincinnati took a sample over a ten-year period 1939–48 based on a total group of 3,274 women and 726 men teachers. According to its report, absences of teachers from illness during that period averaged 2·9 days a year for men and 5·2 days for women. Absences from all causes averaged 3·4 days for men, and 6·1 days for women.

In the report of the British Royal Commission on Equal Pay, the following data were given concerning absenteeism among school teachers:

SHEFFIELD EDUCATION COMMITTEE

(percentage of teachers absent each School Meeting 1943–44)

	Personal Illness	Other Causes	Total
Single women	2·57	0·30	2·87
Married women	2·50	1·16	3·66
Total women	2·55	0·54	3·09
Men	2·40	0·22	2·61
All teachers	2·52	0·48	3·00

LONDON COUNTY COUNCIL

(*average number of working days missed per year*)

Men	Single Women	Married Women
4	8	11

The difference between the absence of single and married women seems largely due to illness of their husbands and children. As can be seen from the above table, they exceed all other categories mainly in absences from 'other causes' rather than personal illness. (Confinement leaves are not included in the above figures.)

When the women teachers in Sweden were campaigning for equal pay, the question of absenteeism was used as a major argument by their opponents. A special investigation was therefore carried out which led to the following results (based on data for 1937):

Table 26

SICK-LEAVE AMONG TEACHERS IN SWEDEN

	Total Number Asked	Percentage having sick-leave during year	Average number of days sick-leave	
			per all teachers	per teacher sick
Men teachers	8,011	12·7	5·5	43·0
Women, unmarried	3,663	23·9	14·1	58·9
,, married	1,889	32·6	14·8	45·4

In the attempt to explain the greater number of sick-leaves of married women, it was noted that it was in fact easier for a married woman, who often has a servant or at any rate a husband to look after her, to stay in bed for a day or two, than it is for a single woman who has to look after herself. The considerably greater proportion of long sick-leaves among the single women teachers was explained by nervous and gastric illnesses or states of deficiency, all of which seem to bear witness to a considerable nervous strain.

We have quoted these figures at some length because it seems to us necessary for a full understanding to appreciate that one of the major objections against the employment of women is based not merely on prejudice but on actual experience. The statistical data are undeniable evidence that, with all due variations as from one type of employment to another, the rate of absenteeism is higher among women than men in each occupational group.

This, however, is only one aspect of the position and other factors need to be considered for a comprehensive and accurate appreciation of the problem. It is, for instance, fair to say that people in more responsible jobs are less prone to absenteeism than those who carry less responsibility; that good labour relations tend to raise attendance records; that more mature women and those with a long employment record are more likely to be regular attenders at work than the younger and more inexperienced women. In 1943 Mr. Ernest Bevin, then Minister of Labour, stated in Parliament, 'from practical experience, where women go in at the middle ages, there is less absenteeism, and greater efficiency'. Mr. Bevin then recalled that at one point at the beginning of his term of office he had to force employers to accept women over 40, and he continued: 'I am very glad I did. Employers have realized since that the steadying influence of the middle-aged woman in the workshop has been a great success and of great benefit to everybody concerned.'

There may also be a good deal of truth in Professor Zweig's contention[1] that married women, and especially those with children at home, really only want part-time jobs and accept full-time employment only because part-time work is not available. They will try, he says, as far as possible to convert a full-time job into a part-time one, and if they are not, as they are in some firms, given at least a half-day free for shopping and other home requirements, they will tend to take time off on their own account in order to avoid overburdening their weekends with domestic chores.

A certain laxity concerning regular full-time attendance may be a symptom of immaturity in some women's attitude to their job. This is, of course, given freer play in a period of full employment. With their husbands at work and earning good wages, and in the knowledge that they can practically always find another job if necessary, many women—unless their work is attractive, or near their homes, or offers other special advantages—feel less constrained

[1] *Op. cit.*, p. 119.

to make an all-out effort than if their livelihood depended on the continuation of their job.

Turnover of Labour

The same factors also influence the turnover of labour, which is very much larger among women than among men, and which is often a serious problem to the employees of female labour. Labour wastage is on an average 50–60 per cent higher among women than among men, sometimes even more than that. It is not unknown, for instance in textile areas employing large numbers of women, for the staff of a factory to be completely renewed within the course of one year, a labour wastage of 100 per cent.[1]

The figures published by the American Department of Labor offer much the same picture as those published by the British Ministry of Labour. The average duration of current employment in U.S.A. was 3·9 years for men and 2·2 years for women (January 1951).[2] While at that time 25 per cent of the men had been with the same employer for at least ten years, only 14 per cent of the women had such a long record of continuous employment. (This is, of course, partly due to the fact that many women have come in only recently.)

Labour wastage is naturally very much larger among the younger women than among the older ones. The median duration of current employment for older women, regardless of marital status, exceeds the average of all workers, and in January 1951 was 4 years for women aged 45–54, and 4·5 years for women aged 55–64.

It is, of course, very much easier for a young girl to find another job than it is for a woman over 40. Therefore the latter will stick to her current job as best she can. To this extent, the differential in wastage between younger and older women reflects supply and demand in the labour market.

The chief reasons, however, for the large wastage of labour among women apply by their very nature mostly to the younger age groups: many girls give up their jobs on marriage, or on having their first baby, or when their husband's position sufficiently improves; some may move to a different place when they marry or when their husband is transferred elsewhere; or they

---

[1] Cf. also Viola Klein, *Britain's Married Women Workers*, London and New York, 1965.
[2] *Facts on Women Workers*, Women's Bureau, Department of Labor, March 1952.

may have to break off their employment because of pregnancy or family cares.

In addition to all these causes, or rather behind most of them, there is the fact that most women as yet lack a sense of career and therefore adopt a somewhat casual attitude towards the continuity of their employment. Many of them think of their jobs merely as temporary occupations before and until they marry. Trusting that they will not have to carry on for very long, and unmindful of the more distant future, they often do not take an interest in a particular sphere of work, but keep being prepared to accept any vacancy which is offered and which appears suitable for the moment—often for fortuitous reasons, such as because it is near home or because a friend of theirs works there or because the job is clean, and so on.

For similarly casual reasons they are often prepared to change their jobs if they do not like the atmosphere, or the foreman, or if they do not get on with their mates, or are bored, or if a better opportunity offers itself. Since there are now many more vacancies for young girls than can readily be filled, it is easy to see why they form such a shifting section of the labour force. Women are as a rule more adaptable to changing circumstances than men; their willingness to vary the circumstances themselves is the reverse side of this same trait. In addition, it must not be overlooked that the lack of a sense of continuity in a career, or absence of loyalty to a chosen occupation, which is often found even among women with high qualifications, is connected with the collective experience of women that their opportunities for advancement are small unless they have quite exceptional abilities of character combined with good fortune. Their continuity at work after marriage is, moreover, discouraged by official policy, e.g. through taxation, in practically all countries. Finally, they cannot but know that, however much in demand they may seem at the moment, in time of crisis they will be the first to be redundant. In this respect they resemble other social groups with similar past experiences, e.g. the coal-miners, who even during a period of full employment are still haunted by collective memories of past depressions. That such fears are not just ghosts of times past is constantly brought home to women. In 1952, for instance, at the first signs of 'retrenchment', a motion was put forward in the British Civil Service Association to re-introduce the marriage bar for women civil servants. This motion, it is true, was defeated after a long and lively debate; but it is certainly symptomatic of their insecurity of tenure that if economic troubles threaten, women should be considered as the first 'ballast' to be shed. This is not surprising while women's earnings are still generally regarded as 'supplementary' to the family income, and the result is that women feel their hold on any career to be tenuous.

Apart from such occasional reminders of their uncertain and unequal position on the labour market, there is also the constant one of being paid at a lower rate than men for the same job. This inequality of reward, which applies to all wages, most salaries, cost of living bonuses, and any collective pay-increases which may be agreed upon between employers and trade unions, perpetuates in women the feeling that their work is not valued fully and that as workers they are not taken as seriously as men. This has the psychological effect that they themselves, consciously or unconsciously, do not feel under an obligation to take their jobs quite as seriously as men do.

In Britain, equal pay in the Civil Service and the teaching profession has been in force since 1957. In the United States, the principle of equal pay for equal work was established by the Classification Act of 1923 and women in the Federal Service—though not in private employment—have been paid on the same basis as men ever since. However, an occupational survey of white-collar workers, made by the Civil Service Commission in 1959, disclosed that 79 per cent of all women employees, compared with 28 per cent of all men employees, were in the five lowest grades; correspondingly, the higher one went up the ladder of promotion, the smaller the proportion of women represented. The median grade of women in non-professional occupations was three grades lower than that of men; in the professions, it was four grades lower.[1] Although legislative measures have since been taken (by Executive Order of the President in July 1962 to eliminate discrimination in the matter of appointments and promotion of women in the Federal Service, and by the Equal Pay Act of 1963 establishing this principle in private industry—it is not yet possible to assess the long-term effects of these measures.

In the French Civil Service equal pay has been accepted for a

[1] For details see *Report of the Committee on Federal Employment* to the President's Commission on the Status of Women, Washington, October 1963.

long time, and since 1946 equal minimum pay has been established by law in all types of employment. Nevertheless, the difference between the average pay of men and women was estimated in 1953 to be as high as 40 per cent, because women tend to be in the lower grades of jobs, or in trades, such as clothing, which are traditionally badly paid.[1]

Thus a vicious circle operates: the unequal remuneration of women reduces their sense of 'career' and contributes to the lack of continuity in their employment, and on the other hand, the lack of continuity in their work is one of the main reasons why they are paid at a lower rate and meet with difficulties in their promotion. For frequent changes of personnel of course increase the running costs of a business, involve loss of time, reduce efficiency and, like absenteeism, lower the morale of other workers.

This greater restlessness of women employees which we have been discussing has far wider implications if seen from a longer perspective. Women's readiness not only to change their jobs but to abandon their careers represents a problem of social and economic waste.

If this is true of all women, it particularly applies to women in jobs which require a long or expensive training. It is, in fact, quite surprising that parents, employers and education authorities have not been more chary of investing time and money in the higher education or specialized training of girls, in view of the short time most of them are likely to make practical use of the qualifications they have acquired. It has been said of women in the Civil Service—with how much justification it is difficult to judge—that during the first years of their employment they are not worth the money they earn and when they start being of full value they leave to get married. A serious study of labour economics should make detailed calculations of the investment in time and money required for training various categories of workers, and of the returns on this investment. The waste by women of their training has certainly given cause for grave criticism and, whether wholly justified or not, seriously limits the chances of promotion of those women who hope to make their own living and get on in their career.

In discussions on equal pay for women, these arguments loom large. It is also argued that women need special supervision and

[1] Cf. M. Guilbert and V. Isambert-Jamati, *op. cit.*

more welfare services than men, thus increasing costs of production, and that, while they expect greater flexibility on the part of management and greater adjustment to the needs of their home life, they themselves are more rigid, e.g. they can less easily be transferred from one place to another and are limited in their movement from one occupation to another—the latter largely because of the traditional division of labour between the sexes which still bars many activities to women. In this respect, however, attitudes have been changing during recent years and the range of jobs open to women has considerably widened. Concerning geographical mobility, however, it is certainly true that women as a rule follow their families and do not break up their households to move on if and when their job demands it. Although a few outstanding women in leading positions form an exception, the greater inflexibility of women is undoubtedly a factor to be reckoned with.

This list of shortcomings of women employees as compared with men gives the general impression that, in economic terms the value of female labour is under present conditions not only lower than that of an equal number of men, but lower also than it might be. One can hardly escape the conclusion that women are as yet not fully integrated in our present economic system.

What immediate Improvements are Possible?

A discussion of the social reforms which will be necessary before women can pull their weight in industry, commerce and the professions, will be found in a later chapter. Here we shall consider what can be done under present conditions to improve the productivity of female labour.

We cannot do better than quote once more the pamphlet on *The Problem of Absenteeism* by the Ministry of Labour and National Service. 'It would be of advantage for managements', it states, 'to recognize frankly that many workers, especially women, cannot be expected to work five-and-a-half days per week, or long hours, week in week out, if they have to spend in addition two to three hours a day or more on travelling, possibly by a crowded bus or train and in all weathers, or if they have homes and young children to look after. Much could probably be done by redistributing the work and/or the labour force in the factory so that those who need special working hours would be so employed as not to disorganize the work of others. It might be possible, alternatively, in the case of women, to arrange a rota system whereby each worker has one day off per week apart from Sunday. This latter arrangement would clearly be of value to married women especially.'

This was written during the war. No doubts existed then in people's minds about the value of women's contribution to the national effort. Clearly, women were needed, and all possible efforts were made by the Government, by local authorities and by employers to enable them to accept jobs outside their homes. With the approach of peace the attitude to this question became much more half-hearted. Men, in particular, seem to have watched the new development with mixed feelings. They were influenced, partly, by fear of feminine competition during the coming era of uncertain economic development, and partly by their desire to have full-time wives at home.

A sidelight on this attitude was cast by the Man-Power Debate of September 1943 in the British Parliament. The Government had proposed a Bill to call up women between the ages of 45 and 51 for National Service. This question caused a great stir in public opinion and the press, and feelings ran high. But the Debate in the House of Commons revealed an interesting division between the sexes: only among the men were voices heard which conjured up a mother image and waxed sentimental over the home-makers who 'carry the main burden' and do 'the superb job of keeping the homes of this country together', etc. All the women M.P.s supported Mr. Bevin's Bill; Eleanor Rathbone, herself a venerated and venerable woman leader, even came out in favour of recruiting women up to the age of 65.

The divided mind on the question of women's employment shows itself in the half-hearted measures taken after the end of the war to make it easier for married women to accept outside work. True, in all the Western countries some arrangements have been made to accommodate the work of women to their particular needs. But whatever progress there has been is not the result of planned efforts to meet a problem that has been investigated rationally. In Great Britain and in the United States, where the urge to go 'back to normal' was particularly marked immediately after the end of the war, day nurseries were closed, despite continued full employment and shortage of labour; part-time work, though very much sought after, has barely been available, except where labour shortages have become so acute that even half a worker has been felt to be better than none, and some necessary re-organizations have reluctantly been made.

Part-time Work

Compared with the widespread demand, the number of jobs which are available in half-size packages is relatively small, though it has steadily increased in the last 30–40 years. Shortage of manpower has made it necessary, not only during the war, but also during the period of full employment following it, to employ part-time workers in some branches of industry, in domestic service, commerce and some of the professions. For reasons of scarcity the authorities have positively encouraged the employment of part-time teachers and nurses, for instance.

The shortage of nurses has everywhere been such as to force some hospitals to introduce shift-work and to accept married nurses on a part-time basis—a system which by all accounts seems to work satisfactorily. The results of some local experiments in Britain were so successful that the Ministry of Health in collaboration with the Ministry of Labour and National Service gave encouragement and help to local and hospital authorities throughout the country in the organization of part-time recruitment drives with the effect that, in the words of the Report of the Ministry of Health for 1946/47, 'a reserve of professional skill which would otherwise have been wasted has been tapped. Patients have received extra care and the pressure on full-time staff has been relieved.' With the expansion of the National Health Service this pressure has considerably increased and the number of part-time workers has risen year by year. In September 1960 the total number of part-time nurses and midwives employed in hospitals in England and Wales was 44,243, compared with 162,061 full-time nurses and midwives, that is, a ratio of 1:3.[1]

The Women's Bureau of the U.S. Department of Labor published a report[2] after an investigation into part-time work in ten American cities in which the growing importance of part-time

[1] B. A. Bennett, Part-Time Nursing Employment in Great Britain, *International Labour Review*, vol. LXXXV, No. 4, April 1962.

[2] *Part-Time Jobs for Women: A Study in Ten Cities*, U.S. Department of Labor, Women's Bureau Bulletin No. 238, Washington, 1951.

work was stressed; it recorded that two-thirds of the employers and all the women engaged in part-time work expressed their satisfaction with it.

Some types of work lend themselves by their nature to part-time employment. Examples are domestic work in factories, offices and homes, or employment in catering establishments, particularly in works and office canteens where only midday meals are served. A number of social services open new scope for the part-time employment of women as home helps for old or sick people, in connexion with school meals, and so on. Other work in the field of social welfare is particularly well suited to organization on a part-time basis, and this could be used more frequently than it is. There is also an increase in the number of children taken care of in private homes during their mothers' working time. Both in the United States and Sweden many married women who are tied to their homes because of their own small children have found the supervision of an additional number of infants no undue hardship for themselves, and the source of a small income, while the company of other children has been of benefit to their offspring, and has relieved other mothers. In all these occupations women carry out work which is traditionally in women's domain and which was formerly done in their own homes, though it is now often better carried out on a collective basis.

The distributive trades absorb a considerable number of women in part-time jobs to supplement the regular staff during peak periods, and also, of course, in the many instances where women assist in family businesses. The entertainment industry employs largely on a part-time basis, and so do adult education agencies, market surveys, public opinion polls, and the like.

However, apart from these special types of work, employers are on the whole disinclined to employ people on a part-time basis except when driven to it by acute shortage of labour or when there is a temporary need to work extra shifts. Reasons for their aversion are the increased administrative burden, the costs of compulsory insurance schemes, difficulties in the organization of work, and the feeling that the part-time worker always remains an outsider with only half his, or her, interest engaged.

Workers' organizations, too, regard part-time employment with mixed feelings. Provided that trade union terms and conditions are observed they do not actually oppose part-time work and are prepared to regard it as a necessary means of supplementing labour in times of scarcity. But, not unnaturally, they are afraid of weakening their bargaining position, the basis of which is one job per worker, and they fear a situation where people might come to work full-time on half pay.

For all these reasons the number of part-time jobs available is not sufficient to meet the demands of the many women who would like them. A potentially quite considerable source of skilled labour therefore remains untapped.

It would certainly be desirable to create more opportunities for married women to divide their time between domestic and out-side work on a fifty-fifty basis, and greater flexibility on the part of employers and management should make an increase possible. A special register should be kept at employment agencies for part-time work. At present this type of job is most often found through friends or with ex-employers, sometimes with the help of Church or professional organizations, and only very rarely through employment agencies.[1]

The onus of reorganization cannot, of course, be expected to be borne by the employers alone. The problem is complex and affects society as a whole. It must therefore be tackled by a concerted effort in various sectors of society. Government support and encouragement which, as we have seen in the above example, was forthcoming in the case of the National Health Service in order to meet an acute shortage of nursing staff, will have to be given in other fields too. It would also be very desirable for trade unions and employers' organizations to give this matter some serious consideration.

This is, indeed, increasingly being done as the growing number of married women in employment, and the need to draw more heavily on this manpower potential, have focused attention on their special problems.

On an international level, the I.L.O. has produced two reports on 'Women Workers in a Changing World'[2] in preparation for discussions of this topic during its 48th Session in 1964. These led to the adoption of Recommendations[3] concerning the integration

---

[1] *Report on Part-Time Workers*, Women's Bureau of the United States Department of Labor, 1951.   [2] Report VI (1) and (2), I.L.O., Geneva, 1963.
[3] *Recommendations concerning the Employment of Women with Family Responsibilities*, No. 123, Geneva 1965.

of women with family responsibilities into the workforce on an equal footing and without discrimination; they include specific provisions relating to public information and education; child-care services and facilities; education, counselling, training and re-training for the entry, or re-entry, of women into the employment market after comparatively long absence.

Similarly, the Organization of Economic Co-operation and Development—an intergovernmental body committed to an 'active manpower policy' as a means for promoting economic growth —has devoted special attention to the problem of women workers with family responsibilities whom it recognizes as one of the 'groups intermittently or permanently outside the labour force' and in need of special provisions 'to enable them to participate in useful employment'. Under the auspices of its Manpower and Social Affairs Directorate it carried out a survey among Member States to discover, firstly, whether there is any elasticity of working hours to meet the requirements of this type of workers and, secondly, whether some, at least, of their needs are being met—or can be met—by agencies other than the employers. Recommendations, based on this survey,[1] concern such aids as home-help, child-care facilities, adjustment of shopping hours etc., the regularization of part-time work, 'days-off', and adult training and are in line with those adopted by the I.L.O.

By a number of publications, and by reports and discussions in the press, the public has been alerted to the new situation created by the employment, on a large scale, of women with domestic commitments. It has been made aware that various adaptations are needed to accommodate this new type of worker within the existing social framework without causing unnecessary hardships. A gradual, if slow, change of public attitudes is perceptible; but, as usual, there is a time-lag between the facts of social change and their emotional acceptance. Progress is therefore inevitably slow.

[1] Viola Klein, *Women Workers—Working Hours and Services, A Survey in 21 Countries,* O.E.C.D., Paris, 1965.

CHAPTER SEVEN

THE EFFECTS ON CHILDREN

'Children First' is the motto writ large over all discussions of the merits and demerits of married women's employment. Our children are our stake in the future; hence their well-being is of vital concern to society as well as to us personally. And as we have brought them into this world, it is our responsibility to make them, as best we can, fit to live in it happily and successfully.

The quality of the next generation has become of even greater moment since the size of families has shrunk. With a birth-rate at, or only just above, reproduction level we can less than ever afford the risk of failures. To-day we have learned enough about the formation of personality to understand the great extent to which its development depends on maternal care and affection, particularly during the first years of life.

The maxim 'Children First' must therefore be regarded as axiomatic, even though it has very often been used in the past as a means to impede the emancipation of women.

It is rather unfortunate that the rights of children should ever have been put in opposition to the 'Rights of Women'. The two are not mutually exclusive, as we have by now learned from experience.[1]

This is particularly so since the decision whether or not to have a family has now largely become a matter of free choice. People who for one reason or another are not prepared to accept the responsibilities of parenthood need not do so. All the more binding is the duty on those who have children to give them all the care and devotion of which they are capable.

If women with a job and a family feel torn between them, as they very often do, their dilemma is not one of conflicting rights—their own rights as adult individuals versus those of their children—but rather one of conflicting loyalties. They have willingly accepted their two responsibilities as workers and mothers; their problem is how to harmonize the two.

[1] Cf. Béatrice Marbeau-Cleirens, *Psychologie des mères*, Paris, 1966.

Harassed by the pressure of work, as mothers with outside jobs very often are, they also suffer from a sense of guilt because the existing conditions of life and work are such that many of these women fear they may be sacrificing to the Moloch of work what they feel are the just claims of their children.

We are convinced, however, that work and family are not in principle two irreconcilable alternatives; and it is not beyond the means and ingenuity of our society to devise techniques which would reduce the dilemma of working mothers to a tolerable minimum. We shall have more to say on this subject later. For the moment we want first to examine the question whether the employment of married women affects the well-being of their offspring and if so, whether the effect is unfavourable. Only when these two queries have been answered shall we be in a position to discuss possible reforms which might be made in the interests of mothers and children alike.

Since it is women's business not only to bear children but also to take the lion's share in their care and education we shall have to study the effect of women's employment on both these functions if we are to assess its consequences fully. Thus before entering into a discussion of what appears to be the crucial—and what certainly is to-day the most controversial—problem, namely the question of whether, and if so, how the employment of mothers affects the development of their children, we must first briefly consider whether or not it affects the rate of reproduction and whether it has any bearing on the health of infants.

Fertility and the Employment of Women

What rate of reproduction would, in any given society, be most desirable is a matter of opinion on which we cannot expect our readers to agree. There is, however, no need to enter into an argument of this speculative and highly controversial nature. We are concerned here not with ideal but with actual conditions as they exist to-day, and more particularly, with the possibility of a correlation between the employment of married women and the birth-rate.

Whether or not the employment of women has an effect on the birth-rate cannot, however, be decided simply by a comparison of the families of employed and non-employed married women, for a variety of reasons. First of all, married women who go out to work represent a selected group, and childlessness itself is a major selective factor in its composition. In other words, married women without children are for obvious reasons more likely to accept jobs than women with families to look after. This holds particularly in countries where the employment of married women is not a very widespread custom. Where only a minority of married women go out to work they will—taking each social class separately—constitute a selection of those whose home responsibilities are smallest. When the custom spreads and when more facilities become available to relieve mothers of some of their domestic responsibilities, the gap between the number of children of employed and of non-employed married women tends to narrow.

There is, moreover, an inverse relation between the number of children and the duration of women's employment. But on the face of it, it is impossible to decide whether women spend more years in employment because their families are smaller, or whether their families are smaller because they spend a longer period in gainful employment. Under given social conditions the first interpretation seems the more likely of the two, women in most cases giving up their jobs when their first or second child is born.

During the last few decades there has been a consistent increase in the number of women in employment. At the same time there has been an equally progressive decline of fertility in Western countries. This, at least, was the long-term trend up to the middle of the thirties. From then on a period of relative recovery set in which culminated in a quite remarkable rise in the number of births since the end of the second world war, despite the increased participation of women in the labour force.

Whatever the significance of this recent development may be—and it seems primarily to be connected with the growing number of early marriages—public opinion does see a correlation between the decline of the birth-rate and the employment of women. This opinion is supported by statistical evidence and gains strength from a number of facts. Among these, there is the historical coincidence of both phenomena, and the fact that among the wives in employment the number who are childless exceed the corresponding average for women as a whole. Moreover, in big cities there is both a higher proportion of women in employment and a lower birth-rate than in rural areas, which gives the impression that the two are connected. There is also some evidence that among the working classes in textile areas, where a long tradition of female labour exists, the birth-rate is somewhat lower than in the corresponding class in districts where it is less customary for married women to go out to work, though it is by no means certain that other factors are not at work to lower the fertility in these areas.

Here, however, the parallel ends. Comparing, for instance, different social strata, it is at once evident that the class which during this historical period has had the smallest birth-rate is not the one which shows the largest percentage of women in employment. The most prolific group of the population, as is well known, are manual wage-earners, that is, the class which has always had the largest percentage of working wives. The average family of unskilled labourers, married in 1920, in Great Britain, was 3·76 in 1946; corresponding figures for professional men were 2·02, for salaried employees (clerks, etc.) 1·09.[1] It is of interest that the professional class, which up to 1920 was the least fertile, no longer is so, although the gainful employment of married women in this category is becoming rather more frequent than it used to be, and is relatively more widespread than among the lower middle class which now has the smallest families. It is obvious that other factors play an important part in influencing the level of reproduction on the one hand, and the employment of women on the other hand. The two phenomena are interrelated, but cause and effect are difficult to disentangle. They are both symptoms of one historical process which is characterized by industrialization, rationalization, and urbanization. The most important single determinant in this process has been the continued technological progress which has changed the character of work and the way of life of Western society.

To take changes in the method and organization of work first: new inventions have increasingly relegated heavy physical labour to machines both in factories and in homes. This has reduced domestic work and has set women free to accept outside work. Simultaneously it has increased the number of jobs which women can perform because they now require skill rather than great physical strength. Hand in hand with these changes in the methods of production came the growth of the administrative machinery

[1] *Report of the 1946 Family Census*, 1954.

which has created an ever-widening field of professional opportunities for women. A further result of this development is the
growth of commercial services which have taken over many household functions, on the one hand releasing women at home, and on
the other hand employing their services in factories and offices.

Besides, the whole framework of life has changed, and is continually changing. Rising standards of living are a first effect.
With them go stronger demands for education and comfort, and
there is increased mobility, and financial insecurity, each of which
acts in turn as an incentive to greater participation of women in
the fields of economic production and social administration and at
the same time as a deterrent to the creation of large families.

All these tendencies have naturally been more marked in urban
than in rural areas. But growing urbanization, a further result of
industrial development, has spread their effects over a larger proportion of the population.

In view of the manifold and mutual interdependence of social,
economic, and psychological factors it is obviously impossible to
hold any individual social phenomenon responsible for the falling
birth-rate. If remedies are sought to alter the present situation and
people are to be encouraged to have more children, measures
would have to be applied over a very wide field and in many
sectors of the social organization. To blame the employment of
women as the main cause of declining fertility is as absurd as to
call one rainy day the cause of a wet summer.

At one time it was also argued that the employment of women
actually destroyed their biological potentialities. But no evidence
of this has been produced and it seems hardly plausible that modern work in factories and offices should have greater destructive
effects on women's physique than the far heavier work carried on in
the fields, laundries or kitchens of old times. Similarly, the assertion that the nervous pressure of modern work might cause in-
voluntary sterility among career women can also be relegated to
the realm of conjecture. Psychologically conditioned sterility exists,
but its causes are much more deep-seated in the unconscious. They
are, as a rule, to be found in personal factors related to the intimate
sphere of love experience, either in childhood, or marriage, or
both. These factors are at work in a very complex manner, in
some women and in some men, independently of whether they are
employed or not.

THE EFFECTS ON CHILDREN

The number of children in the group of employed women will always remain somewhat lower than the average for married women. Productive work will continue to offer compensatory satisfaction to the childless woman; and return to work after raising a small family will probably become more widely practised than it is now.

In addition, some factors of a more transitory nature may be at work. At the present time, when family limitation is spreading but is not a general pattern, the more alert type of woman who adopts voluntary control of her fertility will often also be the type who is interested in retaining her financial independence and intensely active life. Thus personality traits can act selectively in favour both of planned (and, under present conditions, that means, as a rule, small) families and the gainful employment of women. So long as the trend towards family limitation has not reached its full development, that is, so long as it is not practised by the whole population, this selective principle is likely to continue.[1]

Moreover, child bearing and rearing undoubtedly complicate the life of women and involve a radical change in their daily life and in their plans and outlook. It would seem plausible to expect that among women in employment a greater proportion than among others respond to the foreseeable difficulties by a voluntary limitation of the size of their families.

This does not, of course, imply any assumption that birth-control is practised merely, or mainly, by working women. Such an hypothesis would be contrary to the known facts. Nor should it be inferred that the desire to continue in employment is one of the major causes of family limitation. This is evidently not the case. But, where there are so many other motives working in the same direction, the difficulties of combining motherhood with an accepted and cherished way of life are an additional inducement to reduce the size of families.

We have intentionally characterized these difficulties as transitory. For we are convinced that they result from a temporary maladjustment between family demands and changed social conditions rather than from an inherent contradiction between women's various aims in life. To combine a career with a family may be difficult at present; but it is already less so than it was

[1] For a fuller discussion of this problem see Alva Myrdal, *Nation and Family*, London and New York, 1945.

thirty years ago, and it is likely to become easier as time goes on and technical efficiency increases, in particular if we set our minds to solving the problem.

Is the Health of Infants affected by the Employment of Mothers?

There is not much to be said about the relation between infant mortality and the employment of women. The general reduction in the mortality rate of infants is one of the outstanding achievements of medical science and welfare organization in our time. The success in this field has been striking, even more striking than the extension of life at its latter end. But while society is only just awakening to its responsibilities for the increasing number of old people, there has always been a social awareness of and interest in the health of young children and of the women bearing them. State and voluntary organizations have combined in tackling this problem. In all civilized countries medical, social, and legislative measures have been taken for the protection of the new-born baby and its mother.

Though the problem of infant mortality has thus, fortunately, shrunk to manageable proportions and is continuously being further reduced, some of the earlier studies investigating the connexion between infant mortality and the employment of women continue to figure in bibliographies and even in discussions of contemporary social policy and must therefore at least be mentioned. Studies, for instance, made by the Children's Bureau of the U.S. Department of Labor for the years 1920–5 showed a high infant mortality rate when mothers were employed away from home during pregnancy. If 100 is set as the expected infant mortality rate of the regional, racial and economic group concerned, it was found in one instance that where mothers were not gainfully employed the mortality rate was lower than expected (94 per cent); where mothers were employed away from home the rate was higher (132 per cent), but where mothers were gainfully employed at home the rate was lowest (91 per cent).

In some other cases the latter figure slightly exceeds the first one. But in the cotton trades and in similar industrial occupations studied, the mothers employed away from home, and particularly those working late during pregnancy, showed an infant mortality rate which was higher than the average. This correlation is not surprising, particularly in view of the fact that women who work late during pregnancy are likely to belong to the poorest social strata where undernourishment, difficult living conditions and lack of hygiene are prevalent and contribute to the higher mortality rate and lower resistance of infants to disease. Dr. Baetjer,[1] from whose detailed study these figures are quoted, comes to the conclusion that in view of the contradictory nature of the evidence and the definite relationship between infant mortality and the socio-economic status of the mother, it is impossible at present to state with any certainty what effects industrial work has on pregnancy.

The conditions of women in industry have considerably changed since the investigations quoted above were made. Welfare services in industry, medical services for pre- and post-natal care, systems of family allowances, and the generally improved economic situation of the working classes have greatly strengthened the powers of physical resistance among young women in industry, and diminished the risks to mothers and babies alike. The evidence of this great improvement is too well known to need repetition here. It is an outstanding example of society's showing itself capable of overcoming hardships which were at one time believed to be intrinsic to women's lot.

The same also applies to the physical health of children past the infant age. There are excellent medical and welfare services available and in most Western countries the State takes an active interest in the health of the young by subsidizing milk and other health foods for children, by providing school meals, medical and dental supervision, etc. Moreover, mothers' earnings provide an addition to the family income which is largely spent on improving food and other physical living conditions. Against these positive items has to be set the danger that through the absence of mothers at work their children may be unsupervised, and the risk of accidents at home and on the roads thereby increased. However, no figures are available with which to investigate this.

Effects of Mothers' Employment on the Mental Health of Children

In contrast to the physical health of children, their psychological development depends to a very large extent on factors which no

---

[1] Dr. Anna M. Baetjer, *Women in Industry, op. cit.*

outside organization can supply. Modern psychology has given support and justification to a belief which at some time may have been thought 'old-fashioned': the view that the future happy development of infants is dependent on the loving care of their mothers.

This view that small children need the permanent, stable devotion of one particular person with whom they can form a close attachment was borne out by practical experience, particularly during the second world war with its many enforced separations of mothers and children.[1]

The new insight into the importance of the physical and psychological symbiosis between mother and child in the early phases of life has led, for example, to the practice of keeping mothers and new-born babies together in maternity wards. Women to-day are told to learn the individual rhythms of their children's need for food, sleep, elimination, etc., to establish what has been termed 'self-regulatory schedules', rather than to follow the clock and the time-table according to rules worked out by doctors on the basis of statistical averages.

Obviously, mothers cannot go out to work if they are to live up to these new and exacting standards of motherhood. This has to be accepted as the consequence of the existing knowledge that love and security are essential to the growth of a harmonious personality.

We are less certain how severe the effects are if mothers do not live up to the expectations. Nor do we really know for how many months, or years, this close identification must be kept up, and whether it is disturbed by temporary breaks.

Little research has so far been done (the difficulties it presents are formidable) to investigate more closely when such breaks first become possible, for what length of time they can safely be made, and whether they are equally injurious when they form part of an established regular routine. The studies which exist, and which are ably and conveniently summarized by J. Bowlby in *Maternal Care and Mental Health*,[2] refer to total deprivation of maternal care; that is, they deal with abandoned, adopted, or boarded-out children

---

[1] A. Freud and D. Burlingham, *Young Children in Wartime*, London, 1942; *Infants without Families*, London, 1943.

[2] J. Bowlby, *Maternal Care and Mental Health*, World Health Organization Monograph Series, No. 2, Geneva, 1951.

rather than with children who have daily breaks of some hours away from their mother, in day nurseries, in the care of a maid, etc. Further, in all cases studied, maternal deprivation is the result of some calamity and often accompanied by a sudden shock which itself would be sufficient to upset the emotional and mental balance of the child. It would be scientifically inadmissible to apply conclusions drawn from cases of deprivation caused by emergency situations, such as death, abandonment or cruelty of the mother, or the separation through illness of mother or child, to cases where the mother is absent at regular intervals for a number of hours yet returns to the child each day and provides it with a home. Here is a field of research which is of great social importance, but has received remarkably little attention.

The point that the situation of deprived children is entirely different from that of children intermittently separated from their mothers is borne out by one of the studies quoted by Bowlby. In an investigation carried out in Denmark by K. M. Simonsen[1] the rate of development of children aged between one and four who had spent most of their lives in one of twelve different institutions was compared with that of children in the same age group who attended day nurseries but lived at home. 'The mothers of these children were working and the homes often very unsatisfactory. Even so, the average "Development Quotient" of the family children was normal—102—while that of the institution children was retarded—93. This difference is found consistently at each of three age-levels, namely, children in the second, third and fourth years of life.'[2]

A home, even a bad one, is better than an institution, and the rates of physical and mental development, as far as these are measurable, are found to be not lower than normal in children who spend most of their waking hours in a day nursery while their mothers are out at work. The research which could give truly adequate answers on this question is, however, still awaited.

Margaret Mead has published some reflections on the unsatisfactory state of research in this important field.[3] Attempts at 'scientific' investigation all too often suffer from methodical errors

---

[1] K. M. Simonsen, *Examination of Children from Children's Homes and Day Nurseries*, Copenhagen, 1947.   [2] See Bowlby, *op. cit.*, p. 19.

[3] Margaret Mead, 'Some Theoretical Considerations on the Problem of Mother-Child Separation', *American Journal of Orthopsychiatry*, Vol. XXIV, No. 3, July 1954.

such as over-simplification, insufficiently tested evidence, and exaggerated importance being attributed to single factors while, she says, 'we have evidence we ourselves can trust, that the character formation of the child represents the child's total environmental situation'. All we can do at present is to stress the undeniable fact that maternal love is a decisive element in any equation concerning young children.

Though it is fairly easy to describe what constitutes a bad home, there is no simple definition of a good one. Conformity with the traditional pattern certainly is no guarantee of the happiest results. It cannot be too strongly emphasized that the all-important factor is the attitude and personality of the mother rather than the amount of time she spends with her children. The neurotic, neglectful, or foolish mother is a menace to her children, probably no less if she devotes all her time to them than if she does not. On the other hand, the intelligent, sympathetic, loving mother may be able to give her child a sense of emotional security which is not disturbed by her regular, or even her irregular, absences.

The same conclusion is drawn in an investigation which was carried out on a rather small scale in war-time Britain, and aimed at discovering whether infants cared for in day nurseries showed symptoms of disturbance in comparison with a corresponding group of infants brought up at home.[1] With many married women going out to work during the war the use of day nurseries was fairly widespread, and the separation of mother and child rather longer than is thought desirable—more than 8 hours each day in most cases studied in this pilot project on children aged between 20 and 62 months. Apart from general war-time conditions the situation was further complicated by the fact that more than half the fathers of the nursery children were away in the Services, the proportion being considerably smaller in the home groups studied simultaneously. The investigator expressed her findings in these words: 'The numbers of children with habit disturbances, and of problem children, were found to differ only slightly in the two groups; and since the disadvantageous environmental factors were more numerous for nursery children than for home children, there was no evidence to suggest that children cared for in a day nursery are

---

[1] Netta Glass, 'Eating, Sleeping, and Elimination Habits in Children Attending Day Nurseries and Children Cared for at Home by Mothers', published in *American Journal of Orthopsychiatry*, Vol. XIX, No. 4, October 1949.

more likely by reason of communal care to present developmental problems than are children cared for at home by their mothers. There was, in addition, no confirmation of the belief that nursery care for children under two is especially harmful. Here, however, the numbers are so small that they cannot be used as a basis for generalization. . . . This study suggests that eating, sleeping, and elimination problems, and problem children, were in fact definitely associated with certain parental attitudes and types of personality which were more important in determining good or bad adjustment than was attendance or non-attendance at a day nursery. Mothers who had difficult personalities, whose attitude to their children was unsatisfactory, who took a job because being at home "got them down" (tendencies often aggravated by difficult living conditions, their husband's absence, and so on), were more numerous in the nursery group than in the home group; and this might account for the widely held impression that problem behaviour is more frequent among nursery children than among home children.'

The results of this and other existing studies are inconclusive. It is safer therefore to assume that the higher level of impersonal care which is inevitable when young children are left in the care of institutions, or of changing servants or relatives, may reduce their feeling of security and lead to undesirable results. We therefore support the view that mothers should, as far as possible, take care of their own children during the first years of their lives.

But the question now arises: for how long should the mother be on continuous duty? This question cannot be answered by setting a definite time limit. Generally speaking, the gradual relaxation of the closest ties between mother and child is as important for the development of personality as is the creation of that intimate bond, and sets as serious educational problems.

'At present', writes Margaret Mead,[1] 'the specific biological situation of the continuing relationship of the child to its biological mother and its need for care by human beings are being hopelessly confused in the growing insistence that child and biological mother, or mother surrogate, must never be separated, that all separation even for a few days is inevitably damaging, and that if long enough it does irreversible damage. This . . . is a new and subtle form of antifeminism in which men—under the guise of exalting the importance of maternity—are tying women more tightly

[1] *Op. cit.*, p. 477.

to their children than has been thought necessary since the invention of bottle feeding and baby carriages. Actually, anthropological evidence gives no support at present to the value of such accentuation of the tie between mother and child. On the contrary, cross-cultural studies suggest that adjustment is most facilitated if the child is cared for by many warm friendly people. Clinical studies and anthropological studies support the relationship between strong attachments to single individuals in childhood and capacity for a limited number of intense, exclusive relationships in adulthood. It may well be, of course, that limiting a child's contacts to its biological mother may be the most efficient way to produce a character suited to lifelong monogamous marriage, but if so then we should be clear that that is what we are doing. . . .'

We need not enter here into speculations about the connexion between monogamous marriage and the close mother-infant relationship prevalent in our society, interesting though these may be. Nor need we in our particular context draw on anthropological findings which show that in different social systems the pattern of mother-child relationship differs from our own without harmful effects on the individuals growing up in those societies. We are concerned here with our modern Western civilization and the best means of ensuring that children born into it are made fit to live in it.

We must, however, recognize that societies are shaped in their nurseries, and that the imprint a child receives from its first personal relations within the family will form its character and its ability for human relations as an adult.

The immediate bodily contact which is so necessary during early infancy, when the outside world is mainly experienced by touch, is followed more and more by visual and acoustic experiences. The sight of the mother and her voice becomes connected with the cutaneous experiences of the person who gives bodily warmth and support. In this way the beginnings are made of a more complex relationship to a first human being, and a basic pattern is set for future human relations. Whether a person meets the world around him with confidence or distrust, in a co-operative or defiant manner, is to a large extent determined by these first experiences. The mother should therefore, as far as possible, be available to give these first ministrations and to lay a secure basis for the emotional development of her child.

It needs no scientific confirmation, however, to say that even during the first months short absences of the mother are not harmful to the child. The main thing is that all that is important to the child should be done by one particular person—a person ready to give and receive that love identification from which the child's understanding grows.

Before the end of one year a second person can move within the horizon of the child, and very soon more people. The demand for the round-the-clock presence of the mother is ready to be lessened. It ought to be relaxed in order that the child may go through the normal maturation process.

All through the first few years when the child learns to speak, the presence of the one or two stable human companions is of great importance. It therefore seems very desirable that for the first three years of life mothers should devote their time to their children. They will, in compensation, get a deep personal experience of a kind not to be matched, and they will also train their own faculty for intelligent human understanding. This living with a child takes much more subtlety than is required by the chores of material child care which so often are described in detail in handbooks for mothers. And, not least, it takes a keen sense of how and when to relinquish one or the other of these ties so as to loosen them not before, but just as the children's needs for constant closeness are satisfied.

At about the age of 3 it becomes possible to make without anxiety a more prolonged daily break in the mother-child relationship. At that time the social maturation of the child should have proceeded far enough to enable it to leave its home for some hours a day and start life in a new world, a first society consisting of age-equals. These social contacts meet a fundamental evolutionary need, and it should be recognized that, no matter whether the mother stays at home or not, attendance at a nursery school becomes a beneficial complement to home life for most children. In our modern Western society most of them could not otherwise find an environment which is a rich microcosm, adjusted to their needs, and peopled with children, animals, etc., that is, a world of relationships which they can begin to shape themselves.

If the mother could be absent for work during the same four to six hours a day as the child spends at a nursery school or kindergarten between the ages of 3 to 6, harmony between the interests of mother and child could be created.

What happens in reality is not always such a wisely scheduled evolution from primitive security to gradually maturing independence and individuality, and mistakes are likely to be made at each stage.

The two grave psychological risks which young children normally run are those of 'rejection' and 'over-protection'. With some simplification each might be said to correspond roughly to the type of error which working and homestaying mothers, respectively, are more prone to commit.

The child experiences the lack of love, or simply of insufficient attention, from its mother as 'rejection'; that is, it feels it is not wanted. Although deficient understanding of the children's need at each age level may itself cause emotional and social and perhaps also intellectual underdevelopment, and although a feeling of 'rejection' occurs now and then for reasons which have to do with a mother's personality, whether or not she goes out to work, the risk exists that working mothers, owing to overwork, ambition or worries, may more often cause their children to feel wilfully neglected than women who are about the house all day long. Mothers staying at home run that risk to a lesser degree, even though the so-called 'old-fashioned', i.e. authoritarian, school of child education also gave rise to similar reactions, because parental strictness is often experienced as rejection by children. From these deprivations result many neurotic personalities, insecure, restless, dissatisfied people, both young and old.

At the other end of the scale lies another risk, that of 'over-protection'. This is the fate of children whose mothers do not help them to outgrow their baby needs. Again, personality factors are at play, some mothers being much more unwilling than others, because of their own maladjustment, to give up their dominance over their children, and many more being not sufficiently aware of the emotional needs of their children to see when and how the step to gradual independence should be taken. Mothers staying at home run the greater risk of this mistake, particularly if they have come to feel that the children are 'the meaning of their life'.

In the children's interest it cannot be overstressed that mothers must have other aims in life as well. What they otherwise tend to produce in their offspring is weakness, immaturity and the need for constant reassurance—not to speak of the risk of graver disturbances which often only come to the surface at a later age when the demands of life become more stringent.

Between the Scylla of 'rejection' and the Charybdis of 'over-protection' the education of a child steers an uncertain course. It is probably best for parents not to meditate overmuch on these dangers lest their natural confidence be destroyed by self-consciousness. Since in the field of parental upbringing the extraordinary situation exists that the product is in a position to judge the producer as well as the process of production, it is almost futile to aim at perfection. Once they are old enough to read psychological literature, many children will, anyway, blame their parents for committing one or the other sin or both.

In pointing out some of the chief errors mothers are prone to make, it is obviously not our aim to add to their anxieties. So much has been written and said in recent years about the vital needs of children for maternal affection, and about the dangers of neglect, that many parents, in particular those who take an intelligent interest in the emotional development of their children, are becoming over-anxious on this score. Very little attention has, in comparison, been paid to the effects of over-protection, though these also may cripple the psychological development of the child.

Security and independence are two basic human needs and the two main pillars on which the structure of personality rests. To foster its full growth a balance between them has to be struck. The art of education consists in administering precisely the right quantities of each at the right time. As years go by the measure of independence has gradually to be increased. This can more safely be done if there is a firm foundation of security laid by parental affection.

Children of School and Adolescent Age

Generally speaking, from the beginning of school years, that is at an age around 5 or 6, the companionship of age-equals is of more and more importance to a child and is necessary for its social growth. The attentive understanding of both father and mother continues to be essential for a happy development, but it no longer has to be on call the whole time. The child, if it is normally mature, can well tolerate a certain rationing of parental care. Therefore, from the time when the child begins going to school its interests are no longer incompatible with the mother's desire to do other things. Provided suitable practical arrangements can be made—and the

provision of school meals is an important item of such arrangements—mothers should have very little cause to hesitate to take on
a job during that period. If the psychological dangers which might
be involved are to be evaluated correctly they have to be weighed
against the opposite risks, that is, against the 'occupational diseases' afflicting mothers with no interests outside their family: their
proneness to over-protect or to dominate their children, or to
make too high demands on their affections—in fact to expect their
children to compensate them for the lack of social contacts and
intellectual stimulus from which so many of them suffer.

The effect of these mistakes is not so immediately obvious to
the outsider as are the effects of neglect which often hit the headlines. They are nevertheless often serious. The percentage of
'mother-fixated neurotics' in the U.S. army during the last war has
been described as 'catastrophic' by the army's psychiatric expert,
Professor Edward Strecker.[1] That is the price to be paid for the
image, and the practice, of the 'great American Mom', the youthful person who sacrifices her life for her home.

There are no grounds for the belief that child neglect is the
necessary result of the employment of mothers. This is as mistaken
as it would be to assume that all mothers who devote their whole
time to their families spoil their children. Nevertheless, this view of
the negligent working mother is frequently put forward. Teachers
who, understandably, feel that too heavy a burden of responsibility is put on their shoulders by unco-operative parents are inclined to hit back at the weakest link in the chain—the mother
who goes out to work. In conferences of headmasters, magistrates
of juvenile courts, probation officers and other welfare workers, the
working mother is almost unfailingly brought up as a bogey. She
is blamed for the increase in juvenile delinquency, for shortcomings in contemporary education, and for all sorts of behaviour
problems of the younger generation. The regularity with which
newspapers report on the effects of 'broken homes' under the heading of 'Mothers Who Go Out to Work', and the ease with which
public speakers mix up the two, makes one suspicious of their conscious, or unconscious, motives.

Despite this host of accusations and their strong emotional
appeal, there is little factual evidence to support them. The problem has as yet to be scientifically investigated. One study carried

[1] Edw. Strecker, *Their Mother's Sons*, Philadelphia, 1946.

out in Britain[1] has shown that the rate of delinquency among children whose mothers go out to work is not higher than among those whose mothers stay at home, other conditions being equal.

An investigation made among 1,345 elementary school children in Gothenberg, Sweden, by their medical officer, Dr. Blume-Westerberg, showed no difference in the rates of absenteeism between the children of employed and non-employed mothers. With regard to school results the investigator found that in the first form children of mothers who go to work had lower marks than children of mothers at home; in the fourth form the two groups were level; and in the seventh form the children of working mothers came out top.

Some teachers are known to have observed that children of working mothers are intellectually more alert and socially more independent than others. No conclusive studies of this problem have yet been made, and the assertion still has to be proved. For two reasons, however, it does not seem unplausible: firstly, because children of working mothers are led to take a more active responsibility for their own lives; and secondly, because mothers at home are continually adjusting themselves intellectually to a much lower level of maturity than their own. This is a fact which is even more deplorable for the women themselves than for their children. While at a very early age this adjustment to their infants takes on the character of an instructive as well as imaginative extension of their faculties of understanding, the habitual sharing of women's lives with those of their children far too often brings mothers down from the level of maturity which should be their own to that of their children. The intellectual immaturity of which women have often been accused in the past may have its roots mainly in this situation. The lack of adult stimulus, of new ideas, of varying experience and widening interests leads to a cultural poverty in the family environment which may well enough account for the observation mentioned above, that children of working women are on the whole more alert. Their greater independence may not, of course, be wholly desirable; the question whether independence in children ought to be fostered or suppressed is at the centre of modern educational controversy. How teachers evaluate the qualities of children of working mothers probably largely depends on the side they take in this controversy.

[1] T. Ferguson and J. Cunnison, *The Young Wage Earner*, London, 1951.

In later adolescence the latent conflict between the children's need for independence and their mothers' urge to expect compensation for their single-minded devotion to them often comes to a head. Terrible crises may then shake supposedly harmonious homes. Particularly in our time, when the economic dependence of children continues so long after they have physiologically and psychologically grown up, it takes a rare skill for parents to recede tactfully into the background, and provide without self-effacement the right amount of non-interference which is necessary to build up the young people's self-respect and self-reliance. The guilt feelings created in sons and daughters by the awareness that their mother has 'sacrificed her life' to them—a mother who is still young enough to continue through decades asking for compensation—are a heavy burden to give our young men and women whose adjustment to life is difficult enough as it is.

If a mother can in good conscience make herself independent of her children at the age of 45, or earlier, it should be considered a blessing for the children. It would be the modern equivalent of the gratification parents used to feel when they could stop worrying over their children's livelihood. For the span of life which a woman of 45 to-day has in front of her is not much shorter than that which a young man in his early twenties could expect a hundred years ago. If for these thirty years of life she is capable of emancipating herself from her grown-up children she will benefit herself, her family, and the community.

CHAPTER EIGHT

CONTEMPORARY FEMININE DILEMMAS

Our civilization is full of inner contradictions which are reflected in the intellectual uncertainties of contemporary man. The individual member of society is faced with a great variety of choices, while he is left with few guiding principles to help him in his decisions. It is part of our democratic ideology that everyone should be free to make up his own mind according to his lights; and since many of the ideals of our society are at odds with one another, modern man meets with a host of moral and psychological dilemmas.

Some of the typical conflicts inherent in our culture have been described by Karen Horney in *The Neurotic Personality of Our Time* (1937). Examples are the contrasts between the aggressiveness engendered by competition on the one hand, and the Christian ideals of brotherly love and humility on the other; between the idolization of success and the creed 'the meek shall inherit the earth'; between the belief in freedom and the need for control; between the accepted principle of equality and the prestige of wealth and rank. These and numerous other conflicting values confront and bewilder the contemporary Western mind. Science and religion are in a state of uneasy truce; and the sciences themselves are in the grip of an ethical dilemma which is only too glaringly illustrated by the problems of the atom bomb. Conflicts of loyalty might almost be called the endemic disease of the modern mind.

It is against this background that we must consider the typical inner conflicts from which women to-day suffer. However specifically feminine their dilemmas may be, they are symptoms of a general contemporary malaise.

Many women feel that, as women, they have been singled out by providence to cope with an almost insoluble conflict of aims. Yet their position at the cross-roads is by no means as eternal as it appears to its unfortunate victims. It is not the result of a 'Law of Nature', but of contradictory trends and ideals within our society.

The situation has become so tantalizing for the very reason that there are so many new roads open to men and women to-day; and the problem is particularly important since it affects one half of civilized mankind.

The characteristic feminine dilemma of to-day is usually summarized under the heading 'Career and Family'. The struggle for the right to work is no longer directed against external obstacles; no longer is there the same hostile public opinion to overcome with which our grandmothers had to contend, nor is there a lack of opportunities for women. To-day the conflict has become 'internalized' and continues as a psychological problem which may assume many different variations and shades; and just because there is no longer an absolute 'either—or' to be decided on at the beginning of adult life, the pull in two directions goes on practically throughout a woman's life.

The Dilemma of Vocational Choice

The first critical phase is reached when a girl has to choose a career. This she now must do; for we have come so far along the road of emancipation that no girl can merely sit at home and wait for a husband. She will have to take a job, at least until such time as she marries, and therefore she will have to be educated with this aim in mind. Most girls, like boys, have to make a vocational choice at the age of 15; some school systems force a decision on the child at the age of 11, and a certain amount of training for future jobs is given to most of them during their school days. Even for the daughters of the well-to-do, who do not expect to have to earn their living, 'finishing schools', which provide no vocational training but only teach 'accomplishments', have become almost obsolete. The value of education—and education with a purpose—is so well established in our society that parents to-day would feel they were depriving their daughters of a chance to develop their personalities if they did not allow them as good an education as they can afford.

It is at this early stage of deciding on the most suitable education—for what?—that the dilemma sets in. As the girl is likely to marry, it is an open question whether she will ever put her vocational training into practice. But how can she be sure of this? She may never meet the man with whom she would like to spend the rest of her life; or she may meet him at a later age; or the man she loves may not be in a position to support her. At any rate, the ability to provide for herself gives her the independence to be more selective in the choice of a husband. Thus, even a girl who hopes to marry at the earliest convenient opportunity, to have a family and to live happily ever after, is likely to take advantage of the best education open to her. Moreover, for those who feel so inclined, a university, or a job, may well be the best place to meet congenial young men.

Having chosen what seems to all intents and purposes the most sensible path, and having started training for a job, the young woman may then be afflicted with doubts as to whether she has entered a one-way street, and by starting the fairly long training for a profession, blocked her way to home and family. Statistics that indicate a lower marriage rate among university graduates tend to confirm such fears, although these are no longer justified by the facts of the current situation. Figures available both for the United States and Great Britain show that the difference in the marriage rate of university graduates and of other women, which at the beginning of this century was very marked, has gradually diminished and is now very small. In 1940 30 per cent of American college women between the ages of 45 and 49 were single, compared with 12·5 per cent of high-school graduates and 7·6 per cent of women with a lower education. It is this older group of graduates which depresses the general average.[1] The present marriage rate among women graduates—and, incidentally, that of men graduates also—is only slightly below the mean for the sex. The same is true also of Great Britain, where the marriage rate of women graduates has roughly doubled since 1900.[2]

Fifty years ago the chances for a woman with university education of finding a husband were very low indeed. But in those days the higher education of girls was such a rare phenomenon that those who went to college were a selected group—selected, that is, for qualities of mind and character which made it difficult for them to fit into the then prevailing marriage pattern. Now that university education is so widespread, the girls subjected to it no longer represent a particular personality type. And the present

[1] Ernest Havemann and Patricia Salter West, *They Went to College*, New York, 1952.
[2] 'Graduate Wives', *Planning*, Vol. XX, No. 361, April 1954.

marriage pattern allows for sufficient independence and equality of women to make higher education and professional interests a bar to marriage no longer. After a period of trial and error, and a great number of encouraging precedents, men to-day are no longer afraid of marrying a woman who is their equal in education and experience.

Nevertheless, the old fears born from the experiences of the past generation still persist; so does the ideology which regards job and family as mutually exclusive. It is especially powerful in the middle classes and therefore affects most strongly the girls who receive higher education. In the United States, where it is such a wide-spread practice for young women to go to college, irrespective of any plans they may have made for their future, the dilemma is probably more acute than elsewhere. It is further complicated by the fact that in a highly competitive society, such as that of America, young people aspire not to ordinary adult roles, in the manner, for instance, of their parents, but strive to approximate as nearly as possible to an ideal—and the ideal types approved by society are contradictory. The adult feminine roles of housewife, and of a woman with a job, have been glamorized into those of the attractive 'society hostess' on the one hand, and the successful 'career woman' on the other; the conflict has thus been dramatized. The college girl who tries to get on in the world and to make a success of her life feels she is running in two races at the same time and is never quite sure whether her advance in one field may not be a handicap in the other.

The feeling of insecurity which is thereby created in the girl is enhanced by an equally ambivalent attitude in her surroundings. Her parents and male friends are no less uncertain and inconsistent in their expectations of her. 'My family had expected me to become Madame Curie and Hedy Lamarr wrapped up in one,' said an American girl student,[1] putting in a nutshell what may well be the unavowed ideal of many parents of daughters who are studying.

The young men whom the college girl meets may be an even more difficult problem. Their attitude vacillates between a wish to have a girl-friend who is an intelligent companion and a 'good sport', and a desire for a combination of mother-image plus Venus

[1] 'Cultural Contradictions and Sex Roles', by Myrra Komarovsky, *American Journal of Sociology*, November 1946.

de Milo: a woman for whom they are the sole aim in life and with whom they can be proud to be seen in public. To try to satisfy all of these demands simultaneously is of course to invite defeat at least in some.

Another serious dilemma for the girl who wants to be successful in her work arises from the fact that in our society the pattern of male superiority is still so strong that the pretence, at least, of feminine weakness and intellectual inferiority has to be kept up. The investigation from which we quoted before gives evidence of a very widespread compliance with this pattern. The report is the result of a research carried out in 1942 and 1943 among a group of American girl students of social psychology and based on some 150 interviews and autobiographical documents. Its extensive quotations reveal, to a degree which may surprise many people, that among the present generation the ideology of male superiority is still a very potent factor. It is not a genuine belief in the superiority of men but a convention that masculine illusions in that respect must not be disturbed. Of the students interrogated, 40 per cent 'indicated that they have occasionally "played dumb" on dates, i.e. concealed some academic honor, pretended ignorance of some subject, or allowed the man the last word in an intelligent discussion'. One girl said of her co-educational college that 'a reputation of a "brain" killed a girl socially. I was always fearful lest I say too much in class or answered a question which the boys I dated couldn't answer.' Another admitted: 'In spite of myself I played up to his theories because the less one knows and does, the more he does for you and thinks you "cute" into the bargain.' One girl described a work-camp in which 'the girls did the same work as the boys. If some girls worked better, the boys resented it fiercely. The director told one capable girl to slow down to keep peace in the group.'

There is no reason to doubt that the feelings of insecurity and uncertainty about their adult feminine roles, of which evidence was found in all the college girls interviewed in this American investigation, are very widespread among young women to-day. They may be less acute in countries where competition has not yet permeated all spheres of life; where, for instance, 'competitive dating' is not a practice as prevalent as among the youth of America, and where getting married or engaged as early as possible does not enjoy the same prestige value; but the tendency exists everywhere and the weight of social conventions makes itself felt in the direction of marriage and away from study and career.

Success in her personal relations is, of course, as important to a young woman as success in her work. She cannot well risk sacrificing it in the pursuit of an as yet uncertain career. To strike a balance between the demands made on her time, attention, and energy, in either sphere is more difficult for the girl than it is for the young man, firstly, because in her case the roads to success appear to lead into two opposite directions, and secondly, because in the back of a girl's mind there always lurks the thought that her efforts, even if successful, may lead nowhere. How seriously is she to take herself, even though her interest in her work be sincere? Can she be sure that it will always remain strong enough to hold out against all appeals to her emotions and against the temptation to fall back into the traditional family pattern? There are too many examples of brilliant and promising young students who eventually became quite ordinary housewives for a girl not to have secret reservations even about her own earnest protestations to be serious about a career.

It may be hoped that this dilemma might be lessened by effective vocational guidance; if girls whose main interest is to marry and to have a family could be directed towards jobs which prepare them for this contingency and which call for the same kind of skills and qualities as home-making, while those with a strong interest and ability for one of the traditionally 'masculine' careers could be expected to continue in employment as long, and with as few interruptions, as possible. A great variety of jobs of the first type exist —nursing, teaching, social work, personnel management, catering, etc., and many more such jobs are in need of being developed. There is, therefore, no shortage of professions from which women can choose even though their main hope for the future be marriage. All these jobs have the advantage that the professional skills acquired in their practice do not get lost by disuse during prolonged periods of absence from employment when the woman marries. On the contrary, the experience of having run a home and brought up a family may be a distinct asset for those who want to return to any of these occupations at a later stage.

Correct assessment of personality is a basic requirement for vocational guidance; and young women's attitude to marriage and career is a personality factor of great importance which should be given due consideration by those who advise on the direction their education should take and the jobs best suited for them.

The effectiveness of such guidance is, however, seriously impeded by two obstacles. The obvious one is the unpredictability of the future. Even if people were consistent in their motives, single-minded in their intentions, and consistent in their aims throughout their life-time—which they are not—there are too many unexpected corners to turn to make long-term planning perfectly safe. A girl who at 18 or 20 is dominated by an overriding interest, say, in physics, or in anthropology, and feels sure that she wants to devote her life to it, may yet at 26 have the irresistible urge to set up house with an officer or an insurance clerk. Another one, no less unpredictable, is the course her future married life may take. Any attempt, therefore, to persuade a girl into adopting a career for which she has no strong inclination is fraught with too many risks to be reasonable.

An even greater difficulty, and one which is at the bottom of this problem of 'feminine dilemmas', is presented by the fact that the woman with domestic aptitudes and inclinations, and the woman with an abiding interest in one of the traditionally 'masculine' professions, are not two different character types. The same woman may make an excellent scientist or business woman as well as a first-rate housewife, mother and cook, and may get a great deal of pleasure out of all these activities. The fact that each of us can probably recall half a dozen women who are such combinations—and who look smart and well-groomed into the bargain—shows that it can be and is being done. Miss Florence Horsbrugh, former Minister of Education, once said: 'I have had more satisfaction out of making a good steamed pudding than in any speech I have ever made from the front bench of the House of Commons.' Dr. Edith Summerskill, Minister of Food in a previous government, has made similar statements in regard to her family life. Yet, obviously, each of them had become a politician of her own choice and inclination against considerable odds and it would have been a loss of talent had they been restricted to the use of their housewifely gifts only.

Compulsion to specialize in one particular field would frustrate an intelligent woman's potentialities in others. A choice between domestic and intellectual interests cannot therefore be enforced on a young girl without harm to her further development. Hence the dilemma is still with us and will remain so until society has so adjusted itself, mentally and materially, to the new conditions that it will be possible for women satisfactorily to combine the pursuit of a chosen career with marriage and family life. Only then will emotional factors—the appeal of a traditional role, maternal example, hopes of marriage—cease to be in acute conflict with other more rational considerations.

The most sensible advice that can be given to young girls under present conditions is that they should choose a career best suited to their interests and inclinations, and work on the assumption that they will have to live by it, for marriage is not a panacea. Either for financial reasons or for their emotional satisfaction they may in the future want a job even though they are married; they ought, therefore, to be in earnest about their work; and under any circumstances, even if they get engaged while still at the training stage, they should try at least to complete their education so that they can resume their career later on if they want to or need to.

The Dilemma of Married Women with Careers

Many thousands of women have undertaken a professional training seriously, but this course, needless to say, has pitfalls of its own. While it provides an insurance for the girl who does not marry, or who does not want to marry the first man who offers himself, it undoubtedly adds to the problems of the woman who does marry.

The legal barriers which, until fairly recently, forced women in some professions, such as teaching or the civil service, to resign on marrying have now, for all intents and purposes, been abolished in most Western countries. Hence the question of whether or not to continue in employment after marriage has largely become a matter of personal choice and of agreement between husband and wife. The fact that such a decision may have been taken rationally after due consideration of the pros and cons does not necessarily eliminate doubts and worries on a deeper psychological level.

Even though a couple may have based their life plan on complete companionship, mutual independence in their careers, and equal shares in domestic responsibilities, this plan can be maintained only under stress in the face of a tradition which assumes a division of labour between a bread-winning husband and a domestic wife. Whether they intend it or not, comparisons between their own way of life and the more traditional one will present themselves—and these comparisons will in many respects not be favourable to the working wife.

The woman who is employed outside her home often asks herself whether she is not putting an undue strain on her husband by expecting him to give a hand with domestic chores while other men are free after office hours either to rest, or to enjoy recreation, or to do some work which may help them to advance in their own careers. Is she, perhaps, too absorbed in her own affairs to be the wholehearted and devoted listener he expects? Is she a good enough housewife? The traditional standards of domestic virtues have not changed very much since the days of our grandmothers. The ideal housewife is still thought of as a woman who spends a maximum amount of time and labour at home, doing whatever is possible with her own hands. Though glossy journals may be full of alluring advertisements illustrating luscious dishes prepared in a jiffy out of a tin, there is, nevertheless, still a certain stigma attached to the use of the tin-opener as a kitchen utensil. Obviously a woman who spends her day at an office cannot devote the same amount of care to the preparation of meals as a full-time housewife and her cakes, bought at a shop or made from a 'Ready-Mix', will not compare with those her husband remembers with nostalgia from his mother's home.

If she has children, her doubts and guilt feelings will be doubled. Does she deprive them of much-needed attention? Perhaps, on the contrary, she pampers them to compensate for her bad conscience? Though there may be no evidence of either—will perhaps their future development bring to light her sins of omission? Contemporary psychology has put a very heavy burden of responsibility on the mother's shoulders, and the more educated she is the more conscious she will be of its implications.

If to all these conflicts of conscience we add the fact that the woman with a double responsibility may often feel tired and irritable, and furthermore, that the financial incentive to accept the double work load is often very small or even non-existent, the extra earnings being eaten up by increased expenses for home-help, nursery, increased laundry bills, fares, meals out and taxation; then we may well ask why so many married women nevertheless prefer to carry on and why so many others, who have given up their jobs in order to devote themselves to their homes and families, feel a sense of loss and look forward to the day when their children are older so that they can return to their careers.

Of the sample of 1,165 married graduates surveyed by Judith Hubback,[1] 500, that is nearly one half, definitely stated that they would like to do some kind of work in the future, i.e. when their children are old enough; some others said they would like to do some work but were not yet certain what they wanted to do; only 13 per cent of the graduates (compared with 41 per cent of the non-graduate married women interviewed as a control group) stated that they did not intend to take up any kind of work. Even if these statements are taken only as expressions of intent, they are a clear indication that the desire to accept outside work is strong in many women, particularly in those with higher qualifications, and that, given better opportunities, many of them are ready to put their skills and energies at the service of the community. The present waste of these, clearly, does not correspond with the wishes of a great number of women and is an unnecessary loss to society.

In a previous chapter we have discussed the motives which induce married women to seek employment outside their homes. Some of them, particularly those affecting chiefly skilled and professional women, deserve greater consideration not only because they do credit to the women concerned, but because they give encouragement to those who believe in the effects of education, and disprove the diehards who assert that higher education is wasted on women.

A sense of vocation influences quite a few women in their desire to continue their work after marriage. This may be found in particular among teachers, nurses and other kinds of social workers. Some may be inspired by a very laudable feeling of social responsibility, that, having spent years in preparation and having taken up one of the limited number of places at a university or professional school, they owe it to the community to put into practice what they have learned.

Whether or not such lofty and unselfish motives are the main factors influencing married women to accept outside jobs, they certainly play a part which does not as yet get due attention. More public praise of the women who of their own accord take on

[1] *Wives Who Went to College*, London, 1957.

what, at least at the present phase of social development, is a double burden of work, would undoubtedly help many women to overcome the psychological dilemma in which they are caught to-day.

The Housewives' Dilemma

Two further reasons which induce married women to go out to work are factors which depress the role of the housewife: financial dependence, and the low esteem in which domestic work is held in our society. Both of these have given much cause for bitterness among married women. Various women's organizations in all the countries concerned have in recent years tried to raise the social status of the housewife in both respects: by agitating for salaries, or their equivalent, for women whose job it is to run a home and bring up a family, and, perhaps more practically and successfully, by improving the quality and thereby also the status of domestic work. The latter efforts have so far mainly achieved higher regard and better pay for domestic helpers—to which their scarcity has no doubt contributed a good deal—but it has not greatly affected the social standing of the housewife. Her status is, as always, derived from her husband as a kind of reflected glory, not from the quality of her own work.

To counteract this state of affairs, which many women find depressing, a cult of Homemaking and Motherhood is fostered by press and propaganda. The sentimental glorification which these activities receive may flatter many housewives, but in the long run it does more harm than good, for it encourages them to indulge in an irrational self-pity and prevents them from assessing their situation at its true value.

Sometimes this glorification has a suspicious air of persuasion: as if women needed convincing that their lot is better than they thought. Whether this impression is true or not, the sentimental cult of domestic virtues is the cheapest method at society's disposal of keeping women quiet without seriously considering their grievances or improving their position. It has been successfully used to this day, and has helped to perpetuate some dilemmas of home-making women by telling them, on the one hand, that they are devoted to the most sacred duty, while on the other hand keeping them on a level of unpaid drudgery.

This term will seem an exaggeration in view of the fact that some women obviously do well in spite of their financial dependence. But the spending power of a woman who has no income of her own is naturally dependent on her husband's generosity. There are still all too few cases in which a real partnership in matrimonial finance exists. And in principle, if not in practice, the financial position of a married woman is similar to that of a minor. This state of dependence is more degrading than is willingly admitted and is the cause of much domestic tension and frustration. Since most women to-day have known the independence which a self-earned income, however small, bestows, they find it difficult to have to ask for money and to account for their expenses.

These very important financial considerations apart, many other circumstances worry the woman who has devoted herself entirely to home and family. The more intelligent, lively, and educated woman especially fears that her mind will get narrowed within the confines of her home and stultified by lack of practice. Children and home may be an emotionally satisfying milieu but they are hardly mentally stimulating. Most of all, housewives suffer from social isolation—an isolation which the woman accustomed to contacts through her work feels even more acutely than one who has been born and bred as a housewife. Their work does not naturally lead to social contacts as do other occupations, or as it did in the old days when households were larger and more work was done at home which lent itself to communal activities. Their work does not provide them with the mental stimulus and emotional satisfaction which result from working in a team. Moreover, the housewife particularly has been the victim of that middle-class ideology of privacy[1] which has to-day spread to vast masses of society and which has made 'keeping oneself to oneself' one of the essential virtues in the accepted code of middle-class and lower middle-class proprieties.

Isolated from companionship by her work and from her neighbours by the conventional behaviour pattern of 'reserve', the housewife is normally cooped up within her four walls, her husband being away at work for the greater part of the day, her children, unless too young to be real companions, out at play, at school or at work. As a rule she lives miles away from other members of her family or from any school-friends she may have. Her shopping

[1] Cf. Paul Halmos, *Solitude and Privacy*, London, 1952.

146

expeditions are her 'excursions into the world' and for this reason she tends to expand them in a manner which to non-housewives is often difficult to understand.

This social isolation imposes a two-fold strain: on the one hand, her solitude gives the housewife a feeling of loss and causes dissatisfaction with her role; she feels that life is passing her by.

On the other hand, the decline of other community ties has put an undue strain on her marriage relationship. This is no longer a part in the social fabric—however essential this part may always have been—but has become practically the solitary link the housewife has with the outside world. Participation in civil activities and recreation groups is not always possible, particularly for the woman with small children, for the same reasons as keeping up with her job is difficult. To join any of these outside occupations requires a special mental effort which many a housewife is not able to make. As a rule, her husband is the only source of all her emotional, intellectual and spiritual satisfaction, her one legitimate contact with the 'world at large'. To rely for so much on any individual human relationship means straining it as far as, and sometimes beyond, the limit of its endurance. 'The current divorce rate', says an American sociologist,[1] 'is, in part, an index of the new demands made upon marriage for sociability and leisure by sensitive middle-class couples . . . these demands not only begin high, in the choice of a mate, but . . . include the expectation that each partner grow and develop at approximately the same rate as (the other).'

The situation has been aggravated by the fact that the husband's share in the life of the family, in the daily routine of the home and the bringing up of his children, has been reduced to a minimum by the specialization of labour between husband and wife and the separation of home and workplace. They live in two different worlds and the area in which the two spheres overlap has been emotionally overburdened by the social isolation of the housewife.

In theory, modern means of communication and entertainment have brought the whole world into the home at the mere switch of a knob. In practice, however, only a shadow of the world is cast into the home. The contact thus created is impersonal and devoid of reciprocity. On the radio, to which the housewife listens

[1] David Riesman, *The Lonely Crowd*, New York, 1953.

while she does her housework, disembodied voices offer her news, views and entertainment; television and films project people and actions on a screen without giving any feeling of 'presence'. There is no mutual response between the artist or speaker and the audience, as is the case in 'real life'. Newspapers may publish all sorts of details of the lives of distant and unknown people, but however much journalists may strive to supply the 'human touch', particularly for their women readers, these people remain aloof and any relationship with them one-sided, even if it attains the intensity of identification, as it often does. The isolated woman at home may well be kept 'in touch' with events, but she feels that the events are not in touch with her, that they happen without her participation. The wealth of information which is brought to her without any effort on her part does not lose its vicariousness. It increases rather than allays her sense of isolation and of being left out.

Many investigators have been struck by the fact that to the women at home offices and workshops seem alluring places, full of interest and human contacts, and that many working mothers state that their jobs provide them with an escape which is well worth the extra burden entailed. Many of them have said that the nervous strain produced by isolation and incessant minor worries is reduced by the safety-valve of outside employment, and that domestic troubles assume their proper proportion when seen against the wider background provided by contact with others.

Retrogression is no way out

The obvious discontent among contemporary women has led some people to the conclusion that the emancipation of women is at the root of the evil. Were it not for the success of feminist agitation, so it is sometimes argued, women could still be happy as housewives and mothers with no aspirations outside their homes. Egalitarianism has 'put ideas into their heads' which have done more harm than good.

Statements like this do not stand the test of historical or sociological analysis. They have to be taken as expressions of an irrational longing for times past, born of present discontent. They are on the same level as other nostalgic comparisons between individual contemporary phenomena and their opposites, supposedly characteristic of past ages. Our restlessness is contrasted with the security of faith of the Middle Ages; our democratic 'vulgarity' with the aristocratic elegance of the eighteenth century, and the like. During that very eighteenth century Montesquieu invented his 'unspoilt' Persian, and Rousseau conjured up the ideal 'noble savage' in contrast to the hypocrisy of their own society. Thus the yearning for the better, 'purer', days of the past is not a new thing. The revolt against our machine-made civilization is as old as civilization itself. It has been completely ineffectual in stemming its progress.

Though there is truth in the assertion that refrigerators are no substitute for peace of mind, and that the speed of air travel has increased neither the total amount of human happiness nor the feeling of fraternity between men, such statements are utterly irrelevant. No practical purpose is, or can be, served by singling out isolated phenomena from their social context and making them individually responsible for contemporary ills.

It may well be that women in pre-emancipation days were on the whole happier than their grand-daughters are to-day, though it seems difficult to compare the total amount of existing happiness at any two points in time. With equal justification, however, it might be said that in those pre-industrial days human beings altogether were happier, measured by our present afflictions—that they were less restless, less competitive, more contented in their work, less ambitious and less divided against themselves. On the other hand, more of them died in infancy, in childbirth, as victims of epidemic diseases and starvation; a greater proportion of the population were incurably ill or disfigured by disease; more people were ill-treated by their elders and superiors, and more suffered from dire poverty and harsh injustice. The sum total of such an elusive thing as human happiness defies measurement.

So much, however, can be said: when the economic and social conditions changed with the Industrial Revolution, the dissatisfaction of women with their lot grew to such an extent that it had to find an outlet in the movement for Emancipation, and remedies had to be sought by a series of adjustments in our social system which are still in progress to-day. To undo emancipation and return to the 'three K's', *Kinder, Küche, Kirche*, if it were at all practicable, would only mean a return to a state of tension and unhappiness —unless industrialization and all its social and economic results could simultaneously also be undone. This, however, is clearly fantastic. Even if it were possible to institute retrogression for women only, it would certainly make the tensions between the sexes more unmanageable than ever. But it is no more possible to return to previous states of social development than for an adult to revert to the embryonic state of unconscious bliss or to the irresponsibility of early childhood. The only way open to the social reformer is to smooth out the roughnesses which have occurred as a result of the uneven development in various parts of the social fabric and to help to make social adjustments to new conditions as easy as possible.

An Important Minority

It is true, of course, that many married women have no regret for their past jobs and are happy to have escaped what they feel was equivalent to slavery. It is also true that many of those who continue in employment after marriage do so not of their own choice but forced by economic circumstances. It will certainly be pointed out to us that the psychological tensions and dilemmas which we discussed in this chapter mainly affect a relatively small section of women, namely the educated middle class.

We have quite deliberately devoted more attention to the problems of women who have been trained for a profession than their numbers warrant. We have done so for a variety of reasons. One is simply that problems of choice arise only where there is at least some freedom to choose. The woman who has to go to work in order to support her family need not be troubled overmuch about the psychological effects her absence from home may have on her children. She knows that if she did not earn the money she needs to feed them, her children would go hungry. There is no doubt which is the lesser evil of the two.

Moreover, the educated élite is more articulate and hence its problems are more widely discussed. This minority creates the patterns which are later adopted by the community as a whole. By their successes and failures the outcome of women's emancipation will be judged, and the question of 'how much equality' decided. One woman teacher, social worker or doctor who throws up her career on marriage creates a stronger precedent than dozens of shop assistants, factory girls or shorthand typists who do the same.

Women are still relatively new in the professions and are still on trial; and, as with other minority groups, the actions of each individual member reflect on the whole class. If they make a failure either of their job, which is easily judged by the watchful eyes of others, or of their marriage, great damage is done to the standing of women in society and even to their personal hopes for a happy adjustment to present conditions of life. If the pioneers succeed in combining motherhood and work, all women may take comfort.

It is, of course, true that the value of education cannot be measured in terms appropriate to assessing the material returns from capital investment. Its rewards are too elusive to be shown on any account sheet. There are repeated controversies in the press as to whether the university education of girls is a waste of time and money, in view of the fact that most women give up their careers on marriage. ('Labour Lost through Love' was the heading aptly chosen by *The Economist* for its own contribution to the discussion). The many graduate wives taking part in the discussion usually agree in emphasizing that they are happy to have had the chance to study, that they benefited by it, and that they have not the slightest doubt that it was very worth while. A minority hope to resume their careers when their children are old enough to permit it, and some others have successfully done so at the age of forty-odd. A majority is convinced of the value of university education in broadening the mind, increasing sensibilities and improving the standards of judgment and understanding—all of which, they say, were assets also in their relations with husband and children, so that their education has on no account been wasted even if it has not been used professionally.

This is not to be disputed. Vocational training is certainly only one aspect of university education; the development of character and mental powers is another which must not be underrated. The more people capable of benefiting from a university education are able to do so, the better for society. However, as long as the number of places is limited, and as long as the cost of this education is borne largely by the public, those who administer the funds will regard it as their duty to ensure that the money invested in education gives the maximum return. They cannot be blamed if they expect a social contribution from those who have had the advantage of a university education. Women who have been admitted to universities on equal terms cannot escape comparison with men in this respect and must not be surprised if the production of cultured and enlightened mothers—desirable as this may be—can only be regarded as a by-product, not as the main aim of university education.

CHAPTER NINE

THE NEXT STEPS

There is no overlooking the fact that women do not yet feel 'at home' in both worlds. Their psychological conflicts are symptoms of the underlying uncertainty of their economic and social role. If they are to be integrated more fully into our society than has been the case so far, changes in individual attitudes of both men and women, adjustments in the labour market, and action by public authorities, will all be necessary.

It is a hopeful sign that under all three headings adaptations to the changing social needs are in continuous progress, albeit often in a hesitant and unco-ordinated way. Measures already taken offer the most convenient starting points for further development, because they are often steps in the right direction, and because they provide us with a stock of experience on which to draw. We propose therefore to survey them briefly.

Individual Adjustments Needed

The requisite changes in the outlook of women have been stated, or implied, in many parts of this book. They can here be briefly summarized under the headings of planning for different phases of a life-span, attitude to work, and choice of career.

PLANNING FOR A LONG AND FULL LIFE. In the long life which women can expect under normal circumstances to-day, bringing up a family will in most instances occupy barely more than a third of their adulthood. It is therefore suggested that women should visualize their life-span as a succession of three phases, each dominated mainly by one function: a period of training and education, followed, if possible, by years devoted to raising a family; these, in turn, being succeeded by a period during which past training and experience are put to wider social use. Education, family and work can be blended to a harmonious whole in one life-time if each is given its own place in a chronological sequence.

In practice this precept is nowadays very often acted upon. The pattern is, however, establishing itself more out of the desire of women in their middle years for a useful and interesting field of activity than as part of a deliberate design for living. The pattern is too new yet to be accepted as a natural rhythm.

Yet if women had this cycle in mind from the outset they could plan their lives more rationally than they do at present. They would not be caught unprepared in middle life. And they would avoid many worries and feelings of frustration if they were not trying to do too many things at the same time—or, doing one thing, being unhappy that they are missing another. Instead, they could devote themselves to the task in hand, conscious that a long life is waiting for them in which they can fulfil all their aims in a rhythm best adjusted to their age and constitution.

WOMEN'S ATTITUDE TO WORK. If women want to play a part in society commensurate with their abilities, one of the essentials is that they should adopt a more realistic attitude towards their careers. They will only be taken seriously in their work when they have learned that taking a job is not only a matter of temporarily earning a living but, literally, of *gagner sa vie*, as the French say.

In an extremely interesting study[1] of the professional status of women in France and its connexion with the persistence of the traditional ideology concerning women's role, the authors discuss the fact that despite the very considerable participation of French women in industry, commerce, civil service and the professions, women are largely to be found in the lowest ranks. They point to the fact that in training centres (*centres d'apprentissage*) the number of girls in 1950 was 55,000 in comparison with 86,000 boys, and of those 55,000 girls 35,000 were being trained in dress-making, and 11,000 for office jobs. In the metal industry, where women are 13 per cent of all persons employed, girls constitute only 0·37 per cent of those being apprenticed in mechanics and 0·63 per cent of those apprenticed in electrical engineering. In most industries, therefore, women are doing unskilled and semi-skilled work, chiefly because their jobs, and their earnings, are regarded as accessory to their role in the family.

A striking example of the waste of skill and training which goes

[1] By M. Guilbert and V. Isambert-Jamati, *op. cit.*

on currently is provided by pharmacologists in France. Among the students of this subject women form the majority (53·5 per cent in 1950); yet among the practising dispensing chemists they are only 22 per cent. Even though the present generation of students may show better results, the return for the labour of professors and the provision of expensive laboratory equipment is extraordinarily disappointing in a field which constitutes a public utility.

The first point, therefore, to be impressed on young girls—a point which should be particularly stressed by those who offer them vocational advice—is that they must take their future work seriously rather than rely on the mental reservation: 'Of course, I can always get out of it when I marry.' Women would constitute a much more valued element on the labour market, and would, accordingly, have much better prospects, if more of them devoted themselves sincerely to their jobs for the better part of their lives, even allowing for an interruption of some years.

CHOICE OF VOCATION. A second point of equal importance is that in future women will have to do more heart-searching when choosing a career. Their choice must, of course, in the first place depend on their abilities and interests and on the opportunities open to them. Within this margin, however, young girls have more than boys to view their prospects against the background of future family responsibilities. This postulate is dictated by practical common sense—disappointing though it may be to many an idealist who had hoped for complete and unconditional equality between the sexes. If the discrimination against women which still exists in many fields of employment is to be abolished, women must be able to compete with men on equal terms. Among these the ability to make long-term plans, to pursue a chosen vocation, and to offer returns for the time and money invested in their training, are important items.

Women could circumvent a crucial handicap on their road to emancipation if they chose occupations which they will be able to continue after marriage or resume after an interval of a few years.

This need not amount to a new division of labour between the sexes. Even less does it mean the abandonment of the feminist ideal of equality, for 'equal opportunity' is part and parcel of our democratic ideology. But it is no use shutting our eyes to the facts of life in pursuit of an abstract ideal. It may well be, in the light of past and present experience, that feminist ideals are in need of some qualification to-day. Women's emotional needs, for instance, were not given enough consideration by the early feminists. Their claim for women's right to work and to own property has over-shadowed the equally important right of working women to marry and to have a family if they so desire.

The fact has to be recognized and frankly admitted that there are perils attendant upon all of our democratic ideals. Studies equivalent to Erich Fromm's *Fear of Freedom* could, and should, be written about the social and psychological problems inherent in the ideals of Equality and Fraternity as well as of Liberty. The conclusion to be drawn from the realization of the difficulties involved is, surely, not to give up these ideals but to face the risks and to try to overcome them.

Girls with a special talent for, or an overriding interest in, any of the traditionally masculine professions should certainly not be discouraged from following their inclinations. It would be wrong, for instance, to persuade a woman who is eager to become a barrister to be trained as a Froebel nurse instead, simply because she hopes to marry if a suitable opportunity arises and also, if possible, to have children. In this way, a woman who might otherwise have become a competent, or even excellent, lawyer may be doomed for the rest of her life to be a moderate and inwardly dissatisfied kindergarten teacher if her hopes of eventual escape into marriage are not fulfilled. And of the two possible failures it seems that to have pinned all hopes on marriage, and then not to be able to realize them, is a more cruel disappointment than having to throw up a promising career because of family demands.

The majority of girls, however, do not feel an impelling urge for one particular career. Their intelligence and abilities are, as a rule, such that they may be fully realized, and their interest engaged, in any of a variety of fields. These are the girls in need of vocational guidance and they should be advised in the direction here indicated.

If, as a result, many women would think it reasonable to choose some of the traditionally feminine occupations this does not, to us, seem as damaging to the 'Woman's Cause' as it might appear to the more orthodox and ardent feminists.

Obviously, not all jobs lend themselves equally well to a combination with family life. Occupations which necessitate a lot of travel, demand long or irregular hours of work, or involve highly delicate skills which may be lost in periods of disuse, are unsuitable in this respect. Professions such as that of a surgeon or a diplomat would be very difficult to reconcile with family responsibilities.

Yet there is a wide range of variations between one kind of job and another. The type of work which claims complete devotion of time, day in, day out, for many years, is at one end of the scale. If these occupations are sometimes chosen by men regardless of the fact that they leave hardly any margin for family life, they can be chosen by women, too, but only if they are willing to work on the same conditions as men.

At the other extreme there are jobs which are so easy to combine with marriage and motherhood that, metaphorically speaking, a woman can practise them almost with one hand at the cradle. Teaching, for instance, particularly in nursery and primary grades, seems next to ideal, because the working hours of mother and children are more or less the same, they can go to school together, their vacations coincide, and a joint interest may help them mutually in their work.

Not many types of work are so cut out for women with young families, but there are various jobs these women can do without hardship to themselves or ill effect on their families, such as running a private nursery, for example, supervising a shop near home, operating a petrol pump, and various kinds of home production —from dressmaking, or the home manufacture of lampshades or industrial parts, or stocking repairs or typing, to proof reading, translating, and literary or artistic creation. It is true, however, that many types of intellectual work require a degree of concentration which is difficult to achieve when concurrent domestic responsibilities also call for attention; although writing, or studying at home may give a woman a better chance than most jobs to look after her young children, unless she has domestic help she will need an iron determination to stick to her working schedule. It is certainly easier to combine motherhood with needlework than with the writing of novels.

Fortunately, in most fields of work, a variety of jobs exists between the two extremes, so that women can choose among them to suit their convenience and their future plans.

Apart from the fairly wide range of traditionally feminine jobs, such as social work, nursing, teaching, dressmaking, cooking, management of hotels, restaurants and institutions, child care, and the like, there are some fields of work, which in most countries are considered typically masculine, such as real estate, housing management and others, which could be relatively easily combined with family duties and which call for a kind of knowledge for which experience in home-making would be an asset. They should therefore commend themselves as jobs for women, particularly for middle-aged women.

Shorthand-typing, on the other hand, which at present absorbs so much female labour, offers only poor long-term prospects for women who intend to marry. It is a skill not used in running a home and one which suffers from a prolonged break; and though a certain amount of free-lance typing or part-time work can be done at times when a full-time secretarial job would be too much to be combined with domestic responsibilities, the amount of work available on such a part-time basis is infinitesimal in comparison to the large numbers of women eager and qualified to undertake it.

KEEPING UP OR IMPROVING VOCATIONAL SKILL. The years women spend at home looking after their families need not be regarded as a loss to the rest of society provided women endeavoured at the same time to keep their professional skill alive. The time they can spare from immediate household chores and from their children could to great advantage be used for study and for the perfection of vocational skills. Lectures, club meetings, subscriptions to professional journals, radio talks, correspondence courses and reading provide useful opportunities although few married women as yet make systematic use of them.

The opportunities are not yet nearly widespread enough, and what is worse, women have not been made aware that they commit a sin against society if they waste the capital of skill invested in them. A growing number of them, however, are waking up to this reality and trying to prepare themselves for a future in which they may want an occupation to fill their time and minds. One of these women summed up her motives for attending evening classes thus: 'The chance of either becoming a shop assistant or else spending my days in women's clubs is too terrifying to be considered. Besides, by the time my children are out of the woods my husband will have developed intellectually miles ahead of me if I don't train my mind to keep up with him.'

If such an approach to the 'home years' became more common, and if women refused to be put on the shelf from the moment they have a family, it would undoubtedly contribute to a more sporting, happy and self-assured attitude among housewives, and among women generally.

Here is a challenge which women's organizations might do well to take up. They could set themselves the task of keeping the vocational spirit alive in married women by advocating and organizing training courses and thereby providing a stimulus for their members to widen their experience and keep up their skills. They would at the same time give an opportunity to those among them who have the qualifications, to impart their own knowledge to others.

Some of these organizations extend up and down the country and have branches also among smaller communities. They are quite well placed for reaching also those women who lack some of the opportunities available only in bigger cities.

Women's colleges and training schools, too, could help not only by inculcating a vocational spirit in their students but also by providing training and refresher courses for 'ex-service mothers', i.e. for women who after several years' interruption wish to resume their careers.

Many adult education institutions exist which give both practical and theoretical training in a great variety of subjects. They would do a service to women and to the community if some of their evening classes catered for the specific needs of married women who want to prepare themselves for the later resumption of skilled occupations. Various organizations have also successfully experimented with family summer schools in which parents can attend lectures while their children are looked after by trained staff. The 'Summer Institute for Family and Community Living' of Vassar College, New York, is perhaps the most widely known and most ambitious venture of this kind. But it is not the only one. A number of family summer schools exist in Great Britain organized by the Workers' Educational Association and by a variety of church organizations. Similar courses for married couples exist in Sweden, teaching a number of general subjects as well as discussing problems of home and family.

These and other courses offer opportunities which deserve to be widely supported by married women who aim at keeping their minds alert and at broadening their outlook. Outstanding examples are the 'Continuing Education Schemes' which many American colleges have set up in recent years. These combine university education with vocational and educational advice, and are specifically designed to meet the needs of married women in search for a 'second chance'.

Trade Unions, too, could play an important part in supporting women's continued interest in their jobs if they provided special programmes for young women on temporary 'family leave'; and if they could be persuaded to adapt their rules so as to allow such women to be associate members on payment of reduced fees. They might thereby well increase women's active interest in trade union organization, which is generally far below that of their male colleagues, though there has been a very considerable increase in women's membership since 1945.

As the demand for skilled personnel increases in all highly industrialized countries, there can be little doubt that the opportunities for vocational training will expand not only for school-leavers but also for women of more mature age.

PARTERNSHIP IN THE HOME. The list of necessary changes in personal attitudes would be incomplete if it did not include some adjustments to be made in the minds and habits of men.

Among these is, first of all, the recognition that the patriarchal family, with its division of functions between a providing and protective father and a home-making, submissive mother, however satisfactory it may have been in its time, has outlived its day. Bread-winning is no longer a monopoly of men, and home-making should no longer be the monopoly of women.

Most men still find it difficult to get used to this idea, and they have not been educated to cope with its practical consequences. Too many of them still feel their self-respect demands that they should be the sole providers for their families; too many rely on female labour for the routine jobs their private lives require. Boys should, like girls, be instructed at school in various aspects of home-making—as is done in Sweden. This is the price at which they can earn their freedom from dependence on a cook, washer up and mender of clothes. And it should be impressed upon them that the home is a joint responsibility of men and women.

We nowadays consider that the relation between husband and wife should be that of a partnership and this is the only pattern consistent with our democratic ideology. But the unholy alliance between an accepted ideal of partnership, on the one hand, and the persistence of the outward forms of the patriarchal family pattern, on the other hand, has led to many frictions and has put the contemporary marriage relationship under a heavy strain. This state of tension will only be overcome when between husband and wife there is a more equitable distribution of work and leisure, a common level of interests, and a joint share of responsibilities for home and family.

The psychological conditions for a changed pattern are growing among the younger couples. Women's employment, together with the shortage of domestic help, has led a great number of married men into kitchen and nursery. This is particularly true of the professional and middle classes.

Working hours being what they are, with often the addition of a considerable time spent in travelling, this new partnership in the home has frequently had to be established under the sign of drudgery and fatigue rather than that of the happy co-operation and 'creative family work' we hope for.

These adverse conditions are, we believe, temporary and symptomatic of the present period of transition. In areas where the employment of married women has a long tradition, such as, for instance, the textile districts, the difficulties are no longer acute even to-day. 'But here the community arrangements are favourable,' wrote Dame Mary Smieton, then Under-Secretary in the Ministry of Labour.[1] 'Community and social life is organized to suit the situation because the employment of married women is widespread and the women and their families are trained unconsciously in suitable methods of household management.' It is plausible to infer that similar adjustments will take place wherever the employment of married women becomes extensive.

Adjustments in the Labour Market

Given continued full employment and present population trends it will be necessary for the nation to draw on whatever labour reserves are available. Among these married women are the

---

[1] 'Problems of Women's Employment in Great Britain', by Dame Mary Smieton, *International Labour Review*, Vol. LIX, No. 1, January 1954.

largest. Many of them are eager to come forward, and many more would be willing if it were made easier for them to combine their family responsibilities with an outside job. They ought to be helped to help themselves.

The economic need is likely in the long run to be more effective than all the social arguments stressed throughout this book in convincing employers and public authorities that something has to be done, in terms of working hours, training courses and the creation of social amenities, to enable married women to accept employment. It should be easier in times of peace than it was during the war to make such arrangements, even though the need for them may be felt with less immediate urgency.

PART-TIME WORK. In view of the very widespread desire of married women to enter gainful employment, part-time work is being advocated by many as the answer to this problem.

Part-time employment has, indeed, a great number of advantages for women. It makes it possible for them to keep in touch with the field of work for which they have been trained. It enables mothers to be back from work when their children come home from school. It breaks the monotony of unrelieved housework while not impinging too heavily on domestic routine. It helps to preserve a certain discipline of work, the lack of which in a housewife's day may make it difficult for her to manage her time and to co-operate with others in doing a job, if she has been away from it for some years.

For all these reasons part-time work seems a good temporary solution for the women who want to resume their careers later on. Regarded thus, as a kind of extended refresher course, part-time employment might be worth some sacrifices not only on the part of women but also on the part of employers. As a more or less permanent pattern of employment for married women, however, part-time work seems to us neither practicable nor desirable; and there is a danger that by the over-emphasis laid in some quarters on this type of employment as being 'the' answer to the problem of married women and work, women may be side-tracked into a blind alley. For most work in our society is so organized as to require a 40 to 48 hours' attendance per week. With the exception of some special types of work where part-time employment meets a real need,[1] it is auxiliary or supplementary to that basic working

---

[1] For examples see pp. 112–13.

week. It may be true that in many types of job, particularly those of a routine character, two people working half a shift each produce more than one person working throughout the day. It would, nevertheless, for reasons given in another context, be unrealistic to expect employers to split the work between two workers as long as they can get one person working full time. The number of part-time jobs available will necessarily always be limited.

Moreover, the social adjustments, so necessary if women are to be enabled to continue in their jobs, are not likely to be made if women continue to be regarded as helping hands rather than as full workers. The difficulties of those married women who attempt to reconcile a career with family life will thereby be perpetuated.

EXTENDED MATERNITY LEAVE. Freeing working women for a period before and after childbirth is an imperative demand on all employers of female labour, and provisions to this effect exist in all countries. They are not quoted here in detail as the differences in length of maternity leave granted in different countries are of no great significance. In all instances they lay down a statutory minimum period which is considered essential to protect the health of mother and baby.

Maternity leave was recently discussed again at the I.L.O. and the Maternity Protection Convention of 1919 was revised, though no recommendation was made to extend to any considerable degree the accepted leave period before and after confinement. What most governments wanted was greater flexibility in the distribution of the 12-weeks leave period that was hitherto, according to the Convention, evenly divided before and after the birth of the child. The quite general recommendation for a major part of the leave to be taken after, rather than before, the confinements reflects a shift in social concern from the pregnant woman, who to-day is generally in quite good health anyway, and receives free ante-natal medical attention, to the well-being of the infant. But this well-being was, even in 1952, seen in terms of the need for breast-feeding rather than the more general claim of babies for their mothers' presence, which may be very desirable for their mental health and happy development.

Looked at from the point of view of the family, these provisions are by no means ideal. Maternity leave of one year, or even a couple of years, would be more appropriate. We do not propose that regulations for leave should be generally extended by law, or that employers should carry such an extra burden; this plea is for consideration in a future state of society in which the interests of the family are included in social calculations. When the interests of the job, the child and the woman are carefully weighed up against each other, longer interruptions of employment than the present statutory minimum will no doubt be considered appropriate.

In France, provisions for unpaid 'special leave' of varying length, in excess of the statutory maternity leave, have been laid down by numerous collective agreements. The most generous one concerns civil servants who can take up to two years unpaid leave, renewable for each child, so that in certain circumstances a mother of four, for instance, can take eight years' consecutive leave.

The analogy of 'sabbatical leave' might be suggested in this connexion. It cannot honestly be claimed, however, that maternity leave of a year or two would have an equally revitalizing effect—though devotion to this creative function may have a beneficial influence on many kinds of work. The regenerative value of a change in occupation, or of different periods of rest, is a subject yet to be studied. It may appear Utopian to believe that women may benefit from the rearing of their children not only in the richness of the experience itself but also in terms of greater efficiency afterwards; yet it may well be worth discussing the question whether a harmony cannot be achieved between the time devoted to family and work duties which would lead to a higher level of efficiency and happiness than is possible under the present régime.

Be that as it may. If it is proved, as recent trends in infant psychology seem to indicate, that children have a definite psychological need of their mothers' presence during a longer period than that awarded by legal provisions for maternity leave, these facts will have to be faced squarely by all who are interested in the welfare of the coming generation and by those responsible for labour conditions.

TRAINING THE OVER-FORTIES FOR RE-EMPLOYMENT. If part-time employment seems to us only a temporary expedient, what are the alternatives under present conditions?

There is, first, continued full-time employment, interrupted only for short breaks when a child is born. Such a course of action may be imposed on many women by economic circumstances. It seems, too, that it is a traditional practice among women in industry in some areas to continue work after the first baby and to leave only when the second arrives.

There are, moreover, women who are so attached to their job that they feel unhappy, sometimes even resentful, when they have to give it up and confine themselves to domesticity. These women would do well, not only in their own interest but also in the interest of their children, to find an adequate substitute at home and to carry on in their job. Otherwise their children may be victimized for their mother's feelings of frustration.

Apart from these cases, however, it is generally thought desirable that mothers should devote themselves whole-time to their children at least until they go to nursery-school, and perhaps longer. This means, with the present size of families and average age at marriage, that most women will be not much below 40 before they can fully resume their interrupted careers.

At that age, however, it is rather difficult to find new employment even to-day, despite shortage of skilled labour and despite official encouragement to employers to adjust age limits to the increasing average age of the population.

This difficulty affects both men and women, but women, perhaps, to an even greater degree. There seems to be a lingering suspicion that middle-aged women are difficult to get on with; and the fact of having been out of practice for some time adds a further handicap to the weight of years.

An answer to this would be the provision of training and refresher courses for rehabilitating people in the higher age groups.

The British Ministry of Health has recently shown itself alive to this need. Prompted by the present shortage of midwives, it has raised the upper age limit for entering midwifery training from 40 to 50 and has instituted refresher courses. In Sweden, some such special courses have been conducted for kindergarten, day nursery and primary school teachers. What is possible in the case of midwives or teachers can, of course, also be done in other professions, though it has not as yet been attempted on a wider scale.

Even where there is no fixed upper age limit for the admission of students, the existing classes which provide professional training are very often over-subscribed so that older applicants may be excluded in the selection of candidates because of their age.

This is particularly deplorable in the field of social work where maturer women with experience in the home might be especially useful. With the coming of the Welfare State and the declining role of voluntary organizations, standard qualifications are required to-day in most types of social work, and it has become essential for anyone entering this field to have the prescribed training. If women of more advanced years have no access to this vocational schooling, many persons with otherwise excellent qualifications are precluded from doing very necessary and useful work. This problem may not arise in twenty years' time when most women of 40 will have been trained for a job and may need no more than a refresher course, but it is of considerable importance to-day.

What is true of the social services applies also, *mutatis mutandis*, to other fields. Rules have been laid down for the recruitment of staff, not only in national and local government service, but also in large business and industrial concerns, and do not allow exceptions. Administrative tidiness and uniformity tend to make the system rigid. The existing trend towards bigger and bigger organizations, while favouring the training and promotion of younger people, leaves little scope for older entrants.

Other factors militating against the recruitment of older people are familiar: the financial disincentives of relatively high initial salaries and of pension and superannuation schemes; the fear that people past their prime may have difficulties in adjusting themselves to a new setting and in assimilating new ideas; and, as far as more highly qualified posts are concerned, the reluctance to appoint outside people over the heads of the existing staff, thereby blocking the promotion of junior members.

These difficulties are of particular concern to women in as far as there is among them a comparatively larger section than among men wishing to make a new start at 40 and over. This is well illustrated by the following American experience.[1]

'When the Child Study Association of America, for example, announced at the beginning of World War II that it was opening

[1] Quoted from S. M. Gruenberg and H. S. Krech, *The Many Lives of Modern Woman*, New York, 1952, a book which presents in popular form some of the issues we are discussing here.

a class to train volunteers for child-care services (women with at least a high school education and some experience with children) those in charge hoped to enrol twenty-five to thirty aides. On the appointed day more than three hundred appeared—former teachers, social workers, trained nurses—and one woman with an M.D. degree. Many of these had children who no longer needed them all day, and they were pitifully eager to do something useful. There was no question of getting paid.'

In Britain, over 300 scientifically trained persons recently answered an advertisement offering research work which people can do in their homes. More than one half of the applicants were married women.

EMPLOYING THE OLDER WOMEN. Employment agencies are facing the problem of placing older people, and particularly older women. (In the United States and in Sweden, labour exchanges have been supplemented by branches specializing in this type of work.) Among the female occupations quite a number are 'age-specific', i.e. some are definitely for the young (e.g. nursing, infant teaching, shorthand typing, 'air hostess', hairdressing, etc.), while in others older women are at a premium. Many executive jobs in hotels, restaurants, laundries are of the latter kind; so are the posts of wardens of hostels, matrons of a variety of institutions, caterers for school meals, canteen managers, housing managers, marriage counsellors, and others. Among the social services now in process of being created there are many which call for abilities that mature women with experience in home management can best supply. It is a fortunate coincidence that the social need for these services has arisen at a time when there are so many older women available and willing to fill the demand.

Among the more conventional types of work in factories, offices and shops, there is also room for the employment of older women; but they should be placed in jobs where the qualities are needed that mature with time; where orderliness, reliability and organizing ability are required rather than speed, flexibility and youthful charm.

In a report on 'The Employment of Older Women Workers', submitted to the Ninth Session of the U.N. Commission on the Status of Women in 1955, the International Labour Office drew up a 'balance sheet' of gains and losses which come with advancing years. The account, no doubt, applies to both sexes, even though the report is specifically concerned with women.

On the debit side, the greatest losses are those on the physical and 'psychomotor' level. Decreases in flexibility, robustness, manual strength, and precision speed, are offset only by a gain in 'regularity' of behaviour.

In the 'moral' category, however, the positions are reversed. No losses appear at all, and gains are seen in punctuality, appreciation of finished work, and care over detail.

On the 'intellectual' level, such qualities as memory, imagination, creative spirit, and adaptability, are expected to deteriorate, against increases in concentration, caution and methodical habits.

Under the heading of 'character', decreased sociability, initiative, diligence, energy, and vitality, are on the debit side of the ledger, compared with increased willingness, patience, discipline, prudence, reliability, and stability, on the credit side.

Commenting on this table and on the 'vast scope' for the employment of older women in skilled and responsible jobs, the I.L.O. report observes that, in fact, prospects of promotion are much more restricted for women than for men, and 'as a consequence, women workers have fewer opportunities of applying the qualities characteristic of middle age in an occupation'.

Attempts are being made, though as yet cautiously, to reverse the long-standing trend towards earlier retirement. The governments in all the countries under discussion are trying to impress upon the public the urgency of the problem and to encourage employers to give work to older people. It may be assumed that under the weight of demographic changes the equivalent modifications in the age composition of our working population will be made. When this happens the problem of employing the older women will be solved as part of a more general adjustment.

In this context it must be said that the facts do not justify an earlier retirement age for women than for men, as is statutory in most countries. These rules were laid down at a time when the frailty of women was a generally accepted axiom, and when working conditions were much severer than they are to-day. Work-places are no longer as insanitary and unpleasant as they used to be in the early phases of industrialization; and the myth of the 'weaker sex' has been debunked by statistics. Though women are weaker in terms of muscular strength or single feats of

vigour, such as lifting weights, high jumping and athletics generally, the figures show that they score over men in endurance,
resistance to disease and fitness for survival. Their prospects of
living in good health to a ripe old age are therefore considerably
better than men's and there is no reason why they should retire at
an earlier age. In 25 years' time one quarter of all women will be
over 60. This fact alone is a sufficient reason to make the extension
of their working life to 65 a matter of urgent public interest.

LOCATION OF EMPLOYMENT. In the past not much thought
was given to the problem of how to employ the wives of working
men. Sites were chosen for factories independent of human considerations, and there was a tendency for certain types to concen-
trate in particular areas, e.g. steel works in one district and textile
mills in another.

During the war, however, governments encouraged a more
rational distribution of factories, and industries were brought
to areas where reserves of labour could be expected. This was
one of the major means of bringing women into the national
effort. Figures of war-time production in different areas show
that the proportion of women among insured workers is always
dependent on the amount of work available for women in the
district.[1]

If, therefore, women are to be encouraged to do outside work,
employers will have to come half-way to meet them in peace-time
no less than in war-time.

It would be desirable, too, if legal provisions could be made, as
is the case in France, to ensure that in the civil service, the teaching profession, etc., the husband or wife of a person already employed in a given district should have a certain priority for posts
in the same area. In the absence of such regulations many women
who would be happy to continue their careers have no alternative
but to resign rather than be separated from their husbands.

A considerable obstacle to the employment of married women
is also the increasing distance between home and work-place which
has resulted from the enormous growth of cities and industrial
centres. The development of motor transport has fostered the
tendency to remove residential districts from the centres of work,
and lengthy journeys usually have to be added to the normal
working hours. This naturally complicates the lives of those who

[1] Cf. 'Employment of Women', *Planning*, Volume XV, No. 285, July 1948.

have to run a home in addition to their employment in offices or factories.

As one means of overcoming this difficulty, it has been suggested that the development of modern transport which has so much contributed to suburbanization might also serve to decentralize manufacture. This dispersal of production would be facilitated by the increased use of small electrically operated machinery which could be installed in private houses. It would enable women to produce goods, or parts of goods, in their homes and it might promote the setting up of local workshops which could be run on a co-operative basis.[1]

The technical facilities to carry out a plan of this kind do in fact exist, but it seems unlikely that it will ever be developed on a large scale. The difficulties of organizing and effectively supervising such a scheme are considerable, and so are the costs of running it. Moreover, organized labour would no doubt view such a plan with the same distrust with which it views all kinds of home industry. And although the hand loom has in recent years regained a certain fashion value, the general trend of our time is towards cheap mass-produced articles.

The answer to our problem seems rather to lie in the sphere of town planning. Its aim, in the words of one planner, is the creation of 'utilities for the collective living not merely of a good social life but of a happy and healthy individual life as well'.[2] For this purpose planning now has to reverse the characteristic trend of the last hundred years towards huge metropolitan areas divided into functionally segregated sections—shopping district, banking centre, theatre area, slum district, dormitory suburb, etc.—all relying on the efficiency of modern transport yet ignoring the loss of time and the nervous strain involved in its extensive use.

This subject, however, no longer comes under the heading of 'Adjustments in the Labour Market' but belongs to the wider field of public responsibilities.

Social Adjustments

HOUSES BUILT FOR WORKING WOMEN. Planners have begun to understand the sociological implications of their task and have

[1] Ralph Borsodi, *Flight from the City: The Study of a New Way to Family Security*, New York, 1933.   [2] Thomas Sharp, *Town Planning*, Harmondsworth, 1945.

awakened to the realization that a community, in the true sense of the word, cannot exist without a *locus* favourable to its development. The new towns which have been built in recent years to relieve the pressure from congested areas are no longer designed as garden suburbs but as complete units for living. They include community centres, schools, playgrounds, shops, and small industries as well as homes. Ideally, a town should include different types of houses for different kinds of families—and some of the best town plans provide for these. One-family houses for the larger families, rows of houses with adjoining garden and a nursery school at the end of the lane for families with small children, blocks of flats with some communal services, such as laundries, etc., and others containing service flats and including restaurants and food lifts. The dependence of the family on the wife and mother as full-time employee in her own home would vary accordingly.

Most plans, however, even the best among them, are hypnotized by the traditional image of a woman devoted solely to domestic cares and available all day long. 'Collective houses', in which such services as cooked meals, laundry, day nurseries, etc., can be obtained at a reasonable price by the families living in them, are being built in most big cities, but they are not yet available in large enough numbers to meet the existing need.

It is no use ignoring the fact that one married woman out of every three has a job outside her home. Moreover, attractive as may be the picture of a well-run home managed with loving care, not all women are good housewives or enjoy domesticity. Obviously, blocks of flats and communal houses are not to everyone's taste, but they are not meant for everyone. What is important is that homes should be available suited to the specific needs of various people and that architects and town planners should not force women to continue in outlived roles.

It is more difficult in the existing older cities to plan for healthier living, not only in the sanitary but also in the social sense, and to distribute residential and business areas more rationally. But a good deal can be done, and is being done, here too. Most local authorities have now become conscious of the possibilities of planning at least to the extent of avoiding the past mistakes of haphazard development, and they receive encouragement from the central government in doing this.

THE DISTRIBUTION OF GOODS. Better planning is also badly

needed in the field of distribution. While seconds are being saved in production through time-and-motion studies and adjustments of machinery, hours are wasted in distribution. Is there anywhere a study of the time actually spent—mostly by women—in travelling to the shops, in waiting, choosing, and carrying? Nobody has cared to investigate it because, housewives' time is not money, and because women are supposed, anyway, to enjoy shopping for the fun of it.

Waste of time and labour could be avoided if housewives could adopt the practice of limiting their shopping to one weekly 'excursion' for their basic household requirements. This would suffice to make them familiar with the goods on the market and their current prices. Thus they could deposit a shopping list and have the goods delivered to their homes. Self-service stores are another step towards shortening the time needed for household shopping.

A great deal of irritation, and many bottlenecks during rush hours, could be eliminated if business hours were arranged so as to allow shopping when the working population is free. This would benefit not only the consumers but be profitable to business interests as well. At present most shops are closed when people who work are free, thus restricting most of the spending to housewives. Only with great difficulty can a man assist his wife in selecting a new piece of furniture or wallpaper for their joint home. Hairdressers have not enough lunch-hours available to accommodate all the working women who need a hair cut and shampoo. To buy herself a new suit or hat is a major operation for a working woman involving, as it usually does, going without lunch more than once, fighting her way through crowded stores and streets, or taking time off work.

Some attempts are now being made to tackle this problem: London West End stores, for instance, keep open until 7 p.m. once a week (and how thronged with people they are during that extra hour), and a few small food shops and launderettes close 1–2 hours later on two evenings weekly. In France, shops open during unorthodox hours, such as evenings and Sunday mornings, and shut on one weekday instead. In the United States, where 'super-markets' have opened up new possibilities of rational food distribution, many food stores keep open until late at night. These are welcome signs of recognition that very many potential customers are tied to their desks or benches during the usual business hours. In these days of social protection and effective trade unions there need be no danger that more variable hours for marketing should mean longer hours for shop assistants.

RATIONALIZING HOUSEWORK. The last decades have witnessed a constant flow of new inventions designed to reduce domestic work. A veritable cornucopia of industrial products has appeared and has been eagerly absorbed: washing machines and vacuum cleaners, electric mixers and immersion heaters, a very wide range of ready-made clothes at all prices, textiles that need no ironing and hardly any mending; canned, frozen and dehydrated food products of excellent quality; cleaned vegetables hygienically wrapped; half-baked bread that only needs a few minutes' oven heat to be ready and crisp; pressure cookers, ready cake mixes, detergents, etc. These and innumerable other, minor household utensils and ingredients should make it possible to run a home effectively in a fraction of the time previously needed.

We have seen in an earlier chapter that this is not what in fact happens and that the average housewife still works more than a 60-hour week. Part of this work is irreducible, particularly that concerned with young children, although even here co-operation with neighbours can give a mother an occasional afternoon off. Cases of such organized mutual aid between women are known to us in Sweden and the United States and they have worked to everyone's satisfaction. More co-operation between housewives would help also to solve a number of other domestic problems, but is impeded by the high value placed in our society on the privacy of the home.

Housework in the narrower sense of the word, however, can be reduced by good management without detriment to the home. Women who go out to work usually succeed, even without domestic help, in keeping their homes up to their normal standard in very much less time than the full-time housewife. Where there are no small children to look after, the number of hours spent in domestic work has become chiefly a question of organization. It is, in addition, of course, also dependent on good equipment—hot-water supply, electricity, central heating, easy floors, a labour-saving kitchen layout. A good deal of scientific research has been done in recent years in this field, and publicity, both through advertising and official encouragement, has made modern housewives alert to the possibilities of rationalizing housework. This alertness, however, is at present mostly to be found among the classes which no longer get the domestic servants they were accustomed to employ.

The means for a considerable reduction of working hours exist to-day, but they are taken advantage of only where there is a positive incentive to do so. However much a housewife may complain about the number of hours she spends on washing, dusting, polishing, shopping, cooking, etc., she will only *do* something about it when she has a definite aim for which it is worth saving time—be this playing tennis, going to the pictures, or having a job. It would seem not only pointless but indefensible in the eyes of many women to reduce their working hours unless they have a more valuable use for their time. Utilitarian as are the values of our society, a gain of leisure is not considered an end in itself by most; it might, on the contrary, be morally disapproved of. As a rule, a housewife will regard it as her duty to save money rather than time, and she will avoid incurring the higher costs of semi-prepared food and other time-saving devices as long as she can provide the same results by expending her own energy and labour.

For these reasons it is mistaken to use the large number of hours which housewives at present spend on domestic work as an argument against the employment of married women, on the assumption that the present average working week is the necessary minimum for the effective running of a home. As a table in another part of this book has shown,[1] the number of extra working hours done by women who run a household as well as having a job is very small in comparison with full-time housewives. It is a graphic illustration of how far domestic work can be reduced if it is done rationally and to a time-table.

For the reasons just mentioned, an appreciable reduction of working hours in the home is not likely to occur automatically, even if yet more and better household gadgets were invented. Housewives will shift the emphasis from one domestic activity to another, or raise their general standard of domesticity to a higher level, rather than spend less time on housework.

By its very nature, housework lends itself like no other occupation to a dissipation of time and energy. Women who never had to discipline themselves to a strict time-table, and have not seen

[1] Cf. p. 35.

at close quarters the example of others who have done it successfully, do not usually know how much can be done in far less time
by efficient organization.

Greater rationalization of housework will, nevertheless, take
place, mainly as the result of a new attitude to work which characterizes our time and which is already beginning to make itself
felt also in the home. For better or for worse, we have become
productivity-minded, that is, we want to see maximum results
for any work done. Unlike our forebears we no longer regard
being busy as a virtue in itself but judge each activity by its
effects.

With the introduction of machinery into housework, which
helps and is helped by the participation of men in domestic work,
this valuation of efficiency is spreading from workshop and factory
into the home. The model housewife is no longer the one who
spends most of the day cleaning and cooking but the woman who
achieves the desired results with a minimum of apparent effort.
In consequence, the prestige of domestic work as a full-time occupation has suffered a further decline. This poor estimation and
the low productivity of their work are not the least causes of the
present discontent among housewives. They feel that there is too
little to show for their many hours of toil. Many of them hope
to find in gainful employment the sense of achievement which they
no longer are able to derive from domestic work.

PUBLIC SERVICES TO RELIEVE THE DOMESTIC WORK LOAD.
The modern housewife is assisted in her traditional tasks by a
number of outside agencies. Most of these have in the past been
commercial services of one kind or another, such as laundries,
window-cleaners, bakeries, repair shops, and a variety of industries
producing ready-made food and clothes.

The provision by State or local authorities of public services
to take over some domestic functions is a fairly new phenomenon
(apart from garbage removal, water supply and, if they may be
included under this heading, schools).

The number of communal services specifically designed to assist
the family and to relieve housewives of some of their burden has
very much increased in recent years, particularly during and since
the 1939 war. Some of the most important ones may be briefly
mentioned here as examples of what may be done.

CANTEEN FACILITIES. To save time, to avoid lunch-time travel and to supplement the domestic larder at a time of scarcity and strict food rationing, the British Government during the war greatly encouraged the provision of works and office canteens. Any firm engaged on Government contracts and employing more than 250 people could be required by the Essential Works Orders to provide a canteen. In addition, a great number of other smaller factories and offices, in other countries as well as in Britain, have instituted canteens for their staff which have proved convenient for all concerned and have therefore been retained in most instances after the war.[1] They help the family not only in providing a cheap midday meal away from home for at least one member of the household, but eventually also in making it possible to shorten the working day by a reduction of the lunch-time interval.

SCHOOL MEALS. Similarly, the younger members of the family can now lunch at school either free of cost or at a nominal charge, so that a midday meal at home has to be prepared only for the housewife herself and her infants; if she has no small children and wants to go out to work she is free of what used to be a major domestic obligation.

The provision of school meals has the longest history in France, where the first school canteen was established as early as 1870. At first designed to bring relief to the most indigent of working-class families, the institution has spread not only in Paris but also in the provinces, ever since 1881, and is now available to rich and poor alike. The earlier need in France for arrangements of this kind is related to the long tradition which the employment of married women has in that country.

Elsewhere the community woke up later to the necessity of providing children at school with food at public expense in order to supplement what often is an inadequate diet at home. In the United States the basis of the federally sponsored school-lunch programme was laid by the legislation of 1935, which authorized the distribution of agricultural products by the U.S. Department of Agriculture for this use. The motives for this legislation were not primarily a desire to advance the welfare of children but rather to achieve a more satisfactory distribution of farm surpluses. Nevertheless, the government-subsidized school-lunch programme

---

[1] For a description of the prevailing conditions in several countries see 'Facilities for Women Workers with Home Responsibilities', *International Labour Review*, Vol. LXIII, No. 3, 1951.

which developed from these beginnings[1] has proved of great value to all families with children, in particular in areas of considerable employment of mothers, and relieves working women of some of the effort to provide adequate meals for their children of school age.

Both in Britain and in Sweden the governments have made the provision of lunches compulsory in all schools. The English Education Act of 1944 included it as a statutory duty of the Local Education Authorities, and school meals are intended as a supplement to family allowances. Owing to difficulties in securing suitable premises, to shortage of building material and labour, etc., not all schools in the country have yet canteen facilities, but the great majority of schools are equipped for the purpose. Similarly in Sweden, where various schemes of providing school meals to necessitous children existed before the war, and were during the war extended to cover all children in 'necessitous municipalities', Parliament decided in 1946 to make the provision of a hot meal (consisting of half the necessary daily calorie intake and a full daily supply of certain vitamins and minerals) in the middle of the day a free service to every child in every school. Subsidies are also available to school districts for the construction of buildings for the purpose. In most schools the scheme is already in operation.

DAY NURSERIES AND NURSERY SCHOOLS. While it is generally agreed that infants should, wherever possible, grow up at home under the personal care of their parents, the stage when children crave for, and benefit from, the company of other children of their own age, is normally reached long before they are old enough to begin their normal school education. In view of the present size of families, the association with other children is possible only if they leave their homes for a few hours each day. To provide facilities for this under the supervision of trained persons, a large number of nursery schools have come into existence, as well as infant and nursery classes added to primary schools.

Crèches and day nurseries are in a different position. They answer certain social needs and have to be regarded in that context.

[1] The National School Lunch Act of June 1946 provides for the allotment, under administration of the Department of Agriculture, of Federal funds to States for food, facilities and servicing of school-lunch programmes. These funds are grants made to States according to the number of children enrolled in schools and the per capita income of the State, and are to be matched by funds raised by the State.

They are doubtless a great help to working mothers, and this was recognized when the participation of women in the national effort was thought to be of paramount importance. In Britain and the United States these day centres for the care of pre-school children were developed during the 1939 war and Government funds were made available for this purpose. With the end of the war the federal funds were withdrawn in the United States, and the grant by the central government to local authorities in Britain was reduced by half. The number of day nurseries has consequently been very considerably reduced. Instances are, however, known to us in both countries where local employers or women's organizations came to the rescue and combined with the local authority to keep the service going. The Nurseries and Child Minders Regulation Act of 1948 has made it a duty on local health authorities to register nurseries and child minders (i.e. persons who receive in their homes children under five years of age to be looked after by the day or any longer period not exceeding six days) and has empowered these authorities to exercise control over them.

Similarly in Sweden the Social Board has sponsored a family day home scheme, under which private homes which receive a certain number of children are registered and placed under the supervision of the local child welfare authorities. An investigation made in Stockholm in 1948 to ascertain what provisions are made for the care of children of working mothers revealed the following figures. Of the 11,000 mothers of children below school age included in the investigation 24 per cent had some kind of job, but only 15 per cent (included in the total of 24 per cent) had full-time employment. Of the working mothers 41 per cent had their children looked after at home by relatives or home helps, 23 per cent had them in the homes of relatives or other persons during the day, and another 23 per cent placed their infants in day-nurseries. The remaining 13 per cent is made up of cases where children accompany their mothers to work, are boarded out, attend nursery-schools for a few hours each day or are accepted at school before the normal school age (which is 7 in Sweden, but can be reduced to 6 for more advanced children).

In France a variety of institutions exist for pre-school children. *Crèches* and *pouponnières* under the supervision of the Ministry of Public Health take charge of infants under the age of 2. In 1949 roughly 650 such institutions between them looked after 20,000 infants (out of a total of 1,305,000 aged 0–2); at the same time there were 3,653 *écoles maternelles*, public institutions under the supervision of the Ministry of Education, for children aged 2–6; jointly, they had about 404,000 children under their charge. In addition there are private kindergartens (*jardins des enfants*), of which the Seine *département* alone had 108 (with 4,400 pupils) in 1949. (The total child population aged 0–7 was 2,600,000 at the time.) [1]

That these institutions are necessary may be seen from the results of opinion polls among women, even more than by the number of mothers actually using them. One such poll [2] showed that the great majority of French women (72 per cent) appreciated and wanted more nurseries. Significantly, more of the women who had used nurseries liked them than of those who had not (14 per cent used them at the time of the inquiry, 12 per cent had used them earlier, and 74 per cent had no experience). Perhaps most interesting from a policy point of view is the following reply: 51 per cent of the mothers in the inquiry who were employed would have been forced to give up their jobs if they had not had recourse to nurseries, and 22 per cent of the non-employed mothers would consider taking up work if they had access to them. [3]

Since it is not generally government policy to encourage the employment of young mothers, it will often be left to local initiative, e.g. from industrial concerns, or women's organizations, or from other interested bodies, in areas where there is an appreciable demand for these services to organize the establishment of day nurseries or play centres. For example, as a consequence of the many student marriages, crèches have been organized at Swedish universities for their children. Given such initiative, the local authorities will not as a rule fail to lend their support.

DOMESTIC HELP. The traditional way of obtaining relief from domestic duties is, or rather was, to engage a housekeeper or maid. For women in employment this would seem an ideal solution.

---

[1] The data are taken from a report issued by the *Organisation Mondiale pour l'Education Préscolaire* (*OMEP*) on pre-school education in France.

[2] See *Population*, Paris, 1948, No. 3.

[3] For a description of the international situation in regard to crèches and day nurseries, see 'Child Care Facilities for Women Workers', *International Labour Review*, Vol. LXII, No. 5, 1950.

From a general point of view, too, it would be a satisfactory division of labour which would enable women to specialize in the field for which they have the greatest ability and interest.

In practice, however, this is hardly possible to-day. It is a common experience in all industrial countries that domestic servants are increasingly difficult to find. Even though conditions of pay and general treatment have greatly improved in our time, the low social status and lack of independence make domestic service unattractive in comparison with other jobs open to young girls. Attempts at remedying this situation by fixing standard wages and hours, and by providing training courses and certificates, all of which aim at raising the status of domestic work to that of a qualified vocation, have not been able to reverse the trend away from domestic service. They have, however, succeeded in reducing the demand for domestic servants through raising the costs of their upkeep.

A further difficulty is that such domestic servants as there are would rather go to the childless families, both because these are able to reward them better financially and also because the work is lighter and the hours often shorter.

Even if conditions could be changed so as to turn domestic service into a job that could compete favourably for the supply of labour (an assumption which at present is purely hypothetical), the question remains open whether, as a matter of sound economy, work in the home is productive enough under current technological conditions to bear the costs of labour. It may well be that setting aside one person for housework in one particular family is not an economic proposition when other means of supplying most of the required services are available.

To this it might, of course, be objected that if housework is worth the time and energy of a housewife, it should also be worth the working energy of somebody else. But housework as such is hardly a full-time job under present conditions, whether it be done by a housewife or by a paid help. In the case of the housewife, however, economic considerations are of minor importance. In addition to the performance of the many menial tasks, the value of her work consists in the intangible creative qualities which turn a household into a home. Such personal functions cannot be delegated to a third person and they have put housewives, as it were, outside our economic system. Because their work is 'priceless' the economic status of housewives is often so depressed, paradoxical as this may sound.

The part-time domestic help, which is the maximum a woman who goes out to work can, as a rule, expect at present, appears altogether the most satisfactory solution. This is so, not only because it is the type of household labour most readily available, but also because it is the most productive use of this labour, seeing that in this way one woman looks after at least two, and sometimes more, homes.

While under normal circumstances any woman, whether employed or not, must trust her own ingenuity to solve her individual problem of help in the home, public services are now available in many countries in cases of emergency or special need. Home aides services are functioning in all the countries under discussion, supplying trained workers for the care of old or sick people in their homes, and taking over domestic work in cases of death, temporary incapacity or absence of the mother, in order to keep homes going for the children. In the United States, 50 to 60 welfare agencies had such services in 1947 as part of their family case work. In Britain, France, and Sweden, organized home help, which was at first also developed by private agencies, has been expanded in recent years and is now part of the social security system. These services are run either by local authorities or by recognized welfare organizations under public control, and uniform standards of employment, training, conditions of work and wages have been established.[1]

Though these services are at present intended mainly for emergency situations, there is no reason, in principle, why a modern organization of domestic service could not be created on a similar basis, whereby a group of well-trained, professionalized, and decently paid home helpers might be made available to working mothers.

This may sound like a plan for women to take in each other's washing. But in fact such a rationalization of housework would not only enable women to devote themselves to the type of work they find most congenial to their temperaments and interests, but it would, at the same time, lead to greater productivity in general.

[1] For descriptions of the Home Aides Services see *International Labour Review*, Vol. XVI, No. 1, 1947 and Vol. LXIII, No. 3, 1951.

RESEARCH IN THE SOCIAL PROBLEMS OF WOMEN AND HOME. We have given an outline of the main types of social services at present available to relieve mothers of some of their domestic burden; and such a description indicates at what points the need of families for outside help has been greatest. It shows, too, that the community has come to the rescue wherever the need has become most apparent. Society has, in fact, taken over many of the functions of the near relatives who in the past were available to most families but now no longer are so.

The existing services are barely sufficient to meet current needs and there is certainly very little margin left under present conditions to provide for ever-increasing demands. They do, however, bear in themselves the seeds for further expansion and can serve as models for the development of other similar services when the need for these, which undoubtedly exists, has become articulate.

What these needs are, and to what extent they are to be met, is a question closely linked with public policy in the matter of married women's work. This policy, so far, has been both ambivalent and ill-informed.

It is an astonishing fact, in itself worth speculating upon, that in this era of social investigations so little systematic research has been done on the vital problems concerning women in contemporary society. Tremendous changes in their way of life, and in their position in family and society, have taken place during the life-time of the present generation.

We are, in fact, the unobservant participants of a social revolution, in spite of having highly developed techniques of social investigation at our disposal. (Whatever little material exists has, as one would expect, mostly been collected in America.)

In writing this book it has been a constant source of surprise and regret that on practically each point in the discussion we have had to look in vain for evidence that had been scientifically collected and examined. More and more statistics of the census type are becoming available, but there are few comprehensive sociological studies, which alone could supply the foundation of details that is required.

There is, for instance, very little information available with which to decide whether there is a correlation between the employment of women and the fertility rate. Not even in the tremendous Indianapolis study,[1] in which twenty-three hypotheses concerning social and psychological factors affecting the size of families were intensively investigated and tested, was attention given to the possible influence of women's actual jobs, or of their desire to keep up work, in different age groups and social strata. If that variable had been introduced among the others, some interesting parallels might have been established and light been thrown on a complex of feminine attitudes.

There are no surveys available on how widespread women's desire is to take up outside employment. The influence of education on their attitude to a job has yet to be investigated. No studies exist on the way in which women between 50 and 65, in general, and widows in particular, spend their lives. Research is badly needed on the influence which the employment of mothers has on the development of their children, and how this is correlated to other factors in their family background.[2] We do not know how much of a mother's time and attention is needed by children at different age levels; or if there is a difference in fatigue between men and women in various jobs, and if so how it is related to home arrangements.

These and a number of other questions need answering if the implications of current trends are to be fully understood and if the existing tensions, arising from piecemeal developments in different parts of the social fabric, are to be reduced.

[1] The *Millbank Memorial Fund Quarterly*, New York, has published a series of reports on the study conducted by the Committee on Social and Psychological Factors Affecting Fertility. See Vols. XXXI, No. 3, 1953, and XXXII, No. 4, 1954.

[2] This deficiency has, partly, been made good by F. Ivan Nye and Lois W. Hoffman, *The Employed Mother in America*, Chicago, 1963.

CHAPTER TEN

LONG-TERM GOALS: SUMMARY AND CONCLUSIONS

It has become evident from the foregoing that the increasing employment of women in all the advanced countries of the West has been a long-term development extending over many years, and not merely a temporary stop-gap due to the emergencies of war, or other sudden calamities. But, except for the incidental adjustments that we have discussed in the last chapter, there has been no fundamental reorganization of our society such as would make this development beneficial to all concerned.

Economic Implications of Women's Increased Employment

As a result of demographic, technological and economic developments a relative manpower shortage has become a chronic state in industrialized countries. The gradual increase of the labour force, which in the past was chiefly due to the growth of populations, has slowed down during the last decades because the proportion of young people in the labour force is declining, owing to extended periods of education and training, while the proportion of old people in the population has been increasing. Women have more and more been called upon to step into the breach in industry, business and the professions, and in the ever-growing administrative apparatus required to keep the wheels of our complex modern society turning.

This long-term trend, starting at first with the employment of 'surplus' women—'surplus', that is, from the family point of view —has been gaining momentum over the years and has reached the point where virtually all unmarried women are either in employment or else in the process of being trained for it. Any further increase in feminine employment can therefore only come from the ranks of married women, and has indeed already done so for some time. This has been made possible by the smaller size of families and the decline of domestic activities.

The living standards of a community depend in a large measure on the proportion of the total population which works, that is, on the ratio of producers to consumers. It would, therefore, obviously be in the general interest to make better use of the latent woman-power—always provided this could be done without causing serious damage to other human values. We can ill afford the failure to use so many potentially productive persons.

The fact that, even to-day, there are many thousands of men willing, yet unable, to find work in some countries does not invalidate our argument. The social disease, of which mass un-employment is a symptom, is not due to the disproportion between a fixed amount of work to be done and an excessive number of people available to do it. It is a defect not in the structure, but in the organization, of society to allow the most important asset of any community, the productive capacity of its members, to go unused. The disastrous consequences of mass unemployment as experienced in the past, and witnessed again in some parts of the world to-day, are apt to underline, rather than to contradict, the economic argument that the welfare of a society is dependent upon the best use being made of its working population, and that the more people take part in its productive processes, the higher the standard of life which the community as a whole is able to enjoy.

The need of society to utilize to the full all available labour resources, male and female, coincides with the under-employment of women. The combination of these two circumstances calls for a revision of the traditional, yet still very widespread view, that marriage is a career for women. The term 'under-employment of women' needs a qualification: of course, not all women are under-employed all the time. Many housewives are sure to protest—and with justification—that looking after a home and a family is a very full-time job indeed under present conditions. This is not to be denied. But, seen in terms of a whole life-time, the period of really full employment at home is relatively short. As we have seen before, many women have themselves a feeling that they are wast-ing their energies, and this is to a large extent responsible for the present state of discontent among housewives. This is so even though most women do not reflect on the implications of their considerably increased expectations of life and health.

Only about one-third of the total labour force are women, although they form more than half the population. If we make a generous estimate that one-fourth of the married women are actively occupied as mothers, or are as productively engaged in their homes as in old times, while one-third of them have proceeded to gainful employment, that still leaves a large reserve of women, mostly middle-aged, and numbering about 4 in 10 of all the married ones, whose energies are at present not available to society.

There can be no doubt that, if the proportion in employment (as exemplified here from U.S.A., France, U.K. and Sweden) could be considerably increased, people in general would be better off economically, as well as better balanced socially and psychologically.

Something must be wrong in a social organization in which men may die a premature death from coronary thrombosis, as a result of overwork and worry, while their wives and widows organize themselves to protest against their own lack of opportunities to work.

A little arithmetic based on existing statistical data will easily show what great effects could be achieved with comparatively little effort. Let us assume that the average age of marriage is 25 —putting it rather higher than recent data warrant—and the retiring age 65, which seems reasonable in view of the generally increased longevity and improved health. This means that at the age of marriage the average woman faces 40 years of adult working life. During these 40 years, two-thirds of all married women are *not* gainfully employed. In terms of an overall average this is equivalent to 13 working years per woman, with roughly 26 years of married life during which no work is done outside the home.

Let us, further, assume that the latter period would be reduced by only six years. The result would be astonishing. The average married woman would still have 20 years to bring up her children, which seems ample. At the same time, the proportion of married women in employment would be increased from 33 to 50 per cent, which in Great Britain would mean an addition of three million people to the labour force, and in the United States about 8.5 million. In fact, it would bring about an increase of roughly $12\frac{1}{2}$ per cent of the working population in any country which is approximately at the same level of industrial and social development as these two.

We could have gone further in our calculation and suggested that married women could give an average of 15, or even of only 10 years to their children instead of 20. The correspondingly

Working and Not-working People in Great Britain, 1951

if half of the married women had been employed

Each figure represents 1 million people

greater increase in the labour force and, as a result, in the total production of goods and the supply of services would be tremendous, and would make possible a considerable rise in the standard of living. If we did not make this suggestion it is because it seems neither practicable nor desirable that mothers of very young children should go out to work. Nevertheless, if some of these mothers did accept employment outside their homes the additional production and services which would result would more than compensate for the extra demands thereby created for such things as laundries, day nurseries and manufactured, as opposed to home-made, children's clothes, etc. At the same time, women would have better chances to specialize in the jobs in which they are interested and for which they have an aptitude—be it cooking, teaching, keeping a shop or conducting an orchestra.

Psychological Implications of Women's Increased Employment

The sociological and psychological effects of women's increased participation in the economic field would be no less far-reaching than the material changes involved, and may well affect the whole mental climate of our society.

Revolutionary as the development towards outside work for married women may appear in some of its consequences, it is a readjustment, under changed conditions, to a more equitable division of labour between the sexes such as existed before the beginning of industrialization. In a sense, therefore, if women are to-day leaving their homes to set out on a new road to work, this is a road which will take them 'back home' to their proper place in the community.

This 'return of the prodigal' is entirely to be welcomed, and is in the interest, not only of women, but of the community as a whole. For the exclusion of women from most economic and scientific pursuits and many social and cultural activities is a factor which has contributed to the lack of social integration and the consequent isolation of the individual so characteristic of contemporary society. It may well be that the non-participation of women is, as A. M. Rose suggests in a discussion of the problems of mass society,[1] a major contributory factor in the feelings of insecurity and mutual estrangement so widespread in modern society. Having lost her previous function as helpmate to her husband in breadwinning and as the chief educator of a large brood of children, Professor Rose says, 'society imposes no demands that she seek substitute functions. She can try her hand at a paid job or at social welfare activity, but usually no one says that she must. And so the modern wife, after her youngest child has started school, is partly functionless, which means that she is likely to raise questions to herself about her very reason for existence and she feels a vague but pervasive dissatisfaction. Since she relates herself to other people at only marginal points, and since

[1] A. M. Rose, 'Social Problems in the Mass Society', published in *The Antioch Review*, September 1950.

she is uncertain as to her role in society, she is a member of a mass, not of an organized (i.e. integrated) society.'

Sharing in the life and activities of the community generates a sense of purpose which is essential to human fulfilment. This is particularly the case in a society like ours, where the obligation to make a constructive contribution to the social effort has become a generally accepted ethos and where this contribution is measured by professional standards and on the basis of tangible results. 'Our definitions of work', writes David Riesman,[1] 'also mean that the housewife, although producing a social work-product, does not find her work explicitly defined and totalled, either as an hour product or as a dollar product, in the national census or in people's minds. And since her work is not defined as work, she is exhausted at the end of the day without feeling any right to be, insult thus being added to injury.'

In the future, it will be as impossible to exempt women in their mature years from the applications of the ideology which exacts a social contribution from everyone in terms of the accepted definition of work, as it was impossible to exclude them from the workings of the democratic ideas of equal rights and opportunities.

A process of unconscious adjustment to this new situation is already taking place in the minds of many women. To quote David Riesman once more: ' . . . middle and upper-middle-class women are no longer welcome as ladies bountiful; the social workers have . . . professionalized the field. . . . Amateurs can no longer help sick people, unless they are willing, as nurses' aids, to help registered nurses be professionals by doing all the dirty work for them. They cannot help others enjoy themselves, because settlement work and recreational activities have also been professionalized. While they can discuss politics and race relations in the League of Women Voters and the Y.M.C.A., they can do so only under the packaged and, in fact, quite excellent programmes provided from central headquarters. . . . Reacting to this situation, the women either sink back in indifference or conclude, like their working-class sisters, that only through a job, a culturally defined job, will they be liberated.'[2]

It is a truism stated many times before that modern mass society suffers from the loss of the community sense which in the past bound people together, expressed their common aims and gave

[1] *Op. cit.*, p. 300.　　　[2] *Op. cit.*, p. 322.

them the security of an assured place in an organic whole. It is not impossible that this loss can and will be made good by people taking a greater share in the working life of society and thereby regaining the sense of a joint purpose. The forming of new associations and new loyalties through one's work may replace the more immediate contacts of past smaller communities, and act as the cement which will once more bind people together into an integrated whole.

As a group, housewives to-day suffer more from social isolation and loss of purpose than any other social group, except, perhaps, the old. Unlike them, however, they cannot look back on a full life and, as a rule, have not had the opportunity to form associations outside their families which would give them a sense of belonging.

If the resumption of interrupted careers at a more mature age became the norm, rather than the exception, among married women, the outlook, and status, of all women—whether young or old, married or single—would undergo a change for the better.

The young would be freed from the psychological stresses and strains which we discussed in a previous chapter. They would, at last, be able to form a consistent long-term plan for their lives and to reap the harvest sown in years of training and study.

Last, but by no means least, many causes of marital friction and unhappiness would be removed if outside contacts and mental stimuli, as well as the whole income-earning power, were not practically the monopolies of one spouse, and if a more even balance could be struck between husband and wife in their interests both inside and outside their joint home.

The emancipation of women is slow and is a process prolific of internal conflicts. The traditional norms of conduct have broken down and have not yet been replaced by new ones. Women to-day can no longer be certain of what is expected of them. There is no longer one accepted feminine role to live up to, but a number of conflicting patterns uneasily existing side by side. It has, for instance, come to light in a number of field studies that surprisingly many professional and business women are afflicted by doubts of their essential femininity. Yet the woman who spends her life at home in the conventional role is no better off; she, too, often wonders whether she has made the right choice and whether she is not neglecting hidden talents or wasting her energies.

This state of widespread inner conflicts and uncertainties is likely to solve itself in the course of social development. The latter, together with technological progress, have made the way 'back to the home' impracticable. There seems therefore really only one way open for further development, and it is well to face these facts and make the best of them.

Re-vitalizing Family Life

It might be argued that the gain in productivity is a small benefit compared with the loss of the free time which women are now privileged to enjoy. Many people, too, feel that some intangible values are lost if family life cannot proceed in an atmosphere of leisure. But is the assumption on which this argument is based correct? Would the employment of married women really mean a loss of leisure to the family?

Let us look at this argument more closely, returning to our hypothesis that married women might devote an average of 20 instead of the present 26 years to their family, and resume outside work after that period. The addition to the labour force which this entails should enable the community to produce $12\frac{1}{2}$ per cent more goods, or the same amount of goods and services in $12\frac{1}{2}$ per cent less time, that is in a working week for all men and women reduced from 48 to 42, or from 40 to 35 hours.

These are long-term possibilities. They are, however, never discussed. So far, all countries seem to be content to let the development take its course, to add to the labour force as women react to the monetary advantages offered, and to make, usually too little and too late, *ad hoc* adjustments to the new situation such as were described in the last chapter.

Although, as said before, the choice would be open between increasing output (and the addition of female labour has so far chiefly been used for this purpose) and reducing working hours, there can be no doubt that women, if they had any say in this matter which is of very personal concern to them, would be in favour of reducing the many hours that modern man spends away from his home and his private interests.

Even with the increased employment of married women suggested here, they would still be mainly responsible, as before, for the upbringing of the young.

It is easy to work out a time-table to show that our hypothetical 20 years are more than sufficient for the upbringing of to-day's average family. Assuming children need their mother's full-time attention until they go to school and require her presence for half the day up to the age of 15, a period of 20 years is a generous estimate of the time needed for the care of the two to three children which are the average to-day.

This schedule may not fit each individual family, but as a pattern it is realistic in the same way that statistics are valid. Deviations from the norm in one direction are cancelled out by deviations in the opposite direction in an equal number of other instances. For the families with more, or more widely spaced, children than the average, there are those with fewer children or none.

The all-round reduction of working hours which might become possible if the employment of married women past the child-rearing age became a widespread practice, would bring about a change in the pattern of home and family life in a direction which seems wholly desirable. Both men and women would have more time and energy left to look after their home, an activity which can be a creative combination of work and leisure if one has neither too much nor too little time for it. A six-hour day for both men and women would then not seem out of reach, corresponding more or less to the time children spend at school. This would make a complete renaissance of home life possible. Even shortening the working day by one hour would help to bring the fathers back to the home. At present, a husband's share in the life of his family tends to be restricted to week-ends and otherwise to receiving his wife's reports on what has been going on during his absence. This amount of 'participation' may, perhaps, be adequate in the relationship between a manager and his staff; it is certainly insufficient to make a family a living community to all its members.

Making husbands, and fathers, full partners in the affairs of their families, instead of mere *'visiteurs du soir'*, seems to us so much to be desired that, with a general shortening of working time in mind, we think the full-time employment of married women preferable to their doing part-time work—although for a period of transition part-time employment may be easier to *do* (it certainly is not easier to *find*).

Discussing similar problems, i.e. the desirability of men having

SUMMARY AND CONCLUSIONS

a greater share in the life of their families, and of married women taking part in outside employment, an American author, Ashley Montague,[1] has suggested a radical revision of our system of work. He proposes a plan according to which all single persons of either sex should work an eight-hour day while all married men and women work only four hours per day. Instead of the old division of labour between the sexes he advocates a differentiation of working hours (though not of the type of work) according to marital status. This would, he feels, help to create harmony between husband and wife by establishing complete equality between men and women: equal shares both in outside and domestic work, and equal responsibilities in the upbringing of children, while giving both of them ample time to devote themselves to home, family and other joint activities.

Desirable as these aims are, it seems to us to be utterly unrealistic to produce a situation in which bachelors would be at a premium, and to expect employers to accept two half-time workers instead of one working full time, or to adjust their staff organization to all changes in the marital status of their employees—not to speak of the employers themselves, or the many professional people, doctors, lawyers, architects, etc., and the independent business men, whose work is of a personal nature and can neither be reduced by half nor be delegated to another person on a fifty-fifty basis.

In contrast, our suggestion to increase the number of working people by including among them married women who are either childless or have ceased to look after small children, does not involve any major changes in the organization of work. It rests mainly on a change in attitudes among the women themselves and on the provision of better services to reduce domestic work. Both of these conditions are already in the process of being fulfilled anyway, and all that is required is that this process should be speeded up gradually, and that it should affect a larger section of the population.

There may possibly be a conflict between the interests of the sexes if a reduction in the average number of hours worked in a week is planned. To shorten the hours worked each day may be attractive to women who want to be at home when their children return from school; to reduce the number of days worked may

[1] Ashley Montague, *The Natural Superiority of Women*, New York, 1953.

appeal more to men and their male trade union representatives who have their eye on sports events. It might indeed be of interest if a survey could be made of the advantages of a shorter working day, in terms of reduced daily fatigue and increased participation in family life, against a shorter working week, in terms of the increased recuperative effect of the 'long week-end'. The attractions of a shorter week will obviously be much greater to workers who spend a long time travelling to and from work, as in London and other big cities.

Among those concerned with the welfare of the population, the view has increasingly gained ground that not only in the homes, but also in the organization of work and leisure pursuits, more account should be taken of the fact that working men and women are not isolated individuals but members of families. The problem is, how best to strike a balance between the economic interests of increased productivity and the social aim of contentment among the workers and their families alike.

The direction in which considered public policy moves has found its most enlightened expression in reports by the Royal Commissions on Population both in Sweden and Great Britain. Their point of departure, it should be noted, was concern not about the status of women, but about means to safeguard the interests of families. Nevertheless, both of them came out decidedly in favour of the employment of married women.

The Swedish Commission of 1935 accused employers of 'social misuse of their power' by hindering married women from obtaining work. It was suggested that punitive legislation should be introduced if the rules of the labour market in this respect were not changed within a reasonable time. In 1938, the Royal Commission proposed a law, promulgated the following year, to the effect that 'employed persons may not be severed from a position on account of marriage, pregnancy or child-bearing'.[1]

The British Royal Commission on Population[2] gave its considered opinion on this question as follows: '*It would be harmful all round, to the women, the family and the community, to attempt any restriction of the contribution that women can make to the cultural and economic life of the nation. It is true that there is often a real conflict between motherhood and a whole-time "career". Part of this conflict is inherent in the*

---

[1] See also Alva Myrdal, *Nation and Family*, London, 1945, p. 415.
[2] Royal Commission on Population Report, Cmd. 7695, 1949.

biological function of women, but part of it is artificial and the persistence of this artificial element tends to depress the status of motherhood into that of an inferior alternative to outside employment or public life. We therefore welcome the removal of the marriage bar in such employments as teaching and the civil service, and we think that a deliberate effort should be made to devise adjustments that would render it easier for women to combine motherhood and the care of a home with outside activities.'[1]

It may be added that the adjustments which are required are not confined to technical and social re-organization. As far as these are concerned, means for improvement can be devised, and we have indicated some of them. Equally important, however, is a change in social attitude, a process which inevitably is much slower and cannot be brought about by mere administrative measures.

This change of attitudes may have incidental consequences, some of which may offend against deeply entrenched social traditions or vested interests and will therefore be unpopular with many people, women no less than men.

To take one example, once the idea is accepted that making a positive contribution to the national economy is a responsibility shared by men and women alike, it is difficult to see why a man should be held responsible for supporting his divorced wife to the end of her life if she is capable of looking after herself. Or, while it is customary now for a woman to give up her job if her husband's occupation requires a change of residence, situations may arise in which it is more opportune for a husband to change his job so that his wife can keep hers. At present, there is a strong emotional prejudice against such a 'reversal of roles'; this can only gradually be removed by people setting an example as the occasion arises.

Fear of wide repercussions, some of them perhaps unforeseeable, must not however be allowed to stand in the way of social reforms which in the present state of technical and economic development have long been overdue and which would be of general benefit to the community.

Social progress always proceeds at an unequal pace in different fields of human activities. It has, as a rule, followed roughly the same pattern, namely that new scientific inventions lead to technical advances which, in their turn, are followed by social adjustments and reorganization; changes in general attitudes and

[1] *Op. cit.*, p. 160.

opinions usually bring up the rear. There is no reason to suppose that in the sphere of women's employment, which has been facilitated, and also made necessary, by contemporary technical developments, the succession of phases should be different, or that prejudices should be allowed to block the road to social advance.

The necessary mental adjustments, however slow to come, are bound to be made in the end, and there are certain symptoms which quite unmistakably indicate that such changes of social attitudes are in progress. While, for instance, there exists at present no ideology demanding that childless married women should accept jobs (except in war-time, when this was a general practice in all countries, and compulsory in some) there also no langer exists a prejudice against it, even in middle- and upper-class circles.

This is in marked contrast to the views and practices of previous generations, and it is a clear indication of the direction in which developments are moving. Attitudes and ideologies are gradually being brought into line with technical and social developments and tend towards greater participation of married women in the economic, political, administrative and cultural activities of the community.

BIBLIOGRAPHY

ABEL-SMITH, BRIAN. *A History of the Nursing Profession* (Heinemann, London, 1960).

ANDREWS, BENJAMIN, R. *Economics of the Household* (The Macmillan Co., New York, 1935).

APPLEBAUM, STELLA B. *Working Wives and Mothers* (Public Affairs Pamphlet No. 188, New York, 1952).

ARREGGER, C. E. (ed.) *Graduate Women at Work* (B.F.U.W., Oriel Press, Newcastle, 1966).

BAETJER, ANNA M. *Women in Industry* (W. B. Saunders Co., Philadelphia and London, 1946).

BANKS, J. A. *Prosperity and Parenthood* (Routledge & Kegan Paul, London, 1954).

BAUR HANSL, EVA VON. 'Part-Time Work—a Sampling from the AAUW Questionnaires' (*Journal of the American Association of University Women*, Vol. 44, No. 3, 1951).

BEAUVOIR, SIMONE DE. *The Second Sex* (transl. from *Le Deuxième Sexe*, Gallimard, Paris, 1949; Jonathan Cape, London, 1953).

BECKERMAN, WILFRED, and SUTHERLAND, JANE. 'Married Women at Work in 1972', (*National Institute Economic Review*, No. 23, February 1963).

BENHAM, ELIZABETH D. *The Woman Wage-Earner* (U.S. Department of Labor, Women's Bureau Bulletin No. 172, 1939).

BENNETT, B. A. 'Part-Time Nursing Employment in Great Britain' *International Labour Review*, Vol. LXXXV, No. 4, April 1962).

BERRY, JANE, and EPSTEIN, SANDRA. *Continuing Education of Women: Needs, Aspirations and Plans* (Univ. of Kansas City, Miss., May 1963).

BORGATTA, E. F., and WESTOFF, C. F. 'Social and Psychological Factors Affecting Fertility, XXV. The Prediction of Total Fertility' (*The Millbank Memorial Fund Quarterly*, October 1954, XXXII, No. 4).

BORSODI, RALPH. *Flight from the City—The Study of a New Way to Family Security* (Harper & Brothers, New York, 1933).

BOWLBY, JOHN. *Maternal Care and Mental Health* (World Health Organization, Geneva, 1951).
Child Care and the Growth of Love (Pelican, 2nd ed., 1965).

BROUGHTON, M. E. 'Children with Mothers at Work' (*Journal of the Royal Institute of Public Health and Hygiene*, May/June 1962).

BRUNTZ, FRANÇOIS. 'The Part-Time Employment of Women in Industrialized Countries (*International Labour Review*, Vol. LXXXVI, No. 5, November 1962).

CHESTER, T. E. 'Growth Productivity and Womanpower' (*District Bank Review*, September 1962).

CHOMBART DE LAUWE, P. H. (ed.). *Images de la femme dans la société* (Editions ouvrières, Paris, 1964).

CHOMBART DE LAUWE, M. J. and P. H., HUGUET, M., PERROY, E., and BOSSERET, N. *La femme dans la société; son image dans les différents milieux sociaux* (Editions du C.N.R.S., Paris, 1963).

CLARK, F. LE GROS. *Woman, Work and Age* (Nuffield Foundation, London, 1962).

CLEPHANE, IRENE. *Toward Sex Freedom* (John Lane, London, 1935).

CURTIS, HELEN, and WILLMOTT, PHYLLIS. *Part-Time Employment and Some Aspects of Recruitment and Training in Social Work—An Enquiry in London* (Assoc. of Part-Time Social Workers, January 1963).

CURTIS, HELEN, and HOWELL, CATHERINE. *Part-Time Social Work* (The National Council of Social Service (Inc.), London, 1965).

DARIC, JEAN. *L'Activité professionelle des femmes en France* (Presses Universitaires de France, Paris, 1947).
'Aperçu général de l'évolution du travail féminin en France' (published in *Avenirs*, Paris, March–April 1951).
'Vieillissement de la population' (published in *Population*, Paris, 1952, No. 1).

DENNIS, LAWRENCE E. (ed.). *Education and a Woman's Life* (American Council on Education, Washington, D.C., 1963).

DOUGLAS, J. W. B., and BLOMFIELD, J. M. *Children under Five* (Allen & Unwin, London, 1958).

DURAND, JOHN D. 'Women in the United States' (*International Labour Review*, December 1943).
'Married Women in the Labour Force' (*American Journal of Sociology*, November 1946).

The Labour Force in the United States, 1890–1960 (Research Monograph, published by the Social Science Research Council, 1948).

DUVERGER, MAURICE. *The Political Role of Women* (UNESCO, 1955).

ELLIOTT, DOROTHY M. 'The Status of Domestic Work in the United Kingdom' (*International Labour Review*, Vol. LXIII, No. 2, February 1951).

ESSIG, MARY, and MORGAN, D. H. 'Adjustment of Adolescent Daughters of Employed Women (*Journal of Educational Psychology*, Vol. XXXVII, 1946).

FERGUSON, T., and CUNNISON, J. *The Young Wage-earner* (Oxford University Press, published for the Nuffield Foundation, London, 1951).

FOLSOM, J. K. *The Family and Democratic Society* (John Wiley & Sons, Inc., New York, and Chapman & Hall, Ltd., London, 1943).

FREUD, ANNA, and BURLINGHAM, DOROTHY. *Young Children in Wartime* (Allen & Unwin, London, 1942).
Infants Without Families (Allen & Unwin, London, 1943).

FREUD, SIGMUND. *The Psychology of Women* ('New Introductory Lectures on Psycho-Analysis', Hogarth Press, London, 1933).

FRIEDAN, BETTY. *The Feminine Mystique* (Gollancz, London, 1963).

GAFAFER, W. M. *Industrial Sickness Absenteeism Among Males and Females During 1950* (U.S. Public Health Reports, Vol. 66, No. 47, November 1951).

GAVRON, HANNAH. *Captive Wives* (Routledge, London, 1966).

GINZBERG, ELI and Associates. *Life Styles of Educated Women* (Columbia University Press, New York and London, 1966).

GLASS, NETTA. 'Eating, Sleeping & Elimination Habits in Children Attending Day Nurseries and Children cared for at Home by Mothers' (*American Journal of Ortho-psychiatry*, Vol. XIX, No. 4, October 1949).

GLICK, PAUL. 'The Family Circle' (*American Sociological Review*, April 1947).

GLUCK, SHELDON and ELEANOR. 'Working Mothers and Delinquency' (*Mental Hygiene*, Vol. XLI, No. 3, 1957).

GOLDSMITH, MARGARET. *Women at War* (Lindsay Drummond Ltd., London, 1943).

GOLDWATER, ETHEL. 'Woman's Place' (published in *Commentary*, New York, December 1947).

GROSS, IRMA H. (ed.). *Potentialities of Women in the Middle Years* (Michigan State Univ. Press, 1956).

GRUENBERG, S. M., and KRECH, HILDA SIDNEY. *The Many Lives of Modern Woman* (Doubleday & Co., New York, 1952).

GUELAUD-LERIDON, FRANÇOISE. *Le travail des femmes en France* Institut National d'Études Démographiques & Commissariat Général du Plan d'Equipement et de la Productivité; Travaux et Documents, Cahier, No. 42, Presses Universitaires de France, Paris, 1964).

GUILBERT, M. *Les fonctions des femmes dans l'industrie* (Études européennes, The Hague, 1966).

GUILBERT, MADELEINE, and ISAMBERT-JAMATI, V. *Statut professionel et rôle traditionnel des femmes* (Cahiers Internationaux de Sociologie, Nouv. Série, XVII, Juillet-Décembre, Paris, 1954).

HALMOS, PAUL. *Solitude and Privacy* (Routledge & Kegan Paul, London, 1952).

HARRIS, E. M. *Married Women in Industry* (Institute of Personnel Management, Occasional Papers No. 4, revised ed., 1960).

HAVEMANN, ERNEST, and WEST, PATRICIA SALTER. *They Went to College* (Harcourt Brace & Co., New York, 1952).

HEINICKE, CHRISTOPH M. 'Some Effects of Separating Two-Year-Old Children from their Parents: A Comparative Study' (*Human Relations*, Vol. IX, 1956).

HERZOG, ELIZABETH. *Children of Working Mothers* (Children's Bureau Publication, U.S. Govt. Printing Office, Washington, 1960).

HEWITT, MARGARET. *The effect of married women's employment in the cotton textile districts on the organisation and structure of the home in Lancashire, 1840–1880* (Ph.D. thesis, London, 1953).
Wives and Mothers in Victorian Industry (Rockliff, London, 1958).

HOOKS, JANET M. *British Policies and Methods in Employing Women in War-time* (U.S. Department of Labor, 1944).
Women's Occupations Through Seven Decades (U.S. Department of Labor, Women's Bureau Bulletin No. 218, Washington, 1951).

HORNEY, KAREN. *The Neurotic Personality of Our Time* (Kegan Paul, London, 1937).

HUBBACK, JUDITH. *Wives Who Went to College* (Heinemann, London, 1957).

BIBLIOGRAPHY

JAMES, EDWARD. 'Women at Work in Twentieth Century Britain' (*The Manchester School of Economic and Social Studies*, Vol. XXX, No. 3, September 1962).

JEPHCOTT, AGNES PEARL. *Girls Growing Up* (Faber & Faber, London, 1942).
Rising Twenty (Faber & Faber, London, 1948).

JEPHCOTT, PEARL, with SEEAR, N., and SMITH, J. S. *Married Women Working* (Allen & Unwin, London, 1962).

KELSALL, R. K. *Women and Teaching* (H.M.S.O., London, 1963).

KELSALL, R. K., & MITCHELL, SHEILA. 'Married Women and Employment in England and Wales' (*Population Studies*, Vol. XIII, Part I, July, 1959).

KINSEY, ALFRED C., POMEROY, W. B., and others, *Sexual Behaviour of the Human Female* (W. B. Saunders Co., Philadelphia and London, 1953).

KISER, CLYDE V., and SCHACTER, N. L. 'Demographic Characteristics of Women in "Who's Who" ' (*The Millbank Memorial Fund Quarterly*, Vol. XXVII, No. 4, October 1949).

KLEIN, VIOLA. *The Feminine Character—History of an Ideology* (Kegan Paul, London, 1946, and International Universities Press, New York, 1948).
Britain's Married Women Workers (Routledge & Kegan Paul, London, 1965).
Women Workers—Working Hours and Services (O.E.C.D., Paris, 1965).

KNEELAND, HILDEGARDE. 'Limitations of Scientific Management in Household Work' (*Jnl. of Home Economics*, 1928, No. 20).
'Woman's Economic Contribution in the Home' (*Annals of the Amer. Academy of Polit. and Social Science*, 1929, No. 143).
Is the Modern Housewife a Lady of Leisure? (Survey Graphic, 1 June 1929).

KOMAROVSKY, MYRRA. 'Cultural Contradictions and Sex Roles' (*American Journal of Sociology*, November 1946).
Women in the Modern World, Their Education and Their Dilemmas (Little, Brown & Co., Boston, 1953).
'Functional Analysis of Sex Roles' (*American Sociological Review*, August 1950).
Women in the Modern World (Little, Brown & Comp., Boston, 1953).

KYRK, HAZEL. *Economic Problems of the Family* (Harper, New York, 1933).

LEPLAE, CLAIRE. *Les femmes universitaires* (Institut de Recherches Économiques et Sociales, Louvain, 1950).

LESER, C. E. V. 'Trends in Women's Work Participation' (*Population Studies*, Vol. XII, Part II, November 1958).

LEVY, DAVID M. *Maternal Over-protection* (Columbia Univ. Press, New York, 1943).

LUETKENS, CHARLOTTE. *Women and a New Society* (Nicholson & Watson, London, 1946).

MEAD, MARGARET. *Male and Female* (Morrow, New York, and V. Gollancz, London, 1949).
'Some Theoretical Considerations on the Problem of Mother-Child Separation' (*American Journal of Ortho-psychiatry*, XXIV, No. 3, July 1954).

MARBEAU-CLEIRENS, BÉATRICE. *Psychologie des Mères* (Editions Universitaires, Paris, 1966).

MEDICAL RESEARCH COUNCIL—INDUSTRIAL HEALTH RESEARCH BOARD. *Hours of Work, Lost Time and Labour Wastage* (Emergency Report No. 2, H.M.S.O., London 1942).
A Study of Absenteeism among Women (Emergency Report No. 4, H.M.S.O., London, 1943).
A Study of Certified Sickness Absence among Women in Industry (Report No. 86, H.M.S.O., London 1945).

MILLER, FRIEDA S. 'Household Employment in the United States' (*International Labour Review*, Vol. LXVI, No. 4, October 1952).

MONTAGUE, ASHLEY. *The Natural Superiority of Women* (The Macmillan Co., New York, 1953).

MYRDAL, ALVA. *Nation and Family* (Harper, New York, and Kegan Paul, London, 1945).

NYE, F. IVAN, and HOFFMAN, LOIS WLADIS. *The Employed Mother in America* (Rand McNally & Co., Chicago, 1963).

PARRISH, JOHN B. 'Professional Womanpower as a National Resource' (*Quarterly Review of Economics & Business*, Univ. of Illinois, February, 1961).
'Top Level Training of Women in the U.S., 1900–1960' (*Journal of the Assoc. of Women Deans and Counsellors*, January, 1962).

PINCHBECK, IVY. *Women Workers and the Industrial Revolution* (Routledge, London, 1930.

RADKE YARROW, M., SCOTT, P. M., DE LEEUW, L., and HEINIG, C. 'Child-Rearing in Families of Working and Non-Working

Mothers' (*Sociometry*, Beacon (N.Y.), Vol. XXV, No. 2, 1962).

RENARD, MARIE-THERÈSE. *La participation des femmes à la vie civique* (Les Éditions ouvrières, Paris, 1965).

RIESMAN, DAVID. *The Lonely Crowd* (A. A. Knopf, New York, 1953). 'Women, Their Orbits and their Education' (*Social Forces*, October, 1951).
Some Continuities and Discontinuities in the Education of Women (Third John Dewey Memorial Lecture, Bennington College, Bennington, 1957).

ROSE, A. M. 'The Adequacy of Women's Expectations for Adult Roles' (*Social Forces*, Vol. XXX, 1951).

RÖSSEL, JAMES. *Women in Sweden*, The Swedish Institute, Stockholm, 1965.

ROUMAN, JACK. 'School Children's Problems as Related to Parental Factors' (*Journal of Educational Research*, Vol. I, 1956–7).

ROYAL COMMISSION ON EQUAL PAY, 1944–46. Report (H.M.S.O. Cmd. 6937, London, 1946).

ROYAL COMMISSION ON POPULATION. Report (H.M.S.O. Cmd. 7695, London, 1949).

SCHAFFER, RUDOLPH, and EMERSON, PEGGY E. *The Development of Social Attachments in Infancy* (Monograph of the Society for Research in Child Development, 1964).

SEEAR, NANCY, and others. *A Career for Women in Industry?* (L.S.E. Publications, 1964).

SMIETON, DAME MARY. 'Problems of Women's Employment in Great Britain' (*International Labour Review*, Vol. LXIX, No. 1, January 1954).

STEINMANN, ANNE. 'Women's Attitudes Towards Careers' (*Vocational Guidance Quarterly*, No. 8, Autumn, 1959).

STEWART, C. M. 'Future Trends in the Employment of Married Women' (*British Journal of Sociology*, March 1961).

STOETZEL, JEAN. 'Une étude du budget-temps de la femme dans les agglomérations urbaines' (*Population*, ed. de l'I.N.E.D., Paris, 1948, No. 1).

STOLZ, L. M. 'Effects of Maternal Employment on Children: Evidence from Research' (*Child Development*, No. 31, 1960).

STOLZ, SIEGEL, HITCHCOCK and ADAMSON. 'Dependence and Independence in Children of Working Mothers' (*Child Development*, December 1959).

STOTT, D. H. 'Do Working Mothers' Children Suffer?' (*New Society*, 19 August 1965).

STRECKER, EDWARD. *Their Mother's Sons* (J. B. Lippincott Co., Philadelphia, 1946).

THOMAS, GEOFFREY. *Women and Industry* (Social Survey, London, 1947).

THOMPSON, B., and FINLAYSON, A. 'Married Women Who Work in Early Motherhood' (*British Journal of Sociology*, Vol. XIII, No. 1, March, 1962).

TITMUSS, R. M. *Essays on the Welfare State* (Allen and Unwin, London, 1958).

WHITE, LYNN, JR. *Educating Our Daughters—A Challenge to the Colleges* (Harper & Brothers, New York, 1950).

WILLIAMS, GERTRUDE. *Women and Work* (Nicholson & Watson, London, 1945).

WILSON, MAUD. *Use of Time by Oregon Farm Home-makers* (Oregon Agricultural Experimental Station Bulletin No. 256, 1929).

WITMER, HELEN. *The Field of Parent Education* (Nat. Council of Parent Education, Vassar College, Poughkeepsie, N.Y., 1934).
'The Influence of Parental Attitudes on the Social Adjustment of the Individual' (*Amer. Sociological Review*, 1937, No. 2).

WOLFE, BERAN, M.D. *A Woman's Best Years* (Garden City, N.Y., Publ. Co. Inc., Garden City and London, 1946).

WOOD, ETHEL M. *Mainly for Men* (V. Gollancz, London, 1943).

WOODHALL, MAUREEN. 'Is it Worth Educating Women?' (*New Society*, 19 August 1965).

YOUNG, LOUISE M. 'Women's Opportunities and Responsibilities' (*The Annals of the Amer. Academy of Political & Social Science*, May 1947).
'The American Woman at Mid-Century' (*American Review*, December 1961).

YUDKIN, SIMON, and HOLME, ANTHEA, *Working Mothers and their Children* (Michael Joseph, London, 1963).

⟋ ZAPOLEON, MARGUERITE. *Occupational Planning for Women* (Harper & Bros., New York, 1951).

ZWEIG, FERDYNAND. *The Worker in an Affluent Society* (Heinemann, London, 1961).
Women's Life and Labour (Victor Gollancz, London, 1952).

BIBLIOGRAPHY

OFFICIAL AND ANONYMOUS PUBLICATIONS

American Women. Report of the President's Commission on the Status of Women (U.S. Govt. Printing Office, Washington, 1963).

The Changing Pattern, Report on the Training of the Older Woman (National Federation of Business and Professional Women's Clubs, London, 1966).

'Child Care Facilities for Women Workers' (*International Labour Review*, Vol. LXII, No. 5, November 1950).

Deprivation of Maternal Care—A Reassessment of Its Effects (Public Health Papers, W.H.O., Geneva, 1962).

'Employment of Married Women and Mothers of Families' (*International Labour Review*, Vol. LXIII, No. 6, June 1951).

'Employment of Women' (*Political and Economic Planning*, Vol. XV, No. 285, July 1948).

Employment of Women in an Emergency Period (U.S. Department of Labor, Women's Bureau, 1951).

'Enquiry on Equal Pay in Sweden' (*International Labour Review*, Vol. LXIII, No. 7, July 1951).

'Facilities for Women Workers with Home Responsibilities' (*International Labour Review*, Vol. LXIII, No. 3, March 1951).

La Femme au Travail (Special issue of ESPRIT, Paris, May, 1961).

15 to 18, A Report of the Central Advisory Council for Education (England) (H.M.S.O., London, 1959).

Graduate Wives (P.E.P. in *Planning*, Vol. XX, No. 361, April, 1944).

Handbook of Facts on Women Workers (U.S. Department of Labor, Women's Bureau Bulletin No. 237, Washington, 1950).

Higher Education, Report of the Committee appointed by the Prime Minister under the Chairmanship of Lord Robbins, 1961–1963 (Cmd. 2154, H.M.S.O., October 1963).

'An International Survey of Part-Time Employment' (*International Labour Review* Vol. LXXXVII, Nos. 4 and 5, October and November, 1963).

Occupations Suitable for Women (U.S. Social Security Board, Bureau of Employment Security, 1942).

Older Women Workers (U.S. Department of Labor, Women's Bureau, 1945).

Part-Time Jobs for Women: A Study in Ten Cities (U.S. Department of Labor, Women's Bureau Bulletin No. 238, Washington, 1951).

People in Production. Enquiry into British War Production (Mass Observation Report, Penguin Special, London, 1942).

Progress of Women in the United States, 1949–1951 (Report prepared by the U.S. Department of Labor, Women's Bureau, for the 7th Assembly of the Inter-American Commission of Women at Santiago, 30 May–14 June 1951).

'Social Contribution by the Ageing' (*The Annals of the Amer. Academy of Political and Social Science*, Philadelphia, Jan. 1952).

The Housewife's Day—a Pilot Survey (*Mass Observation Bulletin* No. 40, London, May/June, 1951).

The Influence of Home and Community on Children Under Thirteen Years of Age (UNESCO, Paris, 1949).

The Problem of Absenteeism (Ministry of Labour and National Service, London, September 1942).

The Outlook for Women in Social Work Administration, Teaching and Research (U.S. Department of Labor, Women's Bureau Bulletin 235–6).

The War and Women's Employment; The Experience of the United Kingdom and the United States (International Labour Office, Montreal, 1946).

Vocational Guidance and Training for Women (*International Labour Review*, Vol. LXVI, No. 1, July, 1952).

The Woman in America (Special edition of DAEDALUS, Jrl. of the American Academy of Arts and Sciences, Spring, 1964).

The Women in the Labour Force, Parts I and II, National Central Bureau of Statistics (Stockholm, 1965, Nos. 5 and 7).

Woman, Wife and Worker, London School of Economics (H.M.S.O., London, 1960).

Womanpower, National Manpower Council (Columbia Univ. Press, New York, 1957).

Women and Top Jobs, An Interim Report (P.E.P. 1967).

Women Want to Work, Some Notes on Prospects, Training and Finding Work for the Older Woman with a Good Educational Background (Women's Employment Federation, London, Spring, 1964).

Women Workers/1963 (Trades Union Congress, 1963).

Women Workers in a Changing World, Reports VI (1) and (2), (International Labour Office, Geneva, 1963).

Womanpower (*Civilian Personnel Pamphlet*, No. 20, published U.S. War Dept., 1945).

Women in the Federal Service. Part I: Trends in Employment, Part II: Occupational Information (U.S. Department of Labor, Women's Bureau Bulletin No. 230—I & II, Washington, 1949 and 1950).

Women in Higher Level Positions (U.S. Department of Labor, Women's Bureau Bulletin No. 236, Washington, 1950).

Women's Jobs: Advance and Growth (U.S. Department of Labor, Women's Bureau Bulletin No. 232, Washington, 1949).

Work in the Lives of Married Women, National Manpower Council (Columbia University Press, New York, 1958).

INDEX

INDEX

INDEX

Summerskill, Edith, 141
Sweden, 7, 8, 24, 31, 32, 133, 160, 194
    absenteeism in, 97
    in Civil Service, 103
    teachers, 104
    average size of families in, 20–2
    day homes in, 178
    employment of women in, 43, 45, 66 ff.
    increase in female labour force, 69
    school meals in, 177
    married women working, 34, 61

Teachers, absenteeism among, 103–4
Teaching, as career, 157–8
    married women in, 53, 58
Town planning, 170
Towns, new, 171
Trade Unions, 113, 160
Training, waste of, 109, 155
Transport, development of, 169
Turnover, labour, 106 ff.

Under-employment of women, 185
Unemployment, 185
United States, 19, 31, 59, 78, 111, 132
    absenteeism in, 95–6, 100
    teachers, 103
    college education for girls, 65
    general education in, 7
    employed wives and husbands' income, 82
    employment of women in, 59 ff.
    increase in female labour force, 80
    labour turnover in, 106

marriage rate of college women, 137
married women working, 34, 60, 61
school meals in, 176–7
shopping facilities, 172
time spent in housework, 36
universal suffrage in, 7
women's occupations, 78
Universities, admission of women, 8, 32
University education, value to women, 151
    graduates, marriage rate, 137
Unskilled occupations, women and, 76, 154
U.S.S.R., *see* Russia

Vocation, difficulties of choice, 136 ff.
    sense of, 144

Wars, world, effects of, 3, 39, 51
Washing machines, 81, 173
Welfare services, children's, 123, 176 ff.
West, P. S., 137n.
Widowhood, 24
Widows, in labour force, 39
Work, right to, 7, 9
    varying attitude to, and social strata, 9
Working conditions, reorganization of, 53
Working time and marital status, 193
    possible reduction of, 191
Workplace and home, separation of, 27, 169

Zweig, F., 83, 97, 98, 105

The International Library of
Sociology
and Social Reconstruction

Edited by W. J. H. SPROTT
Founded by KARL MANNHEIM

ROUTLEDGE & KEGAN PAUL
BROADWAY HOUSE, CARTER LANE, LONDON, E.C.4

CONTENTS

PRINTED IN GREAT BRITAIN BY HEADLEY BROTHERS LTD
109 KINGSWAY LONDON WC2 AND ASHFORD KENT

GENERAL SOCIOLOGY

Brown, Robert. Explanation in Social Science. *208 pp. 1963. (2nd Impression 1964.) 25s.*

Gibson, Quentin. The Logic of Social Enquiry. *240 pp. 1960. (2nd Impression 1963.) 24s.*

Goldschmidt, Professor Walter. Understanding Human Society. *272 pp. 1959. 21s.*

Homans, George C. Sentiments and Activities: Essays in Social Science. *336 pp. 1962. 32s.*

Jarvie, I. C. The Revolution in Anthropology. *Foreword by Ernest Gellner. 272 pp. 1964. 40s.*

Johnson, Harry M. Sociology: a Systematic Introduction. *Foreword by Robert K. Merton. 710 pp. 1961. (4th Impression 1964.) 42s.*

Mannheim, Karl. Essays on Sociology and Social Psychology. *Edited by Paul Keckskemeti. With Editorial Note by Adolph Lowe. 344 pp. 1953. 32s.*

Systematic Sociology: An Introduction to the Study of Society. *Edited by J. S. Erös and Professor W. A. C. Stewart. 220 pp. 1957. (2nd Impression 1959.) 24s.*

Martindale, Don. The Nature and Types of Sociological Theory. *292 pp. 1961. (2nd Impression 1965.) 35s.*

Maus, Heinz. A Short History of Sociology. *234 pp. 1962. (2nd Impression 1965.) 28s.*

Myrdal, Gunnar. Value in Social Theory: A Collection of Essays on Methodology. *Edited by Paul Streeten. 332 pp. 1958. (2nd Impression 1962.) 32s.*

Ogburn, William F., and **Nimkoff, Meyer F.** A Handbook of Sociology. *Preface by Karl Mannheim. 656 pp. 46 figures. 38 tables. 5th edition (revised) 1964. 40s.*

Parsons, Talcott, and **Smelser, Neil J.** Economy and Society: A Study in the Integration of Economic and Social Theory. *362 pp. 1956. (3rd Impression 1964.) 35s.*

Rex, John. Key Problems of Sociological Theory. *220 pp. 1961. (3rd Impression 1965.) 25s.*

Stark, Werner. The Fundamental Forms of Social Thought. *280 pp. 1962. 32s.*

FOREIGN CLASSICS OF SOCIOLOGY

Durkheim, Emile. Suicide. A Study in Sociology. *Edited and with an Introduction by George Simpson. 404 pp. 1952. (3rd Impression 1965.) 35s.*

Socialism and Saint-Simon. *Edited with an Introduction by Alvin W. Gouldner. Translated by Charlotte Sattler from the edition originally edited with an Introduction by Marcel Mauss. 286 pp. 1959. 28s.*

Professional Ethics and Civic Morals. *Translated by Cornelia Brookfield. 288 pp. 1957. 30s.*

Gerth, H. H., and **Mills, C. Wright.** From Max Weber: Essays in Sociology. *502 pp. 1948. (5th Impression 1964.) 35s.*

Tönnies, Ferdinand. Community and Association. *(Gemeinschaft und Gesellschaft.) Translated and Supplemented by Charles P. Loomis. Foreword by Pitirim A. Sorokin. 334 pp. 1955. 28s.*

SOCIAL STRUCTURE

Andrzejewski, Stanislaw. Military Organization and Society. *Foreword by Professor A. R. Radcliffe-Brown. 226 pp. 1 folder. 1954.*

Cole, G. D. H. Studies in Class Structure. *220 pp. 1955. (3rd Impression 1964.) 21s.*

Coontz, Sydney H. Population Theories and the Economic Interpretation. *202 pp. 1957. (2nd Impression 1961.) 25s.*

Coser, Lewis. The Functions of Social Conflict. *204 pp. 1956. (2nd Impression 1965.) 25s.*

Dickie-Clark, H. F. Marginal Situation: A Sociological Study of a Coloured Group. *240 pp. 11 tables. 1966. 40s.*

Glass, D. V. (Ed.). Social Mobility in Britain. *Contributions by J. Berent, T. Bottomore, R. C. Chambers, J. Floud, D. V. Glass, J. R. Hall, H. T. Himmelweit, R. K. Kelsall, F. M. Martin, C. A. Moser, R. Mukherjee, and W. Ziegel. 420 pp. 1954. (2nd Impression 1963.) 45s.*

Kelsall, R. K. Higher Civil Servants in Britain: From 1870 to the Present Day. *268 pp. 31 tables. 1955. (2nd Impression 1966.) 25s.*

Marsh, David C. The Changing Social Structure in England and Wales, 1871-1961. *1958. 272 pp. 2nd edition (revised) 1965. 35s.*

Ossowski, Stanislaw. Class Structure in the Social Consciousness. *212 pp. 1963. 25s.*

SOCIOLOGY AND POLITICS

Barbu, Zevedei. Democracy and Dictatorship: Their Psychology and Patterns of Life. *300 pp. 1956. 28s.*

Crick, Bernard. The American Science of Politics: Its Origins and Conditions. *284 pp. 1959. 32s.*

Hertz, Frederick. Nationality in History and Politics: A Psychology and Sociology of National Sentiment and Nationalism. *432 pp. 1944. (5th Impression 1966.)*

Kornhauser, William. The Politics of Mass Society. *272 pp. 20 tables. 1960. (2nd Impression 1965.) 28s.*

Laidler, Harry W. Social-Economic Movements: An Historical and Comparative Survey of Socialism, Communism, Co-operation, Utopianism; and other Systems of Reform and Reconstruction. *864 pp. 16 plates. 1 figure. 1949. (3rd Impression 1960.) 50s.*

Lasswell, Harold D. Analysis of Political Behaviour. *324 pp. 1947. (4th Impression 1966.) 35s.*

Mannheim, Karl. Freedom, Power and Democratic Planning. *Edited by Hans Gerth and Ernest K. Bramstedt. 424 pp. 1951. (2nd Impression 1965.) 35s.*

Mansur, Fatma. Process of Independence. *Foreword by A. H. Hanson. 208 pp. 1962. 25s.*

Martin, David A. Pacificism: an Historical and Sociological Study. *202 pp. 1965. 30s.*

Myrdal, Gunnar. The Political Element in the Development of Economic Theory. *Translated from the German by Paul Streeten. 282 pp. 1953. (4th Impression 1965.) 25s.*

Polanyi, Michael. F.R.S. The Logic of Liberty: Reflections and Rejoinders. *228 pp. 1951. 18s.*

Verney, Douglas V. The Analysis of Political Systems. *264 pp. 1959. (3rd Impression 1965.) 28s.*

Wootton, Graham. The Politics of Influence: British Ex-Servicemen, Cabinet Decisions and Cultural Changes, 1917 to 1957. *320 pp. 1963. 30s.*
The Worker, Unions and the State. *160 pp. 1966. 25s.*

FOREIGN AFFAIRS: THEIR SOCIAL, POLITICAL AND ECONOMIC FOUNDATIONS

Baer, Gabriel. Population and Society in the Arab East. *Translated by Hanna Szöke. 228 pp. 10 maps. 1964. 40s.*

Bonné, Alfred. State and Economics in the Middle East: A Society in Transition. *482 pp. 2nd (revised) edition 1955. (2nd Impression 1960.) 40s.*
Studies in Economic Development: with special reference to Conditions in the Under-developed Areas of Western Asia and India. *322 pp. 84 tables. 2nd edition 1960. 32s.*

Mayer, J. P. Political Thought in France from the Revolution to the Fifth Republic. *164 pp. 3rd edition (revised) 1961. 16s.*

Schlesinger, Rudolf. Central European Democracy and its Background: Economic and Political Group Organization. *432 pp. 1953. 40s.*

Trouton, Ruth. Peasant Renaissance in Yugoslavia 1900-1950: A Study of the Development of Yugoslav Peasant Society as affected by Education. *370 pp. 1 map. 1952. 28s.*

CRIMINOLOGY

Ancel, Marc. Social Defence: A Modern Approach to Criminal Problems. *Foreword by Leon Radzinowicz. 240 pp. 1965. 32s.*

Cloward, Richard A., and **Ohlin, Lloyd E.** Delinquency and Opportunity: A Theory of Delinquent Gangs. *248 pp. 1961. 25s.*

Downes, David. The Delinquent Solution. A Study in Sub-cultural Theory. *304 pp. 1965. 42s.*

Dunlop, A. B., and **McCabe, S.** Young Men in Detention Centres. *192 pp. 1965. 28s.*

Friedländer, Dr. Kate. The Psycho-Analytical Approach to Juvenile Delinquency: Theory, Case Studies, Treatment. *320 pp. 1947. (6th Impression 1961.) 28s.*

Glueck, Sheldon, and **Eleanor.** Family Environment and Delinquency. *With the statistical assistance of Rose W. Kneznek. 340 pp. 1962. (2nd Impression 1966.) 40s.*

Mannheim, Hermann. Comparative Criminology: a Textbook. *Two volumes. 416 pp. and 360 pp. 1965. (2nd Impression with corrections 1966.) 42s. each.*

Morris, Terence. The Criminal Area: A Study in Social Ecology. *Foreword by Hermann Mannheim. 232 pp. 25 tables. 4 maps. 1957. (2nd Impression 1966.) 28s.*

Morris, Terence and **Pauline,** assisted by **Barbara Barer.** Pentonville: a Sociological Study of an English Prison. *416 pp. 16 plates. 1963. 50s.*

Spencer, John C. Crime and the Services. *Foreword by Hermann Mannheim. 336 pp. 1954. 28s.*

Trasler, Gordon. The Explanation of Criminality. *144 pp. 1962. 20s.*

SOCIAL PSYCHOLOGY

Barbu, Zevedei. Problems of Historical Psychology. *248 pp. 1960. 25s.*

Blackburn, Julian. Psychology and the Social Pattern. *184 pp. 1945. (7th Impression 1964.) 16s.*

Fleming, C. M. Adolescence: Its Social Psychology: With an Introduction to recent findings from the fields of Anthropology, Physiology, Medicine, Psychometrics and Sociometry. *271 pp. 2nd edition (revised) 1963. (2nd Impression 1964.) 25s.*
The Social Psychology of Education: An Introduction and Guide to Its Study. *136 pp. 2nd edition (revised) 1959. (3rd Impression 1965.) 11s.*

Fleming, C. M. (Ed.). Studies in the Social Psychology of Adolescence. *Contributions by J. E. Richardson, J. E. Forrester, J. K. Shukla and P. J. Higginbotham. Foreword by the editor. 292 pp. 29 figures. 13 tables. 5 folder tables. 1951. 25s.*

Halmos, Paul. Towards a Measure of Man: The Frontiers of Normal Adjustment. *276 pp. 1957. 28s.*

Homans, George C. The Human Group. *Foreword by Bernard DeVoto. Introduction by Robert K. Merton. 526 pp. 1951. (5th Impression 1965.) 35s.*
Social Behaviour: its Elementary Forms. *416 pp. 1961. (2nd Impression 1966.) 32s.*

Klein, Josephine. The Study of Groups. *226 pp. 31 figures. 5 tables. 1956. (4th Impression 1965.) 21s.*

Linton, Ralph. The Cultural Background of Personality. *132 pp. 1947. (6th Impression 1965.) 16s.*

Mayo, Elton. The Social Problems of an Industrial Civilization. With an appendix on the Political Problem. *180 pp. 1949. (5th Impression 1966.) 18s.*

Ottaway, A. K. C. Learning Through Group Experience. *180 pp. 1966. 25s.*

Ridder, J. C. de. The Personality of the Urban African in South Africa. A Thematic Apperception Test Study. *196 pp. 12 plates. 1961. 25s.*

Rose, Arnold M. (Ed.). Mental Health and Mental Disorder: A Sociological Approach. *Chapters by 46 contributors. 654 pp. 1956. 45s.*
Human Behaviour and Social Processes: an Interactionist Approach. *Contributions by Arnold M. Ross, Ralph H. Turner, Anselm Strauss, Everett C. Hughes, E. Franklin Frazier, Howard S. Becker, et al. 696 pp. 1962. 60s.*

Smelser, Neil J. Theory of Collective Behaviour. *448 pp. 1962. 45s.*

Stephenson, Geoffrey M. The Development of Conscience. *128 pp. 1966. 25s.*

Wolfenstein, Martha. Disaster: A Psychological Essay. *264 pp. 1957. 23s.*

Young, Professor Kimball. Personality and Problems of Adjustment, *742 pp. 12 figures. 9 tables. 2nd edition (revised) 1952. (3rd Impression 1959.) 40s.*
Handbook of Social Psychology. *658 pp. 16 figures. 10 tables. 2nd edition (revised) 1957. (3rd Impression 1963.) 40s.*

SOCIOLOGY OF THE FAMILY

Banks, J. A. Prosperity and Parenthood: A study of Family Planning among The Victorian Middle Classes. *262 pp. 1954. (2nd Impression 1965.) 28s.*

Chapman, Dennis. The Home and Social Status. *336 pp. 8 plates. 3 figures. 117 tables. 1955. 35s.*

Gavron, Hannah. The Captive Wife: Conflicts of Housebound Mothers. *192 pp. 1966. (2nd Impression 1966.) 25s.*

Klein, Josephine. Samples from English Cultures. *1965.*
1. Three Preliminary Studies and Aspects of Adult Life in England. *447 pp. 50s.*
2. Child-Rearing Practices and Index. *247 pp. 35s.*

Klein, Viola. Britain's Married Women Workers. *176 pp. 1965. 28s.*

Myrdal, Alva and **Klein, Viola.** Women's Two Roles: Home and Work. *238 pp. 27 tables. 1956. (2nd Impression 1962.) 25s.*

Parsons, Talcott and **Bales, Robert F.** Family: Socialization and Interaction Process. *In collaboration with James Olds, Morris Zelditch and Philip E. Slater. 456 pp. 50 figures and tables. 1956. (2nd Impression 1964.) 35s.*

THE SOCIAL SERVICES

Ashdown, Margaret and **Brown, S. Clement.** Social Service and Mental Health: An Essay on Psychiatric Social Workers. *280 pp. 1953. 21s.*

Bracey, Howard. In Retirement: Pensioners in Great Britain and the United States. *304 pp. 1966. about 40s.*

Goetschius, George W. and **Tash, Joan.** Working with the Unattached. *528 pp. 1966. about 60s.*

Hall, M. Penelope. The Social Services of Modern England. *416 pp. 6th edition (revised) 1963. (2nd Impression with a new Preface 1965.) 30s.*

Hall, M. P., and **Howes, I. V.** The Church in Social Work. A Study of Moral Welfare Work undertaken by the Church of England. *320 pp. 1965. 35s.*

Heywood, Jean S. Children in Care: the Development of the Service for the Deprived Child. *264 pp. 2nd edition (revised) 1965. (2nd Impression 1966.) 32s.*

An Introduction to teaching Casework Skills. *192 pp. 1964. 28s.*

Jones, Kathleen. Lunacy, Law and Conscience, 1744-1845: the Social History of the Care of the Insane. *268 pp. 1955. 25s.*

Mental Health and Social Policy, 1845-1959. *264 pp. 1960. 28s.*

Jones, Kathleen and **Sidebotham, Roy.** Mental Hospitals at Work. *220 pp. 1962. 30s.*

Kastell, Jean. Casework in Child Care. *Foreword by M. Brooke Willis. 320 pp. 1962. 35s.*

Rooff, Madeline. Voluntary Societies and Social Policy. *350 pp. 15 tables. 1957. 35s.*

Shenfield, B. E. Social Policies for Old Age: A Review of Social Provision for Old Age in Great Britain. *260 pp. 39 tables. 1957. 25s.*

Timms, Noel. Psychiatric Social Work in Great Britain (1939-1962). *280 pp. 1964. 32s.*

Social Casework: Principles and Practice. *256 pp. 1964. (2nd Impression 1966.) 25s.*

Trasler, Gordon. In Place of Parents: A Study in Foster Care. *272 pp. 1960. (2nd Impression 1966.) 30s.*

Young, A. F., and **Ashton, E. T.** British Social Work in the Nineteenth Century. *288 pp. 1956. (2nd Impression 1963.) 28s.*

SOCIOLOGY OF EDUCATION

Banks, Olive. Parity and Prestige in English Secondary Education: a Study in Educational Sociology. *272 pp. 1955. (2nd Impression 1963.) 28s.*

Bentwich, Joseph. Education in Israel. *224 pp. 8 pp. plates. 1965. 24s.*

Blyth, W. A. L. English Primary Education. A Sociological Description. *1965.*
1. Schools. *232 pp. 30s.*
2. Background. *168 pp. 25s.*

Collier, K. G. The Social Purposes of Education: Personal and Social Values in Education. *268 pp. 1959. (3rd Impression 1965.) 21s.*

Dale, R. R., and **Griffith, S.** Down Stream: Failure in the Grammar School. *112 pp. 1965. 20s.*

Dore, R. P. Education in Tokugawa Japan. *356 pp. 9 pp. plates. 1965. 35s.*

Edmonds, E. L. The School Inspector. *Foreword by Sir William Alexander. 214 pp. 1962. 28s.*

Evans, K. M. Sociometry and Education. *158 pp. 1962. (2nd Impression 1966.) 18s.*

Foster, P. J. Education and Social Change in Ghana. *336 pp. 3 maps. 1965. 36s.*

Fraser, W. R. Education and Society in Modern France. *150 pp. 1963. 20s.*

Hans, Nicholas. New Trends in Education in the Eighteenth Century. *278 pp. 19 tables. 1951. (2nd Impression 1965.) 30s.*

Comparative Education: A Study of Educational Factors and Traditions. *360 pp. 3rd (revised) edition 1958. (4th Impression 1964.) 25s.*

Holmes, Brian. Problems in Education. A Comparative Approach. *336 pp. 1965. 32s.*

Mannheim, Karl and **Stewart, W. A. C.** An Introduction to the Sociology of Education. *208 pp. 1962. (2nd Impression 1965.) 21s.*

Musgrove, F. Youth and the Social Order. *176 pp. 1964. 21s.*

Ortega y Gasset, Jose. Mission of the University. *Translated with an Introduction by Howard Lee Nostrand. 88 pp. 1946. (3rd Impression 1963.) 15s.*

Ottaway, A. K. C. Education and Society: An Introduction to the Sociology of Education. *With an Introduction by W. O. Lester Smith. 212 pp. Second edition (revised). 1962. (3rd Impression 1965.) 21s.*

Peers, Robert. Adult Education: A Comparative Study. *398 pp. 2nd edition 1959. 42s.*

Pritchard, D. G. Education and the Handicapped: 1760 to 1960. *258 pp. 1963. (2nd Impression 1966.) 28s.*

Simon, Brian and **Joan** (Eds.). Educational Psychology in the U.S.S.R. *Introduction by Brian and Joan Simon. Translation by Joan Simon. Papers by D. N. Bogoiavlenski and N. A. Menchinskaia, D. B. Elkonin, E. A. Fleshner, Z. I. Kalmykova, G. S. Kostiuk, V. A. Krutetski, A. N. Leontiev, A. R. Luria, E. A. Milerian, R. G. Natadze, B. M. Teplov, L. S. Vygotski, L. V. Zankov. 296 pp. 1963. 40s.*

SOCIOLOGY OF CULTURE

Eppel, E. M., and **M.** Adolescents and Morality: A Study of some Moral Values and Dilemmas of Working Adolescents in the Context of a changing Climate of Opinion. *Foreword by W. J. H. Sprott. 256 pp. 39 tables. 1966. 30s.*

Fromm, Erich. The Fear of Freedom. *286 pp. 1942. (8th Impression 1960.) 21s.* The Sane Society. *400 pp. 1956. (3rd Impression 1963.) 28s.*

Mannheim, Karl. Diagnosis of Our Time: Wartime Essays of a Sociologist. *208 pp. 1943. (8th Impression 1965.) 21s.*

Essays on the Sociology of Culture. *Edited by Ernst Mannheim in co-operation with Paul Kecskemeti. Editorial Note by Adolph Lowe. 280 pp. 1956. (2nd Impression 1962.) 28s.*

Weber, Alfred. Farewell to European History: or The Conquest of Nihilism. *Translated from the German by R. F. C. Hull. 224 pp. 1947. 18s.*

SOCIOLOGY OF RELIGION

Argyle, Michael. Religious Behaviour. *224 pp. 8 figures. 41 tables. 1958. (3rd Impression 1965.) 25s.*

Knight, Frank H., and **Merriam, Thornton W.** The Economic Order and Religion. *242 pp. 1947. 18s.*

Stark, Werner. The Sociology of Religion: A Study of Christendom. *Volume 1,* Established Religion. *232 pp. 1966. 35s.*

Watt, W. Montgomery. Islam and the Integration of Society. *320 pp. 1961. (3rd Impression 1966.) 35s.*

SOCIOLOGY OF ART AND LITERATURE

Beljame, Alexandre. Men of Letters and the English Public in the Eighteenth Century: 1660-1744, Dryden, Addison, Pope. *Edited with an Introduction and Notes by Bonamy Dobree. Translated by E. O. Lorimer. 532 pp. 1948. 32s.*

Misch, Georg. A History of Autobiography in Antiquity. *Translated by E. W. Dickes. 2 Volumes. Vol. 1, 364 pp., Vol. 2, 372 pp. 1950. 45s. the set.*

Schucking, L. L. The Sociology of Literary Taste. *112 pp. 2nd (revised) edition 1965. 18s.*

Silbermann, Alphons. The Sociology of Music. *224 pp. 1963. 28s.*

SOCIOLOGY OF KNOWLEDGE

Hodges, H. A. The Philosophy of Wilhelm Dilthey. *410 pp. 1952. 30s.*

Mannheim, Karl. Essays on the Sociology of Knowledge. *Edited by Paul Kecskemeti. Editorial note by Adolph Lowe. 352 pp. 1952. (3rd Impression 1964.) 35s.*

Stark, W. America: Ideal and Reality. The United States of 1776 in Contemporary Philosophy. *136 pp. 1947. 12s.*
  The Sociology of Knowledge: An Essay in Aid of a Deeper Understanding of the History of Ideas. *384 pp. 1958. (2nd Impression 1960.) 36s.*
  Montesquieu: Pioneer of the Society of Knowledge. *244 pp. 1960. 25s.*

URBAN SOCIOLOGY

Anderson, Nels. The Urban Community: A World Perspective. *532 pp. 1960. 35s.*

Ashworth, William. The Genesis of Modern British Town Planning: A Study in Economic and Social History of the Nineteenth and Twentieth Centuries. *288 pp. 1954. (2nd Impression 1965.) 32s.*

Bracey, Howard. Neighbours: Neighbouring and Neighbourliness on New Estates and Subdivisions in England and the U.S.A. *220 pp. 1964. 28s.*

Cullingworth, J. B. Housing Needs and Planning Policy: A Restatement of the Problems of Housing Need and "Overspill" in England and Wales. *232 pp. 44 tables. 8 maps. 1960. (2nd Impression 1966.) 28s.*

Dickinson, Robert E. City and Region: A Geographical Interpretation. *608 pp. 125 figures. 1964. 60s.*
  The West European City: A Geographical Interpretation. *600 pp. 129 maps. 29 plates. 2nd edition 1962. (2nd Impression 1963.) 55s.*

Dore, R. P. City Life in Japan: A Study of a Tokyo Ward. *498 pp. 8 plates. 4 figures. 24 tables. 1958. (2nd Impression 1963.) 45s.*

Jennings, Hilda. Societies in the Making: a Study of Development and Redevelopment within a County Borough. *Foreword by D. A. Clark. 286 pp. 1962. 32s.*

Kerr, Madeline. The People of Ship Street. *240 pp. 1958. 23s.*

Mann, P. H. An Approach to Urban Sociology. *240 pp. 1965. 30s.*

Morris, R. N., and Mogey, J. The Sociology of Housing. Studies at Berinsfield. *232 pp. 4 pp. plates. 1965. 42s.*

Rosser, C., and Harris, C. The Family and Social Change. A Study of Family and Kinship in a South Wales Town. *352 pp. 8 maps. 1965. 45s.*

RURAL SOCIOLOGY

Bracey, H. E. English Rural Life: Village Activities, Organizations and Institutions. *302 pp. 1959. 30s.*

Infield, Henrik F. Co-operative Living in Palestine. *With a Foreword by General Sir Arthur Wauchope, G.C.B. 170 pp. 8 plates. 7 tables. 1946. 12s. 6d.*

Littlejohn, James. Westrigg: the Sociology of a Cheviot Parish. *172 pp. 5 figures. 1963. 25s.*

Williams, W. M. The Country Craftsman: A Study of Some Rural Crafts and the Rural Industries Organization in England. *248 pp. 9 figures. 1958. 25s. (Dartington Hall Studies in Rural Sociology.)*
The Sociology of an English Village: Gosforth. *272 pp. 12 figures. 13 tables. 1956. (3rd Impression 1964.) 25s.*

SOCIOLOGY OF MIGRATION

Eisenstadt, S. N. The Absorption of Immigrants: a Comparative Study based mainly on the Jewish Community in Palestine and the State of Israel. *288 pp. 1954. 28s.*

Humphreys, Alexander J. New Dubliners: Urbanization and the Irish Family. *Foreword by George C. Homans. 304 pp. 1966. 40s.*

SOCIOLOGY OF INDUSTRY AND DISTRIBUTION

Anderson, Nels. Work and Leisure. *280 pp. 1961. 28s.*

Blau, Peter M., and Scott, W. Richard. Formal Organizations: a Comparative approach. *Introduction and Additional Bibliography by J. H. Smith. 328 pp. 1963. (2nd Impression 1964.) 28s.*

Jefferys, Margot, with the assistance of Winifred Moss. Mobility in the Labour Market: Employment Changes in Battersea and Dagenham. *Preface by Barbara Wootton. 186 pp. 51 tables. 1954. 15s.*

Levy, A. B. Private Corporations and Their Control. *Two Volumes. Vol. 1, 464 pp., Vol. 2, 432 pp. 1950. 80s. the set.*

Levy, Hermann. The Shops of Britain: A Study of Retail Distribution. *268 pp. 1948. (2nd Impression 1949.) 21s.*

Liepmann, Kate. The Journey to Work: Its Significance for Industrial and Community Life. *Foreword by A. M. Carr-Saunders. 230 pp. 40 tables. 3 folders. 1944. (2nd Impression 1945.) 18s.*
   Apprenticeship: An Enquiry into its Adequacy under Modern Conditions. *Foreword by H. D. Dickinson. 232 pp. 6 tables. 1960. (2nd Impression.) 23s.*

Millerson, Geoffrey. The Qualifying Associations: a Study in Professionalization. *320 pp. 1964. 42s.*

Smelser, Neil J. Social Change in the Industrial Revolution: An Application of Theory to the Lancashire Cotton Industry, 1770-1840. *468 pp. 12 figures. 14 tables. 1959. (2nd Impression 1960.) 40s.*

Williams, Gertrude. Recruitment to Skilled Trades. *240 pp. 1957. 23s.*

Young, A. F. Industrial Injuries Insurance: an Examination of British Policy. *192 pp. 1964. 30s.*

ANTHROPOLOGY

Ammar, Hamed. Growing up in an Egyptian Village. *336 pp. 1954. (2nd Impression 1966.) 35s.*

Crook, David and **Isabel.** Revolution in a Chinese Village: Ten Mile Inn. *230 pp. 8 plates. 1 map. 1959. 21s.*
   The First Years of Yangyi Commune. *288 pp. 12 plates. 1965. 42s.*

Dube, S. C. Indian Village. *Foreword by Morris Edward Opler. 276 pp. 4 plates. 1955. (5th Impression 1965.) 25s.*
   India's Changing Villages: Human Factors in Community Development. *260 pp. 8 plates. 1 map. 1958. (3rd Impression 1963.) 25s.*

Fei, Hsiao-Tung. Peasant Life in China: a Field Study of Country Life in the Yangtze Valley. *Foreword by Bronislaw Malinowski. 320 pp. 14 plates. 1939. (5th Impression 1962.) 30s.*

Firth, Raymond. Malay Fishermen. Their Peasant Economy. *420 pp. 17 pp. plates. 2nd edition (revised and enlarged 1966.) 55s.*

Gulliver, P. H. The Family Herds. A Study of two Pastoral Tribes in East Africa, The Jie and Turkana. *304 pp. 4 plates. 19 figures. 1955. (2nd Impression with new preface and bibliography 1966.) 25s.*
   Social Control in an African Society: a Study of the Arusha, Agricultural Masai of Northern Tanganyika. *320 pp. 8 plates. 10 figures. 1963. 35s.*

Hogbin, Ian. Transformation Scene. The Changing Culture of a New Guinea Village. *340 pp. 22 plates. 2 maps. 1951. 30s.*

Ishwaran, K. Tradition and Economy in Village India: An Interactionist Approach. *Foreword by Conrad Arensburg. 176 pp. 1966. 25s.*

Little, Kenneth L. Mende of Sierra Leone. *308 pp. and folder. 1951. Revised edition in preparation.*

Lowie, Professor Robert H. Social Organization. *494 pp. 1950. (3rd Impression 1962.) 35s.*

Maunier, René. The Sociology of Colonies: An Introduction to the Study of Race Contact. *Edited and translated by E. O. Lorimer. 2 Volumes. Vol. 1, 430 pp. Vol. 2, 356 pp. 1949. 70s. the set.*

Mayer, Adrian C. Caste and Kinship in Central India: A Village and its Region. *328 pp. 16 plates. 15 figures. 16 tables. 1960. (2nd Impression 1965.) 35s.*

Peasants in the Pacific: A Study of Fiji Indian Rural Society. *232 pp. 16 plates. 10 figures. 14 tables. 1961. 35s.*

Osborne, Harold. Indians of the Andes: Aymaras and Quechuas. *292 pp. 8 plates. 2 maps. 1952. 25s.*

Smith, Raymond T. The Negro Family in British Guiana: Family Structure and Social Status in the Villages. *With a Foreword by Meyer Fortes. 314 pp. 8 plates. 1 figure. 4 maps. 1956. (2nd Impression 1965.) 35s.*

DOCUMENTARY

Meek, Dorothea L. (Ed.). Soviet Youth: Some Achievements and Problems. *Excerpts from the Soviet Press, translated by the editor. 280 pp. 1957. 28s.*

Schlesinger, Rudolf (Ed.). Changing Attitudes in Soviet Russia.

1. The Family in the U.S.S.R. *Documents and Readings, with an Introduction by the editor. 434 pp. 1949. 30s.*

2. The Nationalities Problem and Soviet Administration. Selected Readings on the Development of Soviet Nationalities Policies. *Introduced by the editor. Translated by W. W. Gottlieb. 324 pp. 1956. 30s.*

Reports
of the Institute
of Community Studies

(*Demy 8vo.*)

Cartwright, Ann. Human Relations and Hospital Care. *272 pp. 1964. 30s.*

Jackson, Brian. Streaming: an Education System in Miniature. *168 pp. 1964. 21s. Paper 10s.*

Jackson, Brian and **Marsden, Dennis.** Education and the Working Class: Some General Themes raised by a Study of 88 Working-class Children in a Northern Industrial City. *268 pp. 2 folders. 1962. (3rd Impression 1965.) 32s.*

Marris, Peter. Widows and their Families. *Foreword by Dr. John Bowlby. 184 pp. 18 tables. Statistical Summary. 1958. 18s.*
Family and Social Change in an African City. A Study of Rehousing in Lagos. *196 pp. 1 map. 4 plates. 53 tables. 1961. 25s.*
The Experience of Higher Education. *232 pp. 27 tables. 1964. 25s.*

Mills, Enid. Living with Mental Illness: a Study in East London. *Foreword by Morris Carstairs. 196 pp. 1962. 28s.*

Runciman, W. G. Relative Deprivation and Social Justice. *344 pp. 1966. 40s.*

Townsend, Peter. The Family Life of Old People: An Inquiry in East London. *Foreword by J. H. Sheldon. 300 pp. 3 figures. 63 tables. 1957. (2nd Impression 1961.) 30s.*

Willmott, Peter. Adolescent Boys in East London. *232 pp. 1966. about 28s.*
The Evolution of a Community: a study of Dagenham after forty years. *168 pp. 2 maps. 1963. 21s.*

Willmott, Peter and **Young, Michael.** Family and Class in a London Suburb. *202 pp. 47 tables. 1960. (3rd Impression 1965.) 25s.*

Young, Michael. Innovation and Research in Education. *192 pp. 1965. 25s.*

Young, Michael and **Willmott, Peter.** Family and Kinship in East London. *Foreword by Richard M. Titmuss. 252 pp. 39 tables. 1957. (3rd Impression 1965.) 28s.*

The British Journal of Sociology. *Edited by Terence P. Morris. Vol. 1, No. 1, March 1950 and Quarterly. Roy. 8vo., £2 10s. p.a.; 12s. 6d. a number, post free.*

All prices are net and subject to alteration without notice